Cognitive Behavior Therapy of DSM-IV-TR Personality Disorders

Cognitive Behavior Therapy of DSM-IV-TR Personality Disorders

Second Edition

Highly Effective Interventions for the Most Common Personality Disorders

LEN SPERRY

Routledge
Taylor & Francis Group
New York   London

Routledge is an imprint of the
Taylor & Francis Group, an informa business

Routledge
Taylor & Francis Group
270 Madison Avenue
New York, NY 10016

Routledge
Taylor & Francis Group
2 Park Square
Milton Park, Abingdon
Oxon OX14 4RN

© 2006 by Taylor & Francis Group, LLC
Routledge is an imprint of Taylor & Francis Group, an Informa business

Printed in the United States of America on acid-free paper
10 9 8 7 6 5 4 3 2 1

International Standard Book Number-10: 0-415-95075-9 (Hardcover)
International Standard Book Number-13: 978-0-415-95075-6 (Hardcover)

Visit the Taylor & Francis Web site at
http://www.taylorandfrancis.com

and the Routledge Web site at
http://www.routledgementalhealth.com

TABLE OF CONTENTS

Foreword to the Second Edition   ix
Foreword to the First Edition   xiii
Preface   xvii

PART I
COGNITIVE BEHAVIOR THERAPY OF
PERSONALITY DISORDERS   1

1   **Cognitive Behavior Therapy of Personality Disorders:**
        Basic Considerations   3

        Changes in the Conceptualization of Personality Disorders   4
        Changes in Diagnostic Criteria for Personality Disorders   5
        Changes in the Assessment of Personality Disorders   6
        Changes in the Treatment of Personality Disorders   7
        Basic Premises About Effective Treatment of Personality Disorders 10
        An Effective Treatment Strategy for Personality Disorders   14
        Summary   19

2   **Cognitive Behavior Therapy Interventions with**
        Personality Disorders: I   21

        Character   21
        Schema   22
        Cognitive Behavioral Treatment Approaches for
            Personality Disorders   25
        Other Cognitive Behavioral Methods   37

3
**Cognitive Behavior Therapy Interventions with
Personality Disorders: II** 39

The Brain and Temperament Modulation 40
Dimensions of Temperament 40
Skills, Skill Deficits, and Skills Training 41
Structured Treatment Interventions for Personality Disorders 42
Summary 69

**PART II
CBT STRATEGIES FOR SPECIFIC
PERSONALITY DISORDERS** 71

4
Avoidant Personality Disorder 77

DSM-IV Description and Criteria 78
Engagement Strategies 79
Pattern Analysis Strategies 81
Pattern Change Strategies 83
Pattern Maintenance and Termination Strategies 89
Case Example 90
Summary 94

5
Borderline Personality Disorder 97

DSM-IV Description and Criteria 98
Engagement Strategies 99
Pattern Analysis Strategies 102
Pattern Change Strategies 104
Pattern Maintenance and Termination Strategies 119
Case Example 121
Summary 126

6
Dependent Personality Disorder 129

DSM-IV Description and Criteria 130
Engagement Strategies 131
Pattern Analysis Strategies 133
Pattern Change Strategies 135
Pattern Maintenance and Termination Strategies 138

Case Example   140
Summary   144

7

Narcissistic Personality Disorder   147

DSM-IV Description and Criteria   148
Engagement Strategies   149
Pattern Analysis Strategies   151
Pattern Change Strategies   153
Pattern Maintenance and Termination Strategies   157
Case Example   158
Summary   162

8

Histrionic Personality Disorder   165

DSM-IV Description and Criteria   166
Engagement Strategies   167
Pattern Analysis Strategies   169
Pattern Change Strategies   170
Pattern Maintenance and Termination Strategies   174
Case Example   176
Summary   180

9

Obsessive-Compulsive Personality Disorder   183

DSM-IV Description and Criteria   184
Engagement Strategies   185
Pattern Analysis Strategies   187
Pattern Change Strategies   189
Pattern Maintenance and Termination Strategies   193
Case Example   195
Summary   200

References   203
Index   213

FOREWORD TO THE SECOND EDITION

Cognitive Behavior Therapy (CBT) is not a singular model. Initially representing the work of Ellis, Beck, Lazarus, and Meichenbaum, it now includes the works of these pioneers and the second and third generations of their students and the students of those initially trained by these pioneers. CBT has become a meeting ground for therapists from diverse backgrounds ranging from the psychodynamic to the behavioral. Some, like Len Sperry, have the added advantage of coming from an Adlerian background. Adler was, after all, probably the first of the cognitive therapists.

The term cognitive behavioral therapy is often misleading inasmuch as it implies that the major modalities are either cognitive (dealing with information processing content and style) and behavioral (dealing with the acquisition of skills). These two aspects have often been seen as mutually exclusive and have become the rallying points for various groups. CBT looks at many factors, all of which are relevant as contributions to the development of problems, the maintenance of problems, and the resolution of problems.

In 1977 I started working at the Center for Cognitive Therapy at the University of Pennsylvania with Dr. Aaron T. Beck. It was to become one of the defining moments in my professional life. The Center had another name in those days. We were part of the Hospital of the University of Pennsylvania and we were the "Mood Clinic." (Just as the hospital had an asthma clinic, a foot clinic, etc., we were the experts on mood.) We treated patients with depression. If a patient had a primary anxiety problem, we might refer him or her to another professional for treatment. If a patient had a character disorder (personality disorders and the DSM criteria for diagnosis were not available until DSM III in 1980) we would certainly refer him or her out. It wasn't until the mid to late 1980s that we started applying the basic CBT model to the treatment of personality disorders. In the last 30 years CBT has grown into a broad spectrum model that has been applied to just about every patient group, clinical setting, problem, and professional discipline.

It seemed to us a rather logical step for us to treat patients with the range of personality disorders. If we look at the basic elements of CBT, it is ideal for the treatment of personality disorders that might range from mild to severe. These elements include: CBT is active, directive, structured, dynamic, collaborative, data centered, problem oriented, solution focused, psychoeducational (skill building), outcome directed, socioculturally relevant and informed, integrative, time-limited, and takes a here-and-now focus. This model seems tailor-made for treating those patients with personality disorders.

When Bob Dylan sang about the time "a-changing'" he could easily be describing the shifts in psychotherapy over the past 30 years. From the days when it was a badge of honor to call oneself a psychoanalyst, it seems that everyone now either endorses a CBT perspective ("CBT is what I do") or has taken specific points from CBT and uses them in a more general and nonspecific manner ("I use many CBT techniques in my work").

Given the growth and availability of CBT literature on the treatment of personality disorders, the following experience was still a surprise to me. While presenting a workshop on the cognitive behavioral (CBT) treatment of patients with personality disorders recently, I described an assessment protocol and the treatment plan that followed the data collection. As part of the treatment planning, the patient, a 22-year-old woman, asked for her diagnosis. I recounted for the workshop participants my discussion with the patient about her diagnosis of Borderline Personality Disorder. Immediately upon my saying that, a workshop participant's hand shot up and she asked in a most upset way, "You mean that you told her that she was BORDERLINE?" The surprise, vehemence, and clinical concern were all very powerful. This clinician, with many years of experience, was aghast at my behavior. Why would I tell a patient the diagnosis, and especially when the diagnosis was that the patient had a borderline personality disorder? This clinician was concerned that I had discussed such a "horrible" diagnosis with the patient and likely damaged the patient in doing so. The discussion in the workshop was akin to my having given a patient a diagnosis of inoperable cancer and that it was done in a very casual manner. I must admit that I was taken aback because I had thought that my behavior was clinically reasonable. My consideration was that this woman had likely heard this diagnosis over the years, but always in hushed tones. For this patient, her diagnosis was made even scarier by the lack of discussion and information from therapists. Her experience was that many euphemisms were used to describe her problems. She was "easily aroused," "impulsive," "had relationship problems," or had "anger issues." What she thought was that everyone was afraid to tell her the awful truth, that she was borderline. This only increased her negative self-view. After all, if the therapists were afraid to tell her, she must really be damaged, flawed, incurable, and destined to suffer forever.

I first tried to place what I had done in sharing the diagnosis with the patient within a CBT context and discussed the importance of collaboration. This collaboration involved the patient having to sign a treatment plan. Should I have used one term for the treatment plan that she signed and another for the record? A second issue is that one is not his or her diagnosis. An individual *has* a borderline personality disorder but is not BORDERLINE. The former suggests that it is something that can be changed, the latter suggests that patients are what they are with a far less optimistic prognosis.

In the last several years I have been amazed at the number of patients who come for therapy having searched the Internet for all possible information about their disorder (or the disorder that they mistakenly believe that they have). For example, one patient came for therapy and in her initial session stated that she had a Borderline Personality Disorder. She had read several books on the topic, had searched the Internet, and had purchased a copy of DSM-IV-TR at a local book shop. As I reviewed her history with her during the evaluation, it seemed quite clear to me that her diagnosis was correct.

Another patient came in with a similar statement regarding his diagnosis as having a Borderline Personality Disorder. He was wrong. His high level of arousal, his impulsive and abusive behavior, and his inability to maintain a relationship were far more diagnostic of intermittent explosive disorder, antisocial personality disorder, and his drug use.

When discussing the issues of assessment, conceptualization, treatment planning, treatment, and follow-up, I find that many clinicians are using unsupported formulations or partial data to support a diagnosis. For example, two psychology interns were describing a patient presently in a psychiatric facility who was, in their view, "very needy." She would ask various staff members for the same things. In the view of these interns, this was a clear example of "splitting," thereby earning this patient the diagnosis of "borderline." When I questioned them regarding where in the diagnostic criteria "splitting" could be found, they were surprised. Didn't everyone know that patients with BPD "split"? Too often, diagnoses are made when the patient meets one or two criteria. It is especially in the areas of conceptualization and case formulation that Sperry's work has been so important.

While the research on personality disorders has grown exponentially over the last several years, the conceptual models for understanding these disorders have remained rather stagnant. For example, Sharon Morgillo-Freeman (2004) has made the observation that most substance abusing patients are given a diagnosis of personality disorder when admitted to a psychiatric facility. When she compared the characteristics of individuals who have substance misuse problems and those that have been diagnosed with a personality disorder, she found a remarkable consonance.

The conventional wisdom seems to be that patients with personality disorders are difficult to treat. This comes from a lack of understanding of the disorder and the available treatments. This group is treated some- how differently from those patients who come to therapy with more typi- cal depressive or anxiety disorders. We can easily make the case that a severely depressed patient may be far harder to treat than a patient with a mild borderline disorder. We seem to forget that personality disorders can be of mild severity (those people that we work with and live with and for whom the personality disorder is an occasional impediment), moderate severity (those who have frequent contact with the mental health system and whose lives are generally negatively impacted by their disorder), and high severity (those who seem unable to function in their families, work environments, or relationships). Again, this is where Sperry shines. His 1995 *Handbook of the Diagnosis and Treatment of the DSM-IV Personality Disorders*, and its 2003 revision, his 1999 first edition of the present volume, *Cognitive Behavior Therapy of DSM-IV Personality Disorders*, and the current revision provide both the student and the practicing profes- sional with some of the best descriptions and clearest CBT treatment conceptualizations available anywhere.

The present volume far exceeds the accepted formula for a second edi- tion. He has taken reviews and critiques of the first volume and added significant new material of both conceptual and therapeutic issues. Hav- ing published several volumes on the topic of personality disorders, I am well aware of the problems and the pitfalls of a revision. Sperry has managed to skirt the crevasse and glide over the speed bumps. What has emerged is a readable, useable, and valuable text. Sperry's clinical experi- ence, his training as both a psychologist and as a psychiatrist, his grasp of the issues involved in the assessment, diagnosis, and treatment of patients with personality disorders is impressive. After describing and discussing the basics of CBT, he spends most of the volume describing the applica- tions of CBT. This is a volume to be read slowly and studied carefully. There are no quick fixes herein. In future editions I would recommend that the publishers provide larger margins so that the reader can take notes and write comments on the valuable insights that the author has offered because this revision has some of the best descriptions and clear- est CBT treatment conceptualizations available anywhere.

Arthur Freeman, Ed.D.
Co-author, *Cognitive Therapy of the Personality Disorders, 2nd ed.*

FOREWORD TO THE FIRST EDITION

We have all had the experience of taking a mid-morning coffee break and meeting colleagues in the coffee room only to find them staring into their cups. When we ask what they are experiencing they would respond, "I just saw three patients with severe depression in a row. I really feel down and need this coffee to pick me up." Or we might see colleagues in the coffee room in a state of high arousal and question them about their agitation. They might respond, "I just saw three patients with severe panic disorder in a row, and need the coffee to calm me down." Or we might take a mid-morning break and on our way to the coffee room we find colleagues wandering aimlessly through the corridors on their way to get coffee. We take them by the arm and guide them to the coffee room because we know that they have just seen three patients with severe personality disorder.

Given the long-term nature of patients with severe personality disorders, their general avoidance of psychotherapy, their frequent referral through family pressure or legal remand, and their seeming reluctance or inability to change, they are often the most difficult patients in a clinician's caseload. They generally require more work within a session, a longer time for therapy, and more therapist energy than do virtually any other patients. All of this expenditure occurs without the same rate of change and satisfaction as is gained with other patients.

These individuals typically come for therapy with presenting issues other than personality problems, most often with more typical Axis I complaints of depression and anxiety. The reported problems may be separate and apart from the Axis II patterns or derived and fueled by the Axis II personality disorder. For the combination of Axis I and Axis II diagnoses, the course of treatment is far more complicated than for the typical non-Axis II patient with the same presenting Axis I complaints. The duration of treatment, frequency of treatment sessions, goals and expectations for both therapist and patient, and the available techniques and strategies need to be altered in the treatment of patients who are diagnosed with personality disorders.

Personality-disordered patients will often see the difficulties that they encounter in dealing with other people or tasks as outside of them and independent of their behavior. Their behavior is generally ego-syntonic. Their behavior somehow makes sense to them and serves as part of their long-standing survival and coping strategies. Their style of behaving and responding seems normal and reasonable to them and they generally see the problems that they encounter in life as a product of other people's inappropriate behavior or ill will.

Patients with a personality disorder may have little idea about how they got to be the way they are, how they contribute to their life problems, or how to change. They are often referred by family members or friends who recognize a dysfunctional pattern or who have reached their personal limit in attempting to cope with this individual. Still other patients are referred by the judicial system. This latter group is often given a choice; for example, to go to prison or go to therapy. Other personality disordered patients are very much aware of the self-defeating nature of their personality problems (e.g., overdependence, inhibition, excessive avoidance) but are at a real loss as to how to change these patterns. Still other patients may have the motivation to change but do not have the skills to change.

The therapy of patients with various disorders of character or personality has been discussed in the clinical literature since the beginning of the recorded history of psychotherapy. The general literature on the psychotherapeutic treatment of personality disorders has emerged more recently and is growing quickly. The main theoretical orientation in the psychotherapeutic literature has been psychoanalytic. More recently, cognitive-behavioral therapists have offered a structured, active, and directive treatment approach and have advocated using a wide range of cognitive and behavioral techniques depending on the level of severity of the dysfunction. This is the first book I know of that convincingly emphasizes the clinical importance and relevance of the temperament dimension in the treatment of personality disorders.

Whereas some personality disorders are diagnosed rather early in treatment, a clinician may not be aware initially of the characterological nature, chronicity, and severity of the patient's personality problems. Early diagnosis is essential to appropriate triage and treatment. Following the assessment, the therapist must make sure that there is socialization or education of the patient to the treatment model. The ideas of what therapy involves, the goals and plans of the therapy, and the importance of therapeutic collaboration must be stressed. The initial therapeutic focus may be on relieving the presenting symptoms, that is, anxiety or depression. In helping the patient to deal with his or her anxiety or depression, the therapist can teach the patient the basic cognitive therapy skills that are going to be necessary in working with the more difficult personality disorder. If the therapist can help the patient become less depressed or less anxious, the patient may accept that this therapy may have some value after all, and it may be worthwhile continuing to work in therapy.

This book clearly articulates the distinction between the character and temperament dimensions of personality disorders. It then provides a variety of specific, clinically potent interventions for both sets of dimensions. Sperry emphasizes the affective, behavioral, and cognitive temperament "styles" each of us develop. In some cases, the Axis II disorder has been functional in life. Witness the style of the hard-driving executive who was up at 5:00 each morning and worked until 7:00 in the evening (behavioral style). Having worked so hard to be successful, financially secure, and a good provider for his family, he is at a loss to explain his difficulty at retirement. He feels himself to be a failure, on the basis of his lack of productivity (cognitive style). The same schema that drove him to be successful now drives him to depression and despair (affective style).

As another example, a 66-year-old man, diagnosed as both obsessive-compulsive and avoidant (behavioral style), stated, "The best time in my life was when I was in the army. I didn't have to worry about what to wear, what to do, where to go, or what to eat (cognitive style). I was really happy then (affective style)." We know that individuals with dependent personalities are sometimes ideal for service in the military, government bureaucracies, or large corporations because they are compliant with orders and procedures and follow orders well. However, when these styles stop working, individuals experience the depression and anxiety that may prompt their referral for therapy.

Given the difficulties inherent in working with the personality disorders, these patients can profit from therapy. What is essential is that therapists have a firm theoretical orientation, a reasonable conceptual framework for understanding the individual, and a broad spectrum of cognitive, affective, and behavioral interventions at their disposal. Much of the difficulty has revolved around the lack of a well-defined and articulated approach for treating the individual with a personality disorder. Dr. Sperry has synthesized his broad theoretical base, experience, sensitivity, and a sharp clinical acumen that offers a truly integrative approach to treating individuals with personality disorders. Examining six of the DSM-IV personality disorders, he takes the reader through his clinical thinking in terms of diagnosis, conceptualization, and treatment. Of especial value is the "bridging" nature of this volume. It incorporates psychodynamic, systemic, biological, and cognitive-behavioral formulations. It unashamedly discusses transference and countertransference along with the directive interventions that have demonstrated efficacy and come from the cognitive-behavioral work. Similarly, Sperry discusses the use and value of medication and psychotherapy as cooperative treatments with a goal of treating the patient from a biopsychosocial perspective (rather than as competitive and divisive and treating the patient as a combination of separate and discrete systems).

The real value of this book will be most evident with the more difficult to treat personality-disordered individuals. Sperry provides not only a clinically useful road map of the various phases of the treatment process (engagement, pattern analysis, pattern change, and pattern maintenance), but also an unmatched compilation of treatment resources—individual, group, family, medication, skill training, and combined treatment—all between two covers! This is about as user friendly as a book can be.

Experienced clinicians will appreciate and resonate with the author's general and specific treatment guidelines. For instance, Sperry advocates the use of specific behavioral interventions—sometimes in conjunction with medication—to reasonably modulate a patient's uncontrollable affects (temperament dimension) before attempting to interpret or cogni-tively restructure (character dimension).

In many ways, this is a comprehensive treatment manual for the treat-ment of the patient with a personality disorder. It is an approach to the treatment of personality disorders that is not only based on a sound theoretical framework, but also deftly guides the clinician safely around a variety of potential therapeutic land mines in the treatment process. And it offers the kind of therapeutic strategies that can maximize treat-ment outcomes. This exciting new book may just set the standard for other treatment texts!

Arthur Freeman, Ed.D.
Co-author, *Cognitive Therapy of the Personality Disorders*

PREFACE

When writing the preface to the first edition of this book, I suggested that a paradigm shift was underway in the treatment of personality disorders. Several markers were noted that reflected such a shift, among them a geometric progressive of research studies, articles, workshops, courses, and books promoting methods of treating personality disorders with results that were unimaginable even a few years ago. Today, there is no question that such a shift, as well as a transformation, in theory and research on personality disorders has taken place. There is also no question that the changes and advancements wrought by this shift have impacted clinical practice. Certainly, the most dramatic evidence of this continuing shift has been the degree of sophistication in planning and implementing treatment strategies. The following clinical illustration reflects these changes:

Two individuals presented for clinical treatment at the same time. Both were attractive single females in their late 20s, were college graduates, had similar presenting complaints, and had the same diagnosis: borderline personality disorder. Beyond these commonalities, they were actually quite different. Most notable was the fact that treatment interventions that were appropriate and effective in one case were inappropriate and ineffective in the other.

When Keri A. was brought to the emergency room by her boyfriend, she presented with agitation, dysphoria, and a laceration on her left wrist. Apparently, her boyfriend had been late in returning from an out-of-town business trip, and Keri thought that he was never going to show up for the candlelight dinner she had prepared for him. She became increasingly agitated believing he was out with another woman and slashed her left wrist. The boyfriend arrived at her apartment 20 minutes later and immediately transported her to the nearest hospital emergency room. This was only the second time in her life that this 28-year-old woman had acted out impulsively. Three years ago, she had slashed her wrist in similar circumstances involving her previous boyfriend. She reported a stable work history for the past 6 years following college graduation.

Recently, she was promoted to district manager. Keri described having four relatively close friends, including her roommate, whom she had known since her college days. She apparently related well with her co-workers, including her male boss. Although she maintained regular contact with her family, she admitted that her relationship with her mother was sometimes strained. Her Global Assessment Functioning (GAF) score on admission was 40, with the highest level in the past year estimated at 71. In the emergency room, she was administered a sedative and her wrist was sutured. After denying suicidal ideation and accepting a referral for outpatient psychiatric treatment, she was discharged. Keri began weekly treatment sessions later that week. This was her first adult experience with individual therapy; she had talked to a counselor in high school a few times after breaking up with a boyfriend. Keri responded well to a dynamic-oriented therapy, which involved the therapeutic confrontation method described by Masterson (Masterson & Klein, 1989). Keri's treatment spanned 42 sessions, spaced over a period of 18 months. Following termination of treatment, she married her boyfriend. In a letter she wrote to her clinician 2 years later, Keri indicated that she and her husband had recently given birth to their first child and that things were going quite well for her.

Cindy J. also presented in the emergency room with slashed wrists. She had been brought in by an ambulance called by her landlady. Apparently, after having her social security disability check stolen from her mail box and being "dumped"—her words—by her off-again, on-again boyfriend, she proceeded to get drunk and slashed both her wrists. In the emergency room, she was so angry and combative that she had to be restrained while her wrists were being sutured. Medical records showed that she had a long history of episodes of psychiatric treatment involving three psychiatrists, two social workers, and various medication trials, and there had been three prior suicide attempts (two involving overdosing on prescribed antidepressants). Compliance with clinical appointments during those episodes of care as well as compliance with prescribed medications was poor. She reported that following graduation from college—after 7 years of trying various majors—she worked at several jobs. In most of the positions she had held, she was underemployed, particularly in the past 3 years. She had started receiving social security disability some 18 months before her latest suicide attempt. She indicated that she had never really gotten along with her family, except for her father. Although she felt quite close to him as a child, he had become increasingly emotionally distant from her during her adolescence and continuing to the present. She reported having no real friends and felt rejected by everybody, except her small dog. In the emergency room, her GAF score was estimated to be 28, with her highest level in the previous year at 42. Because she verbalized continued suicidal ideation, she was hospitalized for 3 days and then transitioned into a partial hospitalization program for 6 months and then subsequently into an outpatient aftercare program, where she remained until some 3 years later. Because she had failed to respond to individual weekly therapy sessions in the past, she was referred to a partial hospitalization program with a focused treatment plan for patients with severe personality disorder. The program consisted of occupational therapy, preemployment training, medication groups, symptom management groups, and social skill training groups, in addition to weekly individual therapy sessions. After 6 months in the program, Cindy's GAF was 56. After 18 months, she was working steadily at a part-time job and continuing in a twice-weekly social skills training group and a biweekly medication group. Her GAF was then estimated at 68 when she "graduated" to monthly individual sessions consisting of supportive therapy and medication monitoring. She began working full-time as a department manager for a large retail store and continued in that capacity for the following 11 months without any further hospitalizations or suicide gestures.

Besides some obvious similarities of demographics and diagnosis, the clinical histories and treatment responses of Cindy and Keri were considerably different. The most obvious differences were in the level of symptomatic distress and level of functioning that reflected the extent of temperament dysregulation and adequacy of coping skills in both women. Figure P.1 illustrates the extent of temperament dysregulation for three style dimensions: affective style, behavior and relational style, and cognitive style. Clearly, there was significantly more dysregulation or overmodulation of the three styles in Cindy than in Keri.

Each responded to very different treatment strategies. Cindy would not, and probably could not, have responded—at least initially—to the treatment accorded Keri. Nor would it have been appropriate to offer Keri the treatment accorded to Cindy. Of necessity, much of the course of treatment for Cindy emphasized re-modulation of affective, behavioral/relational, and cognitive styles, whereas there was little such emphasis in Keri's treatment. In both instances, the treatment strategies used were individualized and tailored to the unique needs and circumstances of each patient.

In short, these cases illustrate that two individuals with the same Axis II diagnosis can and do have differential responses to treatment interventions. These cases reflect the new way in which a growing number of researchers and clinicians are conceptualizing and treating personality disorders today. As a result, there is increasing hope that many, if not most, individuals with personality disorders can be effectively treated and managed with focused treatment strategies and interventions. There

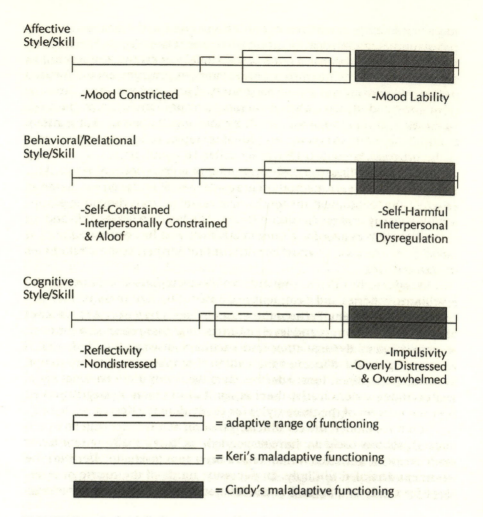

FIGURE P.1. Style/skill dimensions of borderline personality disorder.

is also some speculation that "cure" may some day be an expected treatment outcome.

Whereas it was once assumed that treatment even of milder personality disorders required years of intensive psychotherapy, published case reports and even prospective studies are indicating that shorter term treatment can be effective with even severe disorders, such as borderline personality disorder. Yet, it has not been all that long ago when many clinicians believed that most individuals with borderline personality disorder were untreatable and even unmanageable.

This book reflects the most recent developments in the treatment of personality disorders from a cognitive behavioral perspective. It focuses on how clinicians can increase their effectiveness and efficacy in treating individuals with personality disorders by adopting a focused and tailored treatment strategy. A basic premise underlying this book is that effective treatment is tailored treatment that is focused on both the style or temperament dimensions and the schematic or character dimensions of personality and the degree of severity of a given disorder. Furthermore, effective treatment often requires the use of adjunctive treatment modalities.

This book emphasizes the increasing applicability and effectiveness of a variety of cognitive and behavioral intervention strategies and tactics to treat individuals with personality disorders. Many of these interventions, which appeared after the first edition of this book was published, are included in this edition. These include: schema therapy, cognitive behavioral analysis system of psychotherapy, mindfulness-based cognitive therapy and similar "third-wave" approaches that emphasize mindfulness and acceptance. Also included are new developments in cognitive therapy and dialectic behavior therapy.

This book is divided into two parts. Part I introduces the reader to the paradigm shift that is occurring in clinical practice today with regard to the treatment of personality disorders. The three chapters in Part I provide the reader with an understanding and appreciation of the theory and interventions of cognitive behavior therapy.

Part II describes an integrative and practical approach to the treatment of six personality disorders that are commonly seen in clinical practice. It still is the opinion of many clinicians and researchers that six DSM-IV personality disorders—avoidant, borderline, dependent, histrionic, narcissistic, and obsessive-compulsive—are reasonably "treatable." Treatability means that not only can these six disorders be effectively managed in outpatient settings but, in some instances, might even be cured. The four remaining DSM-IV disorders (schizoid, schizotypal, paranoid, and antisocial personality disorders) are still considered less treatable and are less commonly seen in outpatient settings. Accordingly, they are not included in this edition. In short, the most common personality disorders seen in an outpatient setting are also the ones that are most treatable, and these six disorders are detailed in Part II.

The six chapters in Part II provide a brief overview of the key features of each disorder followed by an easy-to-follow "map" of the treatment process and its various phases: (a) engagement, (b) pattern analysis, (c) pattern change, and (d) termination and pattern maintenance, which includes follow-up and relapse prevention. Although this edition emphasizes the usefulness and effectiveness of cognitive behavioral interventions in the context of individual treatment, various other modalities and intervention strategies are also described. These include medication, group therapy and other group interventions, family interventions, and couples therapy.

The case example at the end of the chapter illustrates the process of treatment for each of these six disorders.

The book is intended as a "hands-on" manual for practicing clinicians as well as for clinicians-in-training. It offers clinicians a hopeful perspective on the treatability of these disorders and highly effective treatment protocols for achieving positive treatment outcomes. I trust it will make a difference in the lives of those who are afflicted with these disorders.

Len Sperry, M.D., Ph.D.

Part

Cognitive Behavior Therapy and Personality Disorders

Part I contains three chapters that lay the foundation for the treatment strategies for the specific personality disorders described in Part II.

Chapter 1, "Cognitive Behavior Therapy and Personality Disorders: Basic Considerations," describes the paradigm shift that is occurring in the conceptualization, assessment, and treatment of personality disorders today. The implications of this paradigm shift for effective treatment of personality disorders are then articulated in terms of basic premises of clinical intervention and the treatment process itself.

Chapter 2, "Cognitive Behavior Therapy Interventions with Personality Disorders: I," describes the character dimension of personality and its evolution and transformation into "schema" language. Schema is discussed with regard to the cognitive behavioral and psychodynamic traditions, and several schemas commonly noted among individuals with personality disorders are described. These schemas will be referred to repeatedly throughout Chapters 4–9. Next, new cognitive behavior therapy (CBT) approaches with particular relevance to personality disorders are described. These include schema therapy, cognitive behavioral analysis system of psychotherapy, mindfulness-based cognitive therapy and similar "third-wave" approaches that emphasize mindfulness and acceptance. Also included are new developments in cognitive therapy and dialectic behavior therapy.

Chapter 3, "Cognitive Behavior Therapy Interventions with Personality Disorders: II," continues the discussion of Chapter 2. It briefly describes the temperament dimension in personality and its revival in the formulation and treatment of personality disorders. Sixteen specific treatment interventions targeted to modifying temperament or style are described. It seems that clinicians who attempt to provide effective treatment to patients with severe personality disorders must have sufficient capability to use these or similar interventions. Because many of these interventions are not commonly used by clinicians, each is described in some detail, along with key references for additional information. These interventions will be referred to repeatedly throughout Chapters 4–9.

CHAPTER

Cognitive Behavior Therapy of Personality Disorders: Basic Considerations

Whether or not clinicians believe that a paradigm shift is occurring in clinical practice, it is difficult to deny that major changes in the treatment of the personality disorders have occurred in the past decade. These changes involve not only radically different treatment methods, but also rather different theories, conceptualizations, criteria, and assessment methods. Not surprisingly, theoretical speculation about personality disorders has greatly increased. However, what is surprising is the growing number of theories on personality disorders that are research based (Clarkin & Lenzenweger, 1996). Language to describe personality disorders has also changed dramatically.

Before 1980, personality disorders were typically conceptualized in "character language," with such terms as "the oral character" or "the obsessive character." In the study of personality, although there was a biological tradition that emphasized temperament, a psychological tradition that emphasized character was in vogue for most of the 20th century. Descriptions of personality disorders in the *Diagnostic and Statistical Manual* (DSM)-I and DSM-II reflected this emphasis on character and psychodynamics. Within the psychoanalytic community, character reflected specific defense mechanisms. Accordingly, the defenses of isolation of affect, intellectualization, and rationalization were common in the obsessive character.

☐ Changes in the Conceptualization of Personality Disorders

Currently, personality disorders are being conceptualized in a broader perspective that includes both character and temperament. Neurobiological and biosocial formulations of personality disorders have attracted considerable attention and have generated a significant amount of research. Millon (1996) and Cloninger (1993) hypothesized that temperament and neurotransmitters greatly influence personality development and functioning. Like many others, both Stone (1993), a psychoanalyst, and Cloninger (2005), a neurobiological psychiatrist, described personality as the confluence of both character and temperament.

Character refers to the learned, psychosocial influences on personality. Character forms largely because of the socialization process, particularly with regard to cooperativeness, and the mirroring process that promotes the development of self-concept and a sense of purpose in life (i.e., self-transcendence and self-responsibility). Another way of specifying the characterological component of personality is with the term *schema*. Whether in the psychoanalytic tradition (Horowitz, 1988; Slap & Slap-Shelton, 1991) or in the cognitive therapy tradition (Beck, 1964; Young, 1990), "schema" refers to the basic beliefs individuals use to organize their view of the self, the world, and the future. Schema has historically been more central to the cognitive tradition and the cognitive-behavioral tradition than to the psychoanalytic tradition, but this apparently is changing (Stein & Young, 1992). Schema and schema change and modification strategies are central to this book.

Temperament refers to the innate, genetic, and constitutional influences on personality. Whereas character and schema reflect the psychological dimension of personality, temperament (or style, as it is used synonymously in this book) reflects the biological dimension of personality. Cloninger (2005) contends that temperament has four biological dimensions (novelty-seeking, harm-avoidance, reward-dependence, and persistence), whereas character has three quantifiable dimensions (self-directedness or self-responsibility, cooperativeness, and self-transcendence). Other researchers have described impulsivity and aggressivity as additional dimensions of temperament (Costello, 1996).

Temperament and character can be assessed by interviews and self-report instruments. The relevance of distinguishing between character and temperament for treatment planning is significant. Insight-oriented psychotherapy may focus on the character dimensions but will have little or no impact on temperament dimensions. For example, in the case of Cindy, who displayed significant dysregulation of temperament (i.e., impulsivity, harm avoidance, and aggressivity), medications and individual psychotherapy were not sufficient to effect change. In addition to these, focused skill training and the structured milieu of a partial hospitalization program were necessary to sufficiently regulate or modulate her affect and behavior; she could then profit from individual and group therapy directed at the character dimensions. On the other hand, in the case of Keri, her temperament was sufficiently modulated that psychotherapy could be the principal treatment directed primarily at the character issues.

☐ Changes in Diagnostic Criteria for Personality Disorders

In the past, criteria for personality disorders were somewhat primitive. DSM-I categorized personality disorders under five headings: personality pattern disturbance, personality trait disturbance, sociopathic personality disturbance, special symptom reactions, and transient situational personality disorders. DSM-II, which appeared in 1968, eliminated the subheadings and streamlined the categorization of personality disorders; however, the descriptions were not based on clinical trials. Although a brief description of each disorder was given, diagnostic criteria were not provided. Furthermore, there was no clear distinction made between symptom disorders (Axis I) and personality disorders (Axis II). This lack of specificity also reinforced some erroneous notions about personality disorders. A notable example is the distinction between obsessive-compulsive disorder and obsessive-compulsive personality disorder. Prior to DSM-III, no distinction was made between these disorders, but today, there is general consensus that these disorders have relatively little overlap (Jenike, 1991). The earlier belief about the inherent similarity of these disorders could be attributed to Freud's description of the case of the Rat Man, in whom both obsessive-compulsive disorder and obsessive-compulsive personality disorder happened to be comorbid conditions. The inference was that these disorders were essentially the same and so treatment should be the same for both. Jenike noted that the chances of co-occurrence of obsessive-compulsive disorder and obsessive-compulsive personality disorder in a patient are small, probably less than 15–18%.

The diagnositic criteria presented in DSM-IV have been considerably refined. However, while these criteria are useful in ruling in or ruling out a personality disorder, they are not particularly useful in planning treatment (Sperry, 2003). For one thing, no weight is given to specific criteria. For another, some criteria seem to reflect character features of disorders, while others reflect temperament features. Because the criteria are not clearly identified or weighted, they have little value in formulating treatment. For instance, among the nine criteria for borderline personality disorder, four seem to reflect temperament features—4 and 5 involve dysregulated cognitive style (impulsivity), 6 and 8 involve dysregulated affective style—whereas the other five reflect character features. DSM-IV requires that *any* five or more criteria—whether they reflect character features or temperament features—are needed to rule in the diagnosis of borderline personality disorder. This lack of specificity is unfortunate.

When we review the cases of Keri and Cindy presented in the preface, we find Keri to meet four character criteria and possibly only one temperament criterion (#5)—her wrist-slashing—which, however, could hardly be considered recurrent suicidal behavior. On the other hand, we would find that Cindy meets all four of the temperament criteria and three of the character criteria. Most clinicians would disagree that Cindy's treatment will be much more complex and challenging than Keri's, largely because of the difficultly in modulating impulsivity, mood lability, and angry outbursts, all of which reflect temperament. In short, it would be clinically useful if future editions of the DSM assigned specific weight and identification to all of the criteria.

□ Changes in the Assessment of Personality Disorders

In the past, assessment of personality disorders was based on clinical interviews and inferred from standardized personality inventories, such as the MCMI (Millon, 1996). Today, there are a number of formal measures of personality disorders. Some,, such as Cloninger's (1993) Temperament Character Inventory (TCI), are based on theory and research. There are a number of semistructured schedules available, for example, the Structured Clinical Interview for DSM-III-R Personality Disorders (SCID-II).

In large part, these assessment measures reflect the increasingly differentiated criteria of DSM-III, DSM-III-R, and DSM-IV. DSM-III subdivided 11 personality disorders—antisocial, avoidant, borderline, compulsive, dependent, histrionic, narcissistic, paranoid, passive-aggressive, schizoid, and schizotypal—into three clusters: odd, dramatic, and anxious. DSM-III-R maintained the essential features of DSM-III but added sadistic and self-defeating personality disorders to the appendix. DSM-IV further differentiated the criteria but dropped the self-defeating and sadistic personality disorders from the group. Passive-aggressive personality disorder was relegated to the personality disorder category "not otherwise specified"

(NOS); depressive personality disorder along with passive-aggressive personality disorder, was placed in Appendix B of DSM-IV.

☐ Changes in the Treatment of Personality Disorders

In comparison with earlier treatments of personality disorders, which were rather generic, current treatment methods tend to be considerably more focused and structured, with the clinician taking a more active role. Many of these treatment approaches and intervention strategies are theory based and have been researched in clinical trials.

Cognitive Behavior Therapies

For the last two decades, behavior therapy, cognitive therapy, and cognitive behavior therapy (CBT) were the treatments of choice for the psychosocial treatment of personality disorders. While research did not consistently support the efficacy of these traditional approaches, it does support that of the newer, more focused approaches, such as dialectic behavior therapy (DBT) and mindfulness-based cognitive therapy (MBCT). Interestingly, DBT and MBCT, along with acceptance and commitment therapy (Hayes, 2004), constitute what is being called the "third wave" of behavior therapy (Hayes, Follette, & Linehan, 2004).

The first wave refers to traditional behavior therapy, which endeavors to replace problematic behaviors with constructive ones through counter-conditioning and reinforcement. Cognitive therapy constitutes the second wave and works to modify problem behaviors by changing the thoughts that cause and perpetuate them. The third wave, in which treatment tends to be more experiential and indirect, utilizes such techniques as mindfulness, dialectics, acceptance, values, and spirituality. More specifically, third-wave approaches are characterized by "letting go of the attempts at problems solving and, instead, standing back to see what it feels like to see the problems through the lens of nonreactivity and to bring a kindly awareness to the difficulty" (Segal, Williams, Teasdale, & Williams, 2004, p. 55). Unlike the first- and second-wave approaches, third-wave approaches emphasize second-order change, that is, basic change in structure and/or function, and are based on contextual assumptions, including the primacy of the therapeutic relationship. These approaches appear to be particularly germane to treating personality disorders. Extended discussions of

DBT and MBCT in the treatment of a wide range of personality disorders appear in Chapters 2 and 3 and are selectively referenced in Chapters 4 through 9.

Psychodynamic Therapies

Fifty years ago, psychoanalysis along with long-term psychoanalytically oriented psychotherapy was considered the treatment of choice for personality disorders. The goal of treatment was to change character structure. Unfortunately, outcomes were mixed, even among patients judged amenable to treatment (Stone, 1993). However, as psychoanalytic treatment has become more focused and specific to personality disorders, this approach appears to be effective. In fact, in head-to-head comparisons, both psychodynamic psychotherapy and CBT are reported to have similar efficacy. Some of these studies are reviewed here.

A recently published meta-analysis of the two approaches included 14 studies of psychodynamic therapy (including 6 randomized controlled trials) and 11 studies of cognitive behavior therapy (including 5 randomized controlled trials). Results indicated that both approaches were effective. Psychodynamic psychotherapy was seen to produce larger effect sizes than did CBT, but it was noted that this was confounded by differences in specific personality disorder diagnoses, measures, treatment durations, and follow-up (Perry, 2004). Results of another meta-analysis showed similar overall findings (Leichsenring & Leibing, 2003).

When specific diagnoses are considered, the results appear to show no differences between the psychodynamic and cognitive approaches. This was noted in a study comparing a short-term dynamic psychotherapy with cognitive therapy for outpatients with Cluster C personality disorders, such as avoidant, dependent, and obsessive compulsive personality disorders. In this study, 50 patients were randomly assigned to receive 40 weekly sessions of short-term dynamic psychotherapy or cognitive therapy. The therapists involved in the study were experienced, full-time clinicians who received manual-guided supervision. Results indicated statistically significant improvements on all measures during treatment and in the 2-year follow-up period, although no statistically significant differences were found between the dynamic and cognitive therapy groups. Two years after treatment, 54% of the patients in the short-term dynamic psychotherapy group and 42% of those in the cognitive therapy group had recovered symptomatically, whereas approximately 40% of the patients in both groups had recovered with regard to interpersonal problems and personality functioning (Svartberg, Stiles, & Seltzer, 2004). It should be pointed out that Cluster C disorders may be more responsive to conventional psychotherapeutic approaches, such as dynamic psychotherapy and cognitve therapy, than Cluster A or B disorders. It could be argued that the results of this study would have been considerably different if the treatment subjects had been individuals with severe borderline personality disorder.

Medication

Traditionally, the use of medication in the treatment of personality disorders was viewed as limited. Medication tended to be utilized only for treating concurrent Axis I conditions or a target symptom, such as insomnia. This view is rapidly changing. Today, a growing number of psychopharmacologists believe that psychopharmacological treatment can and should be directed to basic dimensions that underlie the personality. Psychopharmacological research on treatments for selected personality disorders has grown rapidly in the past few years (Reich, 2002; Sperry, 2003). Until recently, drug therapy of individuals with personality-disorders has been largely empirical, that is, largely on a trial-and-error basis. That is because, generally, there are no specific drug treatments for DSM-IV-TR personality disorders as there are for panic disorder or major depressive disorder. The possible exception is venlafaxine (Effexor), a selective serotonin-norepinephrine uptake inhibitor, which has been particularly effective at reducing avoidant personality traits. Since avoidant personality disorder appears to be only quantitatively different from social phobia, it is possible that the medications that are effective in treating social phobia are likely to be effective with avoidant personality disorder as well (Altamura, et al., 1999; Reich, 2000).

Even though there are currently no specific psychotropic agents for treating specific personality disorders—except as noted above—there appears to be growing confidence that drug treatment can be effective if it focuses on maladaptive personality traits or temperament styles associated with various personality disorders. There is mounting clinical research evidence—including some double-blinded studies—that specific medications can effectively target such maladaptive personality traits as impulsivity, anger and aggression, inhibition, suspiciousness, and mood lability (Reich, 2005).

Combined Treatment

There is growing consensus, among all segments of the psychiatric community, that effective treatment of the personality disorders involves combining treatment modalities and integrating treatment approaches (Sperry, 1995a). Notably, psychoanalytically oriented psychiatrists advocate combined treatment, particularly for severe personality disorders (Gabbard, 2005; Stone, 1993; Winer & Pollock, 1989). Stone suggested combining three approaches: (a) supportive interventions, which are particularly useful in fostering a therapeutic alliance; augmented by (b) psychoanalytic interventions, which are useful in resolving negative transferences at the outset of treatment; and (c) cognitive-behavioral interventions, which are useful in the development of new attitudes and habits. Combining medication with individual and group modalities can also increase effectiveness. Such efforts to integrate various approaches as well as treatment modalities would have been considered heretical just a few years ago. Now, combining treatment approaches is an emerging consensus, which reflects the immensity of the "paradigm shift" that is occurring (Beitman, 2003; Sperry, 2003).

☐ Basic Premises About Effective Treatment of Personality Disorders

The paradigm shift in clinicians' attitudes and practice styles with regard to personality disorders was discussed in terms of conceptualization, assessment, and treatment. Consistent with this paradigm shift, this book provides a number of specific effective intervention strategies based on the following premises.

Premise #1: Maximizing Readiness for Change Is Essential in the Effective Treatment of Personality Disorders

Readiness for treatment and level of functioning reflects a patient's treatability and prognosis (Sperry, 1995a). As will be described in more detail later in this chapter, *patient readiness* refers to the individual patient's motivation and expectations for treatment outcomes and can be assessed in terms of four levels—in addition to past history of treatment compliance and success at efforts to change habits and behavior patterns. Level of functioning can be operationalized in terms of the Global Assessment of Functioning (GAF) scale of Axis IV. High functioning refers to a score of about 65, moderate functioning to 45–65, and low functioning to below 45.

Personality disorders can be classified in *terms of treatability*: (a) *high amenability* includes dependent, histrionic, obsessive-compulsive, avoidant, and depressive personality disorders; (b) *intermediate amenability* includes narcissistic, borderline, and schizotypal personality disorders; and (c) *low-amenability* includes paranoid, passive aggressive, schizoid, and antisocial personality disorders. In addition, because patients show mixtures of various personality features or disorders, prognosis for the low-amenability category is largely dependent on the degree to which features of the disorders are present (Stone, 1993). Prognosis will also depend in part on the prominence of the psychobiological dimensions (Siever & Davis, 1993; Reich, 2005): cognitive/perceptual disorganization; impulsivity/aggression, and affective instability or anxiety/inhibition. To the extent that such dimensions as impulsivity or anxiety respond to medication, concurrent psychosocial intervention efforts should be facilitated.

Premise #2: Combined, Tailored, and Integrative Treatment Modalities Become Increasingly Necessary as the Level of Treatability Gets Lower

Combined treatment refers to adding such modalities as individual, group, couple, and family therapies, either concurrently or sequentially. *Integrative treatment* refers to the blending of different treatment approaches or orientation, such as psychodynamic, cognitive, behavioral, interpersonal, and the like. *Tailored treatment* refers to specific ways of customizing treatment modalities and therapeutic approaches to "fit" the unique needs, cognitive and emotional styles, and treatment expectations of individual patients. Treatments delivered in combination can have an additive, and sometimes synergistic, effect.

On the one hand, the higher the patient's treatability, the less may be the need or immediacy for combining and blending most of the modalities and approaches. On the other hand, the lower the level of treatability, the more the modalities and approaches will need to be combined and blended.

Premise #3: Effective Treatment of Personality Disorders Is Guided by General and Specific Treatment Goals

General treatment goals involving personality disorders can be specified in four levels. First-level goals involve reducing symptoms. Second-level goals involve modulating the temperament dimension of personality. Third-level goals involve reducing impaired social, occupational, and relational functioning. Finally, fourth-level goals involve modifying the character or schema dimension of personality. It should be noted that Level 2 and Level 4 goals involve modification rather than radical restructuring. Stone (1993) used the analogy of the cabinet maker and carpenter to illustrate treatment goals with regard to character and temperament. He likened the clinician working with an individual with a personality disorder to a cabinet maker who sands down the rough edges of a structure, unlike a carpenter, who rebuilds the structure. The patient's character and temperament remain, but treatment renders the individual somewhat easier to work with and live with.

Level 1 and Level 3 goals are easier to achieve than are Level 2 and 4 goals. Medication and behavioral treatments, such as exposure or thought stopping, may quickly remit symptoms. Advice, limit-setting, encouragement, and environmental restructuring are often useful to the patient in achieving higher levels of life functioning. Perhaps the most challenging and time-intensive aspect in the treatment of personality disorders involves modifying character and modulating temperament. Psychotherapeutic interventions are principally used for modifying character, while medication and skill training have been more effective in modulating temperament.

Both clinical experience (Freeman & Davison, 1997; Sperry, 2003) and research (Linehan, Heard, & Armstrong, 1993) suggest that modulation of temperament or styles must come before modification of character structure or schemas. *Modulation* refers to normalizing affective, behavioral, or cognitive style or responsivity that is either excessive or insufficient. Usually, this strategy is required in the case of individuals with lower-functioning personality disorders because under- or over-modulated temperament and acting-out style renders them unready and unprepared for therapies oriented to character modification. It is only when their temperament is adequately modulated that they will have sufficient self-restraint and resources to benefit from standard psychotherapies. Attempting to modify character before modulating temperament can result in negative reactions to therapy. The patient will either act out or regress, which often leads to rehospitalization. The prototypical example is the articulate but lower- to moderate-functioning borderline patient who insists on processing, or goes along with the clinician's desire to process, early abuse issues. Soon thereafter, the clinician is caught by surprise when the patient exhibits a preoccupation with suicidal thoughts or has significantly regressed so that hospitalization becomes necessary (Linehan, 1993). The initial goal of Linehan's dialectical behavior therapy with borderline patients is to achieve an adequate degree of modulation such that the patients are more disposed to continuation of treatment.

Linehan utilized various interventions to modulate patients' affective lability, impulsiveness, and parasuicidal and other acting-out behaviors before shifting the focus to more characterological issues. Her research—a prospective study—indicates that this treatment strategy is significantly better in reducing rehospitalization, parasuicidality, and treatment dropout than is traditional treatment (Linehan, Heard, & Armstrong, 1993).

Effective treatment of personality disorders is guided not only by general treatment goals, but also by specific treatment goals, which will be elaborated on in Chapters 4 through 9. These goals address specific treatment targets. For example, take schema change. In cognitive therapy, specific treatment goals can be stated in terms of the level of schema change that is possible or desirable. There are four levels of schema change, which can range from the maximal level of change, called "schema reconstruction," to the minimal level of change, called "schema camouflage" (Beck, Freeman, Davis, & Associates, 2004). These four levels and their treatment indications and implications are detailed in Chapter 2.

Premise #4: When a Patient Presents with More Than One Personality Disorder, Each Disorder Is Initially Treated Separately

It is not unusual for patients to present with two or more personality disorders (Millon, 1996). In such instances, the manifestations of each disorder usually do not occur simultaneously, nor are the features of the disorders blended. In other words, the characterological and temperament or style manifestations of two personality disorders present more like chocolate-swirled vanilla ice cream than a homogeneous mixture of red and yellow resulting in orange. In other words, both disorders are relatively discrete and intact at any one time.

For example, in the early phases of treatment, the clinician working with an individual who meets the criteria for both obsessive-compulsive personality disorder and narcissistic personality disorder will observe the characteristic drivenness and ambivalence of the obsessive-compulsive personality at some points in the session, and a few minutes later, he may encounter the entitlement and grandiosity of the narcissistic personality.

A suggested overall treatment strategy in working with patients with more than one personality disorder is to focus principally on the character and temperament or style features of the more distressing or troubling disorder. As manifestations of the other disorder(s) become operative, deal with them and then return to the principal focus. A marker of real change in treatment is that the separate manifestations of the different disorders become less pronounced and muted to the point where the features now appear to blend (Sperry, 2003).

For didactic purposes, it has been necessary to focus in each of the chapters of this book—and in the case examples cited—on single disorders. Focusing on a single disorder does not mean that effective treatment for individuals who commonly present with more than one personality disorder is not achievable or that it requires considerably more time or expertise. Rather, the clinician need only attend to this premise and focus treatment on the predominant disorder, recognizing that when manifestations of the other disorder(s) arise, they will be recognized and dealt with accordingly.

☐ An Effective Treatment Strategy for Personality Disorders

The treatment strategy proposed in this book is rather straightforward. Treatment must be specifically planned with regard to the four stages of the treatment process, and it must be specifically tailored on the basis of the patient's needs, style, level of readiness, and expectations of treatment. This section describes the four stages of the treatment process and how treatment should be tailored.

Stages of the Treatment Process

The process of change and the types of interventions required for the effective treatment of personality disorders are similar to the general therapeutic processes and interventions used to treat symptom disorders, but they differ in focus and emphasis. Beitman (1991; 2003) has articulated the general change processes and compatible interventions in both psychotherapy and psychopharmacotherapy. The Beitman model describes four developmental stages of the treatment process: engagement, pattern search, change, and termination. As applied to the treatment of personality disorders, these stages need to be somewhat modified. The stages of engagement, pattern identification, pattern change, and pattern maintenance are described below and will be illustrated in subsequent chapters with regard to specific personality disorders.

Engagement

Engagement is the principal therapeutic process in the early phase of treatment. Engagement requires the patient to trust, respect, and accept the influence of the provider. The building of trust and respect results in psychological connection and commitment. The provider's empathic stance toward the patient is essential to establishing a working therapeutic relationship, or therapeutic bond. Engagement is a necessary prelude to psychotherapy and psychopharmacotherapy, and until it is achieved, little, if any, change is possible. This is not to say that unengaged patients will not attend sessions—they might—but there is little likelihood that any positive movement will occur. One early indication that engagement has been achieved is the patient's willingness to collaborate and take increasing responsibility for making necessary changes in his or her life.

By definition, collaboration means that *both* parties take responsibility. It is for this reason that the clinician must ensure, from the very outset, that the first task of treatment is to develop a collaborative working relationship. In such a relationship, both clinician and patient agree to focus their energies on the same treatment goals and objectives. It is the patient's responsibility to pursue the mutually agreed-upon goals and objectives. And when patients sidestep or move away from an agreed-upon goal, it is the clinician's responsibility to confront the diversion. Therapeutic confrontation is used to return the patient to the treatment goal and refocus the attention on the here and now of the therapeutic transaction. The clinician might say: "Wait a minute! What's going on between us that *we* ended up here? *We* agreed to work on ____. What happened?" Emphasizing the "we" is crucial in a collaborative effort because both need to accept responsibility. Typically, the manner in which the patient with a borderline disorder deviates and moves away from the agreed-upon treatment goal or objective then becomes the focus. Thoughts or discussions about a troubling relationship or a failure to achieve personal goals will result in a move away from the original goal to the extent that the patient feels threatened. The clinician has to process the focus sufficiently until the goals are sufficiently realigned. By definition, individuals with personality disorders find it difficult to cooperate and collaborate, much less take responsibility for their own behavior.

Engagement involves a socialization process that culminates in a formal or informal treatment contract and includes such elements as fee, length of sessions, and duration of treatment, and education about the treatment process. Even more important are clarification and negotiation of expectations, goals, role behaviors, and responsibilities for both patient and clinician for the treatment process.

A critical task of the engagement stage is to assess the patient's readiness and motivation for treatment and, if necessary, increase them. Four levels of readiness for change can be noted (Prochaska & DiClementi, 1982): *precontemplation,* when the patient denies illness or any need for treatment; *contemplation,* when the patient accepts the presence of the illness and the need for treatment but has not decided to make changes; *action*, when the individual has decided to and has begun making changes; and *maintenance,* when the patient sustains the change and avoids relapse. Low readiness for treatment is noted in precontemplation and contemplation is reflected in treatment resistance and noncompliance in various ways: missing or being late for appointments, failure to take the prescribed medications or to complete intersession assignments, or minimal or no progress in treatment. If the patient does not show sufficient treatment readiness, the provider's task is to focus on the readiness issue before proceeding with formal psychotherapy or psychopharmacotherapy. Motivational counseling is a potent strategy for increasing readiness for change (Miller & Rollnick, 1991).

Predictably, transference and countertransference issues emerge in the engagement stage in subtle and not-so-subtle ways. This is particularly true in the treatment of individuals with personality disorders. In the following chapter, transference and countertransference issues for specific personality disorders are noted, along with suggested intervention strategies.

Pattern Analysis

Pattern identification involves the elucidation of the patient's maladaptive pattern that reflects the manner of thinking, acting, feeling, coping, and defending self. In the context of this book, *pattern analysis* refers to the patient's specific schemas or characterological features, style or temperament features, pattern triggers, levels of functioning, and readiness for change: Various assessment strategies can be used to identify the pattern. These include a functional evaluation interview, personality testing, and the elicitation of early recollection or core schemas. To the extent that the clinician understands and appreciates this formulation—particularly the predisposing factors and perpetuating factors unique to the patient—confrontation tactics, interpretations, cognitive restructuring, and behavioral interventions will tend to be more focused and efficacious.

Pattern Change

The purpose of defining underlying maladaptive patterns is to modify or change them. In the case of individuals with personality disorders, the focus on therapeutic change must, of necessity, include both schemas and styles. The treatment goal and process of therapeutic change involve three tasks: (a) the disordered or maladaptive pattern is relinquished; (b) a more adaptive pattern is adopted; and (c) the new pattern is generalized—that is, thoughts, feelings, and actions are maintained. The general treatment strategy is to effect sufficient change or modulation in styles *before* attempting to change or modify schemas. Specific strategies for pattern change target specific disordered styles and schemas.

Disordered or maladaptive schemas are enduring, inflexible, and pervasive core beliefs about self and the world, which greatly impact thoughts and behaviors. The goal of treatment is to effect some measure of change in these beliefs such that they are more flexible and functional. Treatment can either restructure, modify, or reinterpret schemas (Layden, Newman, Freeman, & Morse, 1993).

Disordered styles are either undermodulated or overmodulated, and the goal of treatment is to achieve some measure of modulation. These patients' styles are unmodulated because of their temperaments as well as their failure to learn sufficient self-control. Self-control involves a number of personal and interpersonal skills necessary to function in day-to-day circumstances with some degree of competence. It is necessary to teach the patient the concept of modulation in the context of overmodulation or undermodulation. *Modulation* is the state in which thought precedes action, spontaneity is experienced without pretense or exaggeration, and coping with problems leads to effective and responsible behavior.

Needless to say, many individuals with personality disorders never adequately learned these skills during their formative years. Thus, it is often necessary to reverse these specific skill deficits. These skills are learned and practiced within an individual or group treatment context.

Pattern Maintenance

As the new pattern becomes fixed in the patient's life, the issue of preventing relapse and recurrence needs to be addressed. Formal treatment sessions become less necessary, and the termination of such sessions becomes the next issue to consider. The elements of the termination process are relatively predictable compared with the wide range of possibilities present in the pattern identification and change stages. Patients—and providers—often have difficulty with separation. New symptoms or old ones may appear, prompting requests for additional sessions. Presumably, when difficulty with separation or a sense of abandonment have already been noted in the maladaptive pattern, treatment will have focused on this issue.

Tailoring Treatment

Tailoring treatment involves making treatment selection decisions that provide a reasonably good "fit" between the patient's needs, style, and level of readiness and his or her treatment expectations and the available therapeutic resources. A basic premise of this book is that the lower the patient's level of treatability, the more the treatment must be tailored.

According to Francis, Clarkin, and Perry (1984), the process of treatment selection, no matter how divergent in theory or style, involves decision making in five domains: setting, format, time, approach, and somatic treatment.

Setting refers to the place in which treatment occurs: inpatient or outpatient clinic, private office, day hospital, or a residential treatment center.

Format indicates the context of treatment and is a function of direct participants in the treatment (individual, group, family, couple), medication monitoring, or some combination of modalities, such as: individual–medication, individual–group, individual–couple, medication–group, or even individual–couple–medication.

Time refers to the length and frequency of sessions as well as the duration of treatment. Duration of treatment might be brief or long term, time-limited, open-ended, or discontinuous. Sessions might be scheduled two or more times per week, weekly, biweekly, monthly, bimonthly, or less often.

Approach refers to the treatment orientation, methods, and strategies used by the provider. These range from dynamic to cognitive-behavioral to psychoeducational or supportive.

Somatic treatments typically refer to psychotropic medications or electroconvulsive therapy but also can include nutritional counseling, an exercise prescription, or referral for psychosurgery.

The provider also has a metadecision that overrides the consideration of these five components. That is, should any treatment be provided at all, or should "no treatment" be the recommendation of choice? Francis, Clarkin, and Perry (1984) specified the types of patients at risk for negative therapeutic reaction as well as those at risk for no response to treatment. They also described the relative indications for the "no treatment" option. Not surprisingly, they indicated that the "no treatment" option is most often appropriate for patients with severe personality disorders, particularly those with a diagnosis of borderline personality disorder.

Tailored treatment often involves combining treatment modalities and approaches (Sperry, 2001). Treatments delivered in combination can have an additive, and sometimes synergistic, effect. It is becoming more evident that different treatment approaches are differentially effective in resolving different types of symptom clusters. For example, in major depression, medication is more effective in remitting vegetative symptoms, whereas psychotherapy is better at improving interpersonal relations and cognitive symptoms.

☐ Summary

This chapter has described some of the significant changes that are occurring in the treatment of personality disorders, with particular emphasis on changes in the conceptualization, assessment, and treatment of Axis II disorders. Conceptualizing and assessing personality disorders in terms of the dual dimensions of character and temperament set the stage for introducing the cognitive-behavioral approach to schema or character change and to style or temperament change. The chapter then articulated four basic premises for the effective treatment of personality disorders in an outpatient setting. On the basis of these premises, a treatment strategy that delineates a four-stage approach—engagement, pattern analysis, pattern change, and pattern maintenance—was described. Finally, a second facet of this treatment strategy, tailoring, was briefly described. Chapters 4 through 9 illustrate the two aspects of this treatment strategy— four-stage approach and tailoring—for specific personality disorders.

Cognitive Behavior Therapy Interventions with Personality Disorders: I

This chapter sets the stage for the cognitive behavior therapy (CBT) of specific personality disorders (covered in Chapters 4–9) by emphasizing CBT interventions that are particularly effective in modifying schemas and basic character structure. The chapter begins by discussing the constructs of character and schema. It then articulates how the construct of schema is understood in two psychological traditions: the psychodynamic and the cognitive behavioral. The remainder of the chapter is an overview of recent major developments in the understanding and treatment of the personality disorders within the cognitive behavioral tradition. Besides reviewing revisions in cognitive therapy, schema therapy, and dialectical behavior therapy, it introduces two newer approaches—cognitive behavior analysis system of psychotherapy and mindfulness-based cognitive therapy—that show considerable promise in the treatment of the personality disorders. Furthermore, cognitive coping therapy and structured treatment interventions are briefly described.

☐ Character

Character refers to the learned, psychosocial influences on personality. Because character is essentially learned, it follows that it can be changed through such processes as psychotherapy. Largely because of the influence of Freud and his followers, psychotherapy and psychiatric treatment focused almost exclusively on the dimension of character to the point where personality essentially became synonymous with character. Character forms largely because of the socialization process, particularly with regard to cooperativeness, and the mirroring process that promotes the development of self-concept and a sense of purpose in life (i.e., self-transcendence and self-responsibility). Character can be assessed by both structured interviews and self-report inventories. On the temperament character inventory (Cloninger, 1993), character is measured by three character dimensions: cooperativeness, self-directedness—also called self-responsibility—and self-transcendence. Healthy personality reflects positive or elevated scores on these three dimensions, and personality disorders reflect negative or low scores on them. Furthermore, individuals with low scores on one or more of the character dimensions and increased dysregulation of one or more of the temperament dimensions typically experience either considerable distress or impairment in life functioning or both. For example, the individual with borderline personality disorder would likely rate high in two temperament dimensions but low in character dimensions of self-directedness and cooperation.

☐ Schema

Another way of describing the characterological component of personality is with the term *schema*. Whether in the psychoanalytic tradition (Horowitz, 1988; Slap & Slap-Shelton, 1981) or the cognitive therapy tradition (Beck, 1964; Young, Klosko & Weishaar, 2003), "schema" refers to the basic beliefs individuals use to organize their view of the self, the world, and the future. Although the concept of schema has historically been more central to the cognitive tradition and the cognitive-behavioral tradition than to the psychoanalytic tradition, this apparently is changing (Stein & Young, 1992). Schema and schema change and modification strategies are central to this book. The remainder of this chapter reviews some different conceptualizations of schema and then describes several schemas useful in clinical practice.

Adler first used the term *schema of apperception* in 1929 to refer to the individual's view of the self and the world. For Adler, psychopathology reflected the individual's "neurotic schema" (Adler, 1956, p. 333), and these schemas were central to the individual's lifestyle. Recently, the concepts of *schema* and *schema theory* have emerged as central in the various subdisciplines of cognitive science as well as in the convictions of various psychotherapy schools (Stein & Young, 1992). This section describes the psychodynamic and cognitive-behavioral traditions of schemas.

Psychodynamic Tradition

Whereas classical psychoanalysts focused on libidinal drives, modern analysts have focused instead on relational themes, emphasizing the self, the object, and their interaction, while a number of ego psychology and object relations theorists have emphasized schema theory. Many of these have contributed to the development of schema theories in the psycho-analytic tradition (Eagle, 1986; Horowitz, 1988; Inderbitzin & James, 1994; Slap & Slap-Shelton, 1981; Wachtel, 1982).

A representative example of these theories is the model described by Slap and Slap-Shelton (1991). They described a schema model that con-trasted with the structural model devised by Freud and refined by the ego psychologists and, they contended, fitted the clinical data of psycho-analysis better than the structural model did. Slap and Slap-Shelton's schema model involves the ego and sequestered schema. The ego consists of many schemas that are loosely linked and integrated with one another and are relativity accessible to consciousness. These schemas are based on past experiences but are modified by new experiences. This process forms the basis of adaptive behavior. Sequestered schemas are organized around traumatic events and situations in childhood that were not mastered or integrated by the immature psyche of the child. These schemas remain latent and repressed. To the extent that these sequestered or pathological schemas are active, current relationships may be cognitively processed according to these schemas, rather than treated objectively by the more adaptive schemas of the ego. Essentially, current situations cannot be per-ceived and processed in accord with the reality of the present events but are rather perceived as replications of unmastered childhood conflict.

Treatment consists of helping the patient describe, clarify, and work through these sequestered, pathological schemas. These schemas are exposed to the client's mature, adaptive ego to achieve integration. Patients are helped to recognize how they create and recreate scenarios that reopen their pathological schemas. Repeated demonstrations and the process of working through the traumatic events that gave rise to the pathological schemas engender a greater degree of self-observation, understanding, and emotional growth.

Cognitive-Behavioral Tradition

Like the psychodynamic tradition, the cognitive-behavioral tradition is quite heterogeneous. It is a common belief in this tradition that behavior and cognitions influence each other. Approaches within this tradition include stress-inoculation and self-instructional training (Meichenbaum, 1977), rational emotive therapy (Ellis, 1979), and cognitive therapy (Beck, 1976). Because cognitive therapy has taken the lead in articulating schema theory in the cognitive-behavioral tradition, it will be highlighted. The rest of this chapter and the remainder of this book emphasize the cognitive behavioral treatment of personality disorders.

Schema Assessment

There are various ways of assessing schemas. Basic to a schema is the individual's views of the self and the world. From an Adlerian perspective, schemas are central to an individual's lifestyle (Adler, 1956). Lifestyle, as well as schemas, can be assessed with a semistructured interview that includes the elicitation of early recollections or early memories. The clinician begins the process by asking the patient: "What is your earliest memory?" or "Think back as far as you can, and tell me the first thing you remember." An early recollection must be distinguished from a report. An *early recollection* is a single, specific event that is personally remembered by the individual, whereas a *report* can be of an event that occurred more than once in the patient's life, or one the patient was told about by another, or one the patient knows about by seeing a photo, home movie, or video of it. More memories, from early and middle childhood, are then elicited. From these memories, the clinician searches for patterns related to the patient's views of the self ("I am strong, defective, unloved.") and the world ("The world puts too many demands on me, is a scary place, is unfair.") These views can be summarized and interpreted to reveal the individual's lifestyle themes or schemas (Eckstein, Baruth, & Mahrer, 1992). The case studies in Chapters 8 and 9 illustrate how early recollections are interpreted as schemas.

In the cognitive therapy tradition, schemas are typically identified or derived from the interview process (Beck, Freeman, Davis & Associates, 2003). Young (Young, Klosko & Weishaar, 2003) described several methods for assessing schemas. In the evaluation interview, which is critical in identifying schemas, the clinician elicits presenting symptoms and problems and attempts to formulate a connection among specific symptoms, emotions, life problems, and maladaptive schemas.

During the course of inquiry about life events and symptoms, the clinician endeavors to develop hypotheses about patterns or themes. Issues of autonomy, connectedness, worthiness, reasonable expectations, and realistic limits are probed to ascertain if any of these present significant problems for the patient. The clinician can get useful information by inquiring about "critical incidents," that is, asking the patient to describe a situation or incident that the patient considers indicative of the problem (Freeman, 1992). The clinician listens for specific triggers, patterns indicative of schemas, and specific behavioral, emotional, and cognitive responses. As themes and patterns emerge, the clinician formulates them in schema language, that is, the patient's views of the self, the world, and others. Because schemas are predictable and recurring phenomena, they can be "triggered" in the interview through imagery and by discussing upsetting events in the patient's past or present. This process of triggering helps confirm the clinician's hypothesis about the presence of a specific schema.

In addition to the clinical interview, a number of schema inventories are available, including the Life History Assessment Forms, the Young Schema Questionnaire, the Young Parenting Inventory, the Young-Rygh Avoidance Inventory, and the Young Compensation Inventory. Imagery assessment is another method to assess and confirm operative schemas. (c.f. Young, Klosko & Weishaar 2003 for a description of these inventories.)

The most commonly utilized of these inventories is the Young Schema Questionnaire (Young & Brown, 1994/2001). The long version includes 205 items and is preferable in clinical practice, while the short version contains 75 items and is utilized primarily in research studies.. Both utilize a six-point likert scale. Preliminary reliability and validity data have been reported on both clinical and nonclinical populations (Schmidt et al., 1995; Young & Brown, 2001).

☐ Cognitive Behavioral Treatment Approaches for Personality Disorders

Since the publication of the first edition of this book, there have been a number of promising developments in CBT in the treatment of personality disorders. This section will briefly survey these developments, particularly in cognitive therapy, dialectic behavior therapy (DBT), schema therapy, cognitive behavior analysis system of psychotherapy, mindfulness-based DBT, and mindfulness-based cognitive therapy (MBCT).

Cognitive Therapy

Cognitive therapy for personality disorders was originally presumed to be similar to cognitive therapy for depression in that both focused on a cognitive formulation or case conceptualization, utilized a collaborative relationship, took a problem-solving approach, and actively helped clients learn new skills to cope with problems situations (Beck, Freeman, Davis, & Associates, 2004; Beck, 1997). However, since individuals with personality disorders characteristically have dysfunctional schemas and ingrained interactional patterns, treatment needed to be modified. Unlike patients with Axis I or symptom disorders, those with personality disorders have difficulty complying with treatment protocols, including homework. Their maladaptive beliefs and behavior patterns were found to be extremely resistant to change when only cognitive interventions were used. Besides presenting with problems and symptoms that were often pervasive, vague, and chronic, these patients often had difficulty forming a therapeutic alliance. Therefore, the original model of cognitive therapy needed revision, and Beck and his associates recently offered a revised or reformulated model.

The second edition of their text *Cognitive Therapy of Personality Disorders* (Beck, Freeman, Davis, & Associates, 2004) provides a fuller and reformulated model of personality disorders and its treatment. Notable is the emphasis on identifying and modifying maladaptive schemas. In this text, Beck acknowledges the difficulties in establishing an effective therapeutic relationship with these clients and provides suggestions for focusing "more than the usual amount of attention on the therapist–patient relationship" (Beck, et al., 2004, p. 365). He also suggests not relying primarily on verbal interventions and beginning with interventions that require a minimal degree of client self-disclosure. Furthermore, he advocates helping clients deal adaptively with aversive emotions. Similarly, he considers limit-setting essential to treatment progress (Beck, et al., 2004). The reformulated model of cognitive therapy for patients with personality disorders also recognizes the need to address developmental history issues and presents specialized techniques. Finally, taking into account the proclivity of these clients for relapse, the reformulated model also incorporates relapse prevention techniques (Pretzer & Beck, 2004).

The following sections continue the discussion of cognitive therapy by indicating how schema therapy, DBT, cognitive behavior analysis system of psychotherapy, and mindfulness training (DBT and MBCT) are similar to and different from cognitive therapy.

Schema Therapy

Schema therapy was developed by Young (1990) to help clients with personality disorders who failed to respond adequately to CBT. While Young found that recent revisions of cognitive therapy for personality disorders by Beck and his colleagues (Beck et al., 2004) were more consistent with schema therapy formulations, he contended that there remained significant differences between these approaches, particularly Beck's primary emphasis on conceptual change and the range of treatment strategies. Like Beck's reformulated model, schema therapy has also evolved over the past 15 years. It appears that schema therapy is applicable to all personality disorders; however, Young has emphasized its application to borderline personality disorders (Young, Klosko, & Weishaar, 2003; Klosko & Young, 2004). The following paragraphs provide an overview of the theory and practice of the current model of schema therapy.

Schema therapy is a broad, integrative model, which shares some commonalities with object relations therapy, experiential therapy, DBT, and interpersonal therapy, as well as cognitive therapy and other forms of CBT. Despite the similarities, schema therapy differs from the other approaches with regard to the nature of the therapist–patient relationship, the general style and stance of the therapist, and the degree of therapist activity and directiveness (Young, Klosko, & Weishaar, 2003).

Theory

The four central concepts in the schema therapy model are: early maladaptive schemas, schema domains, coping styles, and schema modes. They are briefly described below.

Early maladaptive schemas are broad, pervasive themes or patterns regarding oneself and one's relationships that are dysfunctional to a significant degree. Schemas comprise memories, emotions, cognitions, and bodily sensations. They begin as adaptive and relatively accurate representations of the childhood environment but can become maladaptive and inaccurate as one grows up. Schemas considerably influence how individuals think, feel, act, and relate to others. They are triggered when an individual encounters an environment reminiscent of the childhood environment that produced them. When this happens, the individual is flooded with intense negative affect. Young reviewed research on the brain systems involved in fear-conditioning and trauma, which, according to him, provide a biological basis for early maladaptive schemas.

Early maladaptive schemas are the result of unmet core emotional needs. These schemas appear to emerge from aversive childhood experiences, such as abuse, neglect, and trauma in early life. Temperament and cultural influences are additional factors. Young and his associates have delineated 18 early maladaptive schemas. Considerable empirical support exists for these schemas (Young, Klosko, & Weishaar, 2003). Schema domains reflect the basic emotional needs of a child. When these needs are not met in childhood, schemas that lead to unhealthy life patterns develop. Currently, the 18 early maladaptive schemas have been grouped into five broad schema domains. Table 2.1 provides a concise description of these schemas and domains.

Coping styles are the ways a child adapts to schemas as well as to aversive childhood experiences. Maladaptive coping styles are mechanisms developed early in life to adapt to maladaptive schemas. Typically, they result in schema perpetuation. There are three common maladaptive coping styles: surrender, avoidance, and overcompensation. Accordingly, some children will surrender to their schemas, some will find ways to block out or escape from pain, and some others will fight back or overcompensate. Coping responses are the specific behaviors through which these three broad coping styles are expressed. There are common coping responses for each schema. An important goal of schema therapy is to help clients reduce their reliance on maladaptive coping styles and replace them with more appropriate coping styles.

A schema mode is a complex construct in schema theory because it encompasses several elements. A schema mode represents an individual's operative schemas, coping responses, or healthy behaviors. It is activated when specific schemas or coping responses flare into strong affects or rigid coping styles that take over and control one's functioning. In short, a schema mode reflects an individual's predominant state at a given point in time, and when an individual shifts from one schema mode into another, several schemas or coping responses that were previously dormant become active. Currently, 10 schema modes have been described and grouped into four general categories: the child mode, the maladaptive-coping mode, the maladaptive-parent mode, and the healthy-adult mode. Some modes are healthy for an individual, while others are maladaptive. One important goal of schema therapy is to teach patients how to strengthen their healthy-adult mode so that they can learn to nurture, navigate, negotiate with, or neutralize their other modes.

Treatment

In general, the basic goals of schema therapy for individuals with personality disorders are the following: identifying early maladaptive schemas, validating the client's unmet emotional needs, changing dysfunctional beliefs and maladaptive schemas to more functional ones, changing maladaptive life patterns and coping styles, and providing an environment for learning adaptive skills. When treating borderline disorders, very specific treatment goals are indicated (Klosko & Young, 2004). These goals are described in Chapter 5, which discusses the treatment of borderline personality disorders.

TABLE 2.1.   Maladaptive Schemas and Schema Domains

DISCONNECTION AND REJECTION	**Abandonment/Instability:** The belief that significant others will not or cannot provide reliable and stable support. **Mistrust/Abuse:** The belief that others will abuse, humiliate, cheat, lie, manipulate, or take advantage. **Emotional Deprivation:** The belief that one's desire for emotional support will not be met by others. **Defectiveness/Shame:** The belief that one is defective, bad, unwanted, or inferior in important respects. **Social Isolation/Alienation:** The belief that one is alienated, different from others, or not part of any group.
IMPAIRED AUTONOMY AND PERFORMANCE	**Dependence/Incompetence:** The belief that one is unable to competently fulfill everyday responsibilities without considerable help from others. **Vulnerability to Harm or Illness:** The exaggerated fear that catastrophe will strike at any time and that one will be unable to prevent it. **Enmeshment/Undeveloped Self:** The belief that one must be emotionally close with others at the expense of full individuation or normal social development. **Failure:** The belief that one will inevitably fail or is fundamentally inadequate in achieving goals.
IMPAIRED LIMITS	**Entitlement/Grandiosity:** The belief that one is superior to others and not bound by the rules and norms that govern normal social interaction. **Insufficient Self-Control/Self-Discipline:** The belief that one is incapable of self-control and frustration tolerance.
OTHER-DIRECTEDNESS	**Subjugation:** The belief that one's desires, needs, and feelings must be suppressed in order to meet the needs of others and avoid retaliation or criticism. **Self-Sacrifice:** The belief that one must meet the needs of others at the expense of one's own gratification. **Approval-Seeking/Recognition-Seeking:** The belief that one must constantly seek to belong and be accepted at the expense of developing a true sense of self.
OVERVIGILANCE AND INHIBITION	**Negativity/Pessimism:** A pervasive, lifelong focus on the negative aspects of life while minimizing the positive and optimistic aspects. **Emotional Inhibition:** The excessive inhibition of spontaneous action, feeling, or communication—usually to avoid disapproval by others, feelings of shame, or losing control of one's impulses. **Unrelenting Standards/Hypercriticalness:** The belief that striving to meet unrealistically high standards of performance is essential to be accepted and to avoid criticism. **Punitiveness:** The belief that others should be harshly punished for their errors.

Schema therapy has two phases: (a) the assessment and education phase, and (b) the change phase. In the first phase, therapists help clients identify their schemas, understand the origins of their schemas in childhood, and relate their schemas to their current problems. In the change phase, therapists integrate several interventions, including cognitive, experiential, behavioral, and interpersonal strategies, to modify the schemas and replace maladaptive coping styles with healthier behaviors (Young, Klosko, & Weishaar, 2003). With regard to borderline disorders, there are three stages of treatment (Klosko & Young, 2004) (see Chapter 5).

It is worth noting that schema therapy is a theory-intense approach, and considerable training and experience are required to practice it appropriately and effectively. However, just as Beck's reformulated model of cognitive therapy for personality disorders was criticized by Young, Young's model is also criticized from the other side: "Although this modification of cognitive therapy [Young's revised model of schema therapy] was a plausible approach to understanding and treating personality disorders, it has the disadvantage of adding considerable complexity" (Pretzer & Beck, 2004, pp. 302–303).

Dialectic Behavior Therapy

Originally developed for the treatment of borderline personality disorders (Linehan, 1993), dialectic behavior therapy (DBT) has been modified and extended for use in the treatment of other personality disorders, as well as Axis I or symptom disorders, such as mood disorders, anxiety disorders, eating disorders, and substance use disorders (Marra, 2005). DBT is an outgrowth of behavior therapy but is less cognitive than traditional CBT because DBT assumes that cognitions, per se, are less important than affect regulation. DBT places more emphasis on emotion regulation than on maladaptive thought processes. DBT recognizes that although cognitions are a factor in behavior, they are not a necessary mediating factor. Rather, it is more likely that cognitions serve to "make sense" of behavior and emotional events after the fact (Marra, 2005).

Theory

There are numerous similarities between DBT and traditional CBT, particularly cognitive therapy. Both require a collaborative relationship between client and therapist. Both utilize learning principles, analyze triggers and environmental prompts, explore schemas and emotions, and utilize modeling, homework, and imagery. Furthermore, both recognize the importance of empathic responding.

However, there are a number of differences between cognitive therapy and DBT in the treatment of personality disorders. Essentially, cognitive therapy posits that the techniques used in eliciting and evaluating automatic thoughts during treatment of depression or anxiety disorders are also used in treating personality disorders (Beck et al., 2004). While cognitive therapy contends that dysfunctional feelings and behaviors are due to schemas that produce consistently biased judgments and a tendency to make cognitive errors through attributional bias, DBT focuses instead on how schemas are initially formed. Accordingly, therapists utilizing DBT explore the schema and the underlying dialectic conflicts that produced them rather than conducting "collaborative experiments" to prove the schema's limited usefulness. Rather than utilizing cognitive restructuring, DBT therapists attempt to connect belief systems to underlying affect and need and then assist clients to reinterpret their belief systems on the basis of greater awareness of their feelings and needs.

Instead of utilizing "guided discovery" to dispute and revise maladaptive beliefs, "...DBT analyzes both the affective and cognitive inference process to determine how the schema was formed in the first place. This involves identifying deprivational emotional states in early development that could have produced fixation or perseveration and attentional constriction that could serve as protection from threatening internal or external cues. It also involves broadly examining the effects of negative reinforcement through emotional escape and avoidance strategies or inadequate psychological coping skills that could have been rewarded through the partial reinforcement effect" (Marra, 2005, p. 141).

Finally, DBT differs from the cognitive therapy for personality disorders by adopting a nonpejorative interpretation of the pathology. The DBT therapist sees behavior and strategy as operant behavior. Like any other person, a client with a personality disorder is attempting to avoid harm and seek pleasure but has difficulty obtaining the desired outcome due to emotional vulnerability. Nevertheless, the DBT therapist assumes that inadequate compromises between competing and contradictory needs and desires form the basis of the patient's personality structure and helps the patient achieve the desired outcome in a nonpejorative way.

Treatment

Linehan (1993) specified four primary modes of treatment in DBT: individual therapy, skills training in a group, telephone contact, and therapist consultation. While keeping within the overall model, the therapist may decide to add group therapy and other modes of treatment, provided that the targets are clear and prioritized. The therapist is the primary provider, and the main work of therapy is carried out in the individual therapy sessions. Between sessions, the client has the option to maintain telephone contact, including out-of-hours telephone contact, although the therapist has the right to set clear limits on such contact. The purpose of telephone contact is not psychotherapy but rather to give help and support to clients to find ways to avoid self-injury as well as to repair any damage in the relationship between the therapist and the client before the next session. To avoid reinforcing self-injury, calls after the self-injury has occurred are not accepted; after ensuring the client's immediate safety, no further calls are allowed for the next 24 hours. Skills training is usually provided in a group context, ideally by someone other that the individual therapist. In skills training groups, clients are taught skills considered relevant to the particular problems of individuals with personality disorders. There are four groups of skills: core mindfulness skills, interpersonal effectiveness skills, emotion modulation skills, and distress tolerance skills. DBT therapists are encouraged to participate regularly in therapist consultation groups. These consultation groups provide emotional support to therapists dealing with difficult clients as well as ongoing training in DBT methods.

Following an initial period of pretreatment involving assessment, commitment, and orientation to therapy, DBT consists of three stages of treatment. Stage 1 focuses on suicidal behaviors, therapy-interfering behaviors, and behaviors that affect the quality of life and helps patients develop the necessary skills to resolve these problems. Stage 2 deals with problems of living, including post-traumatic stress–related problems, and Stage 3 focuses on self-esteem and individual treatment goals. The targeted behaviors of each stage are brought under control before the next phase. In particular, post-traumatic stress–related problems, such as those related to childhood sexual abuse, are not dealt with directly until Stage 1 has been successfully completed. Therapy at each stage is focused on specific targets, which are arranged in a definite hierarchy of relative importance. These include: decreasing suicidal behaviors, decreasing therapy-interfering behaviors, decreasing behaviors that affect the quality of life, increasing behavioral skills, decreasing behaviors related to post-traumatic stress, improving self-esteem, and individual targets negotiated with the client.

The core strategies in DBT are *validation* and *problem-solving*. Attempts to facilitate change are surrounded by interventions that validate the client's behaviors and responses in relation to the client's current life situation and that demonstrate an understanding of difficulties and suffering. Problem-solving focuses on the establishment of necessary skills. Other treatment modalities include contingency management, cognitive therapy, exposure-based therapies, and medication

Practicing DBT therapy is easier in an inpatient, partial hospitalization or residential treatment setting than in private practice. The reason is that as described by Linehan (1993), DBT is better implemented by a treatment team, in which one therapist provides psychosocial skill training, another provides individual therapy, and some others provide consultation; and in such a setting, the therapists have access to a consultation group for support. Recently, Marra (2005) offered suggestions for adapting DBT treatment for private practice settings. He recommends that skills training be provided by another therapist and offers guidelines to follow when that is not possible. He encourages any private practice clinician who anticipates utilizing DBT to have access to a psychotherapy consultant if involvement in a therapist consultation group is not possible.

Cognitive Behavior Analysis System of Psychotherapy

Cognitive behavior analysis system of psychotherapy (CBASP) is a form of CBT that was developed by McCullough (2000). Basic to this approach is a situational analysis that combines behavioral, cognitive, and interpersonal methods to help clients focus on the consequences of their behaviors and to use problem-solving for resolving both personal and interpersonal difficulties. CBASP was initially formulated for the treatment of clients with chronic depression. A national, multisite study launched CBASP as an effective treatment. Clients who met the criteria for chronic unipolar depression, usually both major depressive disorder and dysthymic disorder, were randomly assigned to one of three treatment groups: medication (Serzone) only, psychotherapy (CBASP) only, or a combination of medication and CBASP. While clients in all three treatment groups improved significantly, those receiving the combined treatment improved the most. Over the 12-week study period, 55% of the medication-only group reported a positive response, 52% of the CBASP-only group experienced some treatment response, and 85% of those who received both medication and CBASP had a positive response to treatment (Keller, et al., 2000).

Theory

A basic assumption of CBASP is that clients can learn to analyze specific life situations and then manage daily stressors on their own. The basic premise of CBASP is simple and straightforward: A therapist assists clients to discover why they did not obtain a desired outcome by evaluating the clients' problematic thoughts and behaviors. In short, therapists assist clients in determining which thoughts and behaviors have gotten in the way of achieving what they want. Since there is often a mismatch between what a client wants and what actually occurs in the client's life, the CBASP approach can be utilized to deal with a variety of distressing problems and presentations, ranging from child behavior problems, to couple's conflict, to anxiety disorders and personality disorders, including borderline personality disorders (Driscoll, Cukrowicz, Reardon, & Joiner, 2004). Interestingly, McCullough (2002) noted his reservations with regard to utilizing CBASP to treat adults with severe borderline personality disorders, particularly those with comorbid chronic depression.

Treatment

The overall goal of CBASP is to identify the discrepancy between what clients want to happen in a particular situation and what has happened or is actually happening. By examining their specific circumstances, clients gradually discover the problematic themes and patterns in their lives, as well as ways in which they can achieve what is desired.

There are two phases in CBASP: elicitation and remediation. The elicitation phase consists of six steps that deal with specific questions: (a) How would you describe the situation? (b) How did you interpret the situation? (c) Specifically, what did you do, and what did you say? (d) What did you want to get out of the situation, that is, what was your desired outcome? (e) What was the actual outcome of this situation? (6) Did you get what you wanted?

During the remediation phase, behaviors and interpretations or cognitions are targeted, changed, and revised so that the client's new behaviors and cognitions will contribute to and result in the desired outcome. First, each of the client's interpretations of a situation is assessed to determine whether that interpretation helped or hindered the achievement of the desired outcome. Next, each of the client's behaviors is similarly analyzed to determine whether or not the behaviour helped or hindered the attainment of the desired outcome.

Mindfulness Training: DBT and MBCT

Mindfulness can be defined as paying attention in a particular way, that is, intentionally, in the present moment, and nonjudgmentally (Kabat-Zinn, 1994). This awareness is based on an attitude of acceptance of personal experience, which involves a commitment to living fully in the present moment. Training in mindfulness offers practice in "facing" rather than "avoiding" potential problems and difficulties. This is accomplished through meditative practices, such as the body scan, mindful stretching, and mindfulness of breath, body, sounds, and thoughts. These practices teach the core skills of concentration; mindfulness of thoughts, emotions, feelings, and bodily sensations, as well as being present and letting go; and acceptance of life as it is. This leads to an "aware" mode of being that is characterized by freedom and choice, in contrast to a mode dominated by a habitual pattern of automatic thinking and acting, or "automatic pilot" living. Accordingly, the goal of mindfulness training is to teach individuals how to respond to stressful situations "mindfully"instead of reacting automatically to them.

Of the several approaches to acquiring mindfulness, two—dialectical behavior therapy and MBCT—have particular relevance in the treatment of individuals with personality disorders.

Mindfulness in Dialectical Behavior Therapy

In DBT, mindfulness meditation is considered a necessary skill, as well as an underlying attitude, that has to be developed. Validation is a core strategy that is used to counteract the effects of the invalidating environment and to foster self-validation. DBT therapists search to validate or acknowledge the "wisdom" in patients' experiences. This reflects the Buddhist principle of radical acceptance and the belief that everything is perfect as it is. Patients are encouraged to understand that all behavior can be understood in terms of its consequences. For example, to a patient who reports having slashed his or her wrist in order to avoid shameful feelings, a DBT therapist might say: "It's not surprising that you would want to stop your painful feelings by slashing your wrists, since most of us don't like to experience painful feelings." DBT therapists model an attitude of acceptance toward self and others, and genuine acceptance is an essential element in effective treatment.

Mindfulness is taught as a core skill in the context of skills training (Linehan, 1993b). The training format consists of a year-long program with weekly 2- to 2.5-hour classes of about eight patients and two facilitators. Mindfulness skills make up the first of four skills modules and involve a series of meditative practices for cultivating awareness and acceptance. Patients learn to achieve mindfulness through learning "what" skills and practicing "how" skills. The training involves didactic and experiential learning as well as assigned homework. In contrast to MBCT, which prescribes formal meditation practice, DBT often relies on informal mindfulness practice, such as mindfulness of everyday activities (Linehan, 1993b). This difference is based on the opinion that patients with severe personality disorders, such as borderline personality disorder, are less able to productively engage in meditation practice that requires lengthy sitting.

Finally, empirical support exists for the effectiveness of DBT. Reports of several randomized controlled trials that evaluated the overall effectiveness of a comprehensive DBT treatment have been published (Linehan, et al., 1991; Koons, et al., 2001; Linehan, et al., 2002; Verheul, et al., 2003; Bohus, et al., 2003). When evaluated against treatment-as-usual control conditions, DBT was superior. Unfortunately, no studies have yet examined the specific components of DBT, such as the effect of mindfulness training.

Mindfulness-Based Cognitive Therapy

Mindfulness-based cognitive therapy (MBCT) is an approach that is considered to be part of the "third wave" of CBT. MBCT integrates aspects of cognitive therapy with components of mindfulness-based stress reduction (MBSR), which was developed by Kabat-Zinn (1994). MBSR is a widely used an adjunct to medical treatment for various clinical conditions, as well as a self-help technique for stress management in nonclinical conditions.

Thus, MBCT emphasizes changing the awareness of, and relation to, thoughts rather than changing thought content. It offers participants a different way of living with and experiencing emotional pain and distress. The assumption is that cultivating a detached attitude toward negative thinking provides one with the skills to prevent its escalation at times of potential relapse.

Usually, MBCT skills are taught by one instructor in eight weekly 2- to 3-hour group sessions. In each session, participants engage in various formal meditation practices designed to increase moment-by-moment, nonjudgmental awareness of physical sensations, thoughts, and feelings. Assigned homework includes practicing these exercises along with exercises designed to integrate the application of awareness skills into daily life. Specific prevention strategies derived from traditional cognitive therapy methods are incorporated in the later weeks of the program.

Finally, there is empirical evidence to support the efficacy of integrating mindfulness meditation into cognitive therapy. A comprehensive review of 64 published empirical studies concluded that MBSR can help a broad range of individuals cope with clinical and nonclinical problems (Grossman, Niemann, Schmidt & Walach, 2004). Even though it was noted that there were some methodological problems with the studies, it is interesting to note that both controlled and uncontrolled studies show similar effect sizes of 0.5 ($P < .0001$). A much smaller review of 13 studies (4 controlled and 9 uncontrolled) concluded that MBSR is probably more effective with nonclinical problems than with clinical problems (Bishop, 2002).

☐ Other Cognitive Behavioral Methods

Cognitive Coping Therapy

Cognitive therapy (CT) and cognitive behavior therapy (CBT) have long been used in the treatment of personality disorders (Beck & Freeman, 1990). Cognitive restructuring, wherein maladaptive beliefs or schemas are identified, processed, and challenged, is the most widely known and utilized treatment strategy associated with those approaches. Coping skills methods are commonly an adjunct to cognitive restructuring. Typically, therapists using CT and CBT "first turn to cognitive restructuring to treat the presenting problem and then pull from coping skills therapy specific skills to fill out the treatment plan" (Sharoff, 2002). However, cognitive restructuring has limited utility in complex cases, such as those with chronic depression or anxiety symptoms, low motivation for treatment, emotional lability, and histories of chronic relapse—characteristics common in many individuals with personality disorders. However, cognitive coping therapy has been developed as an alternative treatment to cognitive restructuring and appears to be a particularly promising and potent treatment strategy for personality disorders.

As described by Sharoff (2002), cognitive coping therapy is an active, directive, didactic, and structured approach for treating clients in a short time frame. It is a complete and self-contained approach to treatment, which begins with assessing an individual's coping skills—in terms of skill chains, subskills and microskills—and then goes on to increasing skill competence in targeted areas as needed. Five key skill areas with representative treatment modalities include (a) *cognitive skills:* problem solving, self-instruction training, and self-management; (b) *emotion skills*: emotional containment and compartmentalization; (c) *perceptual skills*: perspective-taking, thought-stopping, and psychological-distance-taking; (d) *physiological skills*: meditation and relaxation-training; and (e) *behavior skills:* communication and assertiveness-training.

Like the structured skill intervention strategies described by Sperry, the cognitive coping therapy approach is also a bottom-up approach; when it is combined with top-down treatment strategies, such as cognitive restructuring, therapeutic confrontation, or interpretation, it can greatly enhance treatment outcomes for individuals with personality disorders.

Structured Treatment Interventions

Unlike schemas, which reflect the psychological dimension of personality, temperament, which is the innate, genetic, and constitutional aspect of personality, reflects its biological dimension. Temperament plays an important role in the regulation or dysregulation of an individual's affective, behavioral and cognitive styles (Sperry, 1999; 2003). Research shows that medication can modulate or normalize dysregulated behaviors; however, a similar modulating effect has been noted for social skills training as well (Lieberman, DeRisi, & Mueser, 1989). Thus, it appears that social skills training is a relatively potent bottom-up treatment strategy for normalizing limbic-system-mediated behaviors, such as impulsivity, aggressivity, and mood lability, to name a few. Sperry (1999; 2003) contends that individuals with personality disorders typically exhibit significant skill deficits and that structured skill training interventions are useful and necessary for successful treatment of moderate to severe personality disorders. Skill deficits can be reversed by the acquisition of requisite skills in individual and group sessions, through practice, modeling, coaching, role-playing, and graded task assignment. Chapter 3 describes and illustrates 16 structured intervention strategies for modifying affective, behavioral, and cognitive temperament styles in individuals presenting with the six most common personality disorders.

3

CHAPTER

Cognitive Behavior Therapy Interventions with Personality Disorders: II

This chapter sets the stage for the cognitive behavioral treatment of specific personality disorders (covered in Chapters 4 through 9) by emphasizing cognitive behavioral therapy (CBT) interventions that are particularly effective in modulating temperament and style. As noted in Chapter 1, temperament primarily reflects the biological dimension of personality, whereas character and schema primarily reflect the psychological dimension of personality. Furthermore, individuals with personality disorders tend to be over- or undermodulated in terms of temperament, and irresponsible, uncooperative, and self-focused in terms of character (Cloninger, Svrakic, & Prybeck, 1993). Accordingly, effective treatment of personality disorders must address both of these disordered dimensions of personality. Unfortunately, therapeutic strategies that are effective in modifying character and schemas tend to be minimally effective in modulating temperament and style (Cloninger, 2004; Young, Klosko, & Weishaar, 2003). However, there are specific treatment interventions, such as medication, social skills training, and other focused behavioral strategies, that are effective in modulating temperament.

This chapter begins with a brief explanation of temperament modulation, which requires certain types of interventions. It then describes the dimensions of temperament in terms of regulation and dysregulation of behavior. Next, it provides a brief overview of skills, skill deficits, and

39

skills training and their role in regulating or modulating the temperament/style dimensions of individuals with personality disorders. Finally, 16 intervention strategies useful in this modulation process are described. Resource citations for each strategy are provided at the end of the chapter. The reader will note that references are made to these strategies in the subsequent chapters of this book.

☐ The Brain and Temperament Modulation

The fact is that psychotherapeutic interventions can and do influence the brain. After noting the differential effects of medication and psychotherapeutic interventions on neuronal functioning and brain circuits, neuroscience researchers have come to conceptualize the treatment process in terms of either "top-down" or "bottom-up" strategies (Sperry, 2006). "Top-down" refers to treatment efforts that primarily focus on and influence cortical structures and neural tracts (top) as well as subcortical circuits, particularly those in the limbic system (down). "Bottom-up" refers to the treatment efforts that largely focus on limbic circuits and also can produce changes in cortical circuits. There is increasing interest in the efforts to normalize the expression of under- and overmodulated maladaptive personality traits with medication and behavioral interventions (Reich, 2000; Reich, 2005). For example, top-down treatment strategies typically utilize standard psychotherapies, that is, cognitive restructuring and dynamic interpretations, to enhance cortical influences on limbic circuits. The goal is to undo negative learning, particularly maladaptive beliefs, and to increase the modulating or normalizing effects of emotional responses. Bottom-up treatment strategies typically involve the use of psychotropic medication in order to modulate harmful and other overmodulated behavior patterns and emotional states by normalizing the activity of limbic structures. However, focused cognitive behavioral therapies appear to be as effective as medication and bottom-up strategies (Fawcett, 2002). It appears that social skills training (Lieberman, DeRisi, & Mueser, 1989), cognitive coping therapy (Sharoff, 2002), dialectic behavior therapy (Linehan, 1993), and cognitive behavioral analysis system therapy (McCullough, 2000) are all effective bottom-up treatments.

☐ Dimensions of Temperament

Cloninger's research (1993; 2004) found that temperament has four biological dimensions—novelty seeking, harm avoidance, reward dependence, and persistence. Other researchers would describe impulsivity and aggressivity as additional dimensions of temperament (Costello, 1996). Harm avoidance or behavioral inhibition can be thought of as inhibition of behavior in response to a stimuli. Thus, the more easily and intensely upset a person is by noxious stimuli, the more likely the person is to avoid it. Reward dependence or behavioral maintenance refers to the ease or difficulty with which a person becomes hooked on pleasurable behavior and the degree to which the behavior remains controlled by it. Finally, novelty seeking or behavioral activation is the heritable tendency toward exhilaration in response to novel stimuli or cues that have previously been associated with pleasure or relief of discomfort. In other words, it involves the activation of behavior in response to potentially pleasurable stimuli. Each of these temperament dimensions is putatively related to a neurotransmitter system: behavioral activation to dopamine, behavioral inhibition to serotonin, and behavioral maintenance to norepinephrine (Cloninger, 1993). As noted in Chapter 1, the influence of temperament is reflected in the individual's basic style: affective style, behavioral/relational style, or cognitive style.

Cloninger (2005) noted that temperament and character can be measured with biological markers and self-report instruments. On Cloninger's (1993) Temperament Character Inventory (TCI), individuals with increased dysregulation of one or more of the temperament dimensions typically experience considerable distress and impairment in life functioning. For example, according to Cloninger's research (1993), the individual with a borderline personality disorder would likely rate high in novelty seeking and harm avoidance, low in reward dependence, and also low on three character dimensions. Just as schema—and its modification—is central to this book, so also is temperament (style)—and its modulation.

☐ Skills, Skill Deficits, and Skills Training

Effective functioning in daily life requires mastery of a number of personal and relational skills. Most individuals begin learning these requisite skills in childhood and further refine them throughout the course of adolescence and early adulthood. Some patients have the requisite skills but, for conscious or unconscious reasons, do not use them. Other patients have never learned or sufficiently mastered these skills. The lack of learning or mastery of a basic requisite skill is called a skill deficit (Lieberman, DeRisi, & Mueser, 1989). It is a basic premise of this book that most individuals with personality disorders have skill deficits. Because of these deficits, these individuals experience, to varying degrees, dysregulation of one or more temperament dimensions, which causes distress to themselves or others. The three temperament or style dimensions emphasized in this book are affective style, behavioral and relational style, and cognitive style. Over- or undermodulation of one or more of these styles can significantly affect the level of symptoms and the level of functioning (i.e., Global Assessment of Functioning or GAF). In other words, requisite skills—including coping skills—have the effect of regulating or modulating temperament or style dimensions, whereas skill deficits make it more difficult, if not impossible, to modulate style dimensions.

Recall the case examples in the Preface. Both Keri and Cindy presented for treatment following a suicide gesture. Although both had the same diagnosis and level of education, Keri's GAF was 40 (with 71 being the highest in the past year) and Cindy's was 27 (with 42 being the highest in the past year). Keri's high level of premorbid functioning suggested that she had mastered most of the requisite skills, including coping skills, to achieve her level of success. Cindy, on the other hand, had significant skill deficits, which explains why her affective, behavioral/relational, and cognitive styles were so overmodulated.

Clinicians can effectively assist patients in reversing such skill deficits by working with them to acquire the personal and relational skills that they had not previously possessed. These skills can be learned directly in individual sessions, through practice, that is, coaching and role playing, and through graded task assignments. When feasible, group treatment settings can be particularly useful for social skills training (Lieberman et al., 1989).

In those patients with personality disorders with significant symptomatic distress and who exhibit significant functional impairment, traditional psychotherapeutic interventions are of limited use. However, medication and structured interventions—called skills training—are quite effective when temperament dysregulation is present. These structured interventions are also effective when skill deficits and reversing these deficits are indicated.

☐ Structured Treatment Interventions for Personality Disorders

The 16 structured interventions to treat personality disorders are listed in Table 3.1. These interventions are referred to throughout the book. Each intervention is described in a stepwise fashion that illustrates its application in the treatment setting. At least one key reference or resource is provided for each of these interventions so that the reader may obtain additional information on using these effective therapeutic interventions.

TABLE 3.1. Structured Intervention Strategies for Personality Disorders

1. Anger Management
2. Anxiety Management Training
3. Assertiveness Training
4. Cognitive Awareness Training
5. Distress Tolerance Training
6. Emotional Regulation Training
7. Empathy Training
8. Impulse Control Training
9. Interpersonal Skills Training
10. Limit-Setting
11. Mindfulness Training
12. Problem-Solving Training
13. Self-Management Training
14. Sensitivity Reduction Training
15. Symptom Management Training
16. Thought-Stopping

Anger Management Training

The purpose of anger management training is to decrease the arousal and expression of hostile affects while increasing the individual's capacity to tolerate and channel this energy in prosocial ways. This is usually a therapist-directed intervention that can be applied in an individual- or group-treatment context. It is then practiced and applied by the individual. Collaboration between the clinician and the individual tends to increase the individual's motivation and compliance. The intervention proceeds in the following fashion.

First, the clinician instructs the patient in the four sets of factors that determine the response of anger in that patient: (a) high-risk circumstances (external, contextual factors, such as individuals, places, or times of day, that can potentially provoke an angry or rageful response in the patient); (b) internal triggering factors (internal factors, such as the patient's feelings, cravings, or level of fatigue, that render the patient more vulnerable to an angry response); (c) patient's self-statements (specific beliefs that can render the patient more vulnerable to an angry response or that can defuse an angry response); and (d) patient's coping skills that neutralize or exacerbate the effects of these internal and external factors.

Second, the clinician instructs/trains the patient in identifying the four sets of factors and develops—with the patient—a checklist, or form, of the most likely factors for that patient. For example, the clinician asks the patient to describe a recent instance of a response of anger and assists the patient in identifying the four specific factors. For instance, he had been stopped for speeding and driving under the influence of alcohol: (a) he left a tavern after four drinks and decided to drive home rather than take a cab (high-risk circumstance); (b) he was tired after a stressful day at work and was disinhibited and feeling upset that someone had just broken his car aerial (internal triggering factor); (c) he was thinking: "Why does this stuff always happen to me?" and "Nobody does this to my car and gets away with it" (self-statement); and (d) he is impulsive and has a "hair-trigger" temper (coping skills), and he speeds off angry and resentful.

Third, the clinician tells the patient to write down each incident in which he felt anger, the four factors, and what he did when he experienced that emotion (i.e., cursed and kicked the side of his car when he noticed the car's aerial was broken). The patient then self-monitors these factors and responses between sessions by using the checklist/form. During subsequent sessions, the clinician and the patient review the form. They analyze the factors, looking for commonalities and specifying coping skill deficits (i.e., the patient is mostly likely to be angry and disinhibited when he is tired, has been stressed at work, or has been drinking).

Fourth, the clinician works with the patient to specify alternatives to these high-risk circumstances (i.e., if he has been drinking, he will take a cab or ask a designated driver to get him home). Then, the clinician helps the patient specify a plan for reducing the various internal triggering factors (i.e., when he is tired and stressed out, he can go jogging rather than go to the tavern).

Fifth, the clinician instructs and assists the patient to learn effective, alternative self-statements to cope with anger-provocation (i.e., "It's too bad this happened, but I don't have to go ballistic over it.").

Finally, the clinician trains the patient in learning relaxation skills (i.e., controlled breathing and counting to 10 before acting, e.g., when he sees that his car has been vandalized) and other coping skills, such as assertive communication as an alternative to anger and rageful responses.

Resources

Novaco, R. (1975). *Anger control.* Lexington, MA: Heath/Lexington Books.
Novaco, R. (1984). Stress inoculation therapy for anger control. In P. Keller & L. Ritt (Eds.), *Innovations in clinical practice: A source book* (pp. 214–222). Sarasota, FL: Professional Resource Exchange.

Anxiety Management Training

The purpose of anxiety management training is to decrease the arousal and expression of distressing affects and to increase the individual's capacity to face and tolerate these affects. This is usually a therapist-directed intervention that can be applied in an individual- or group-treatment context. It is then practiced and applied by the individual. Collaboration between the clinician and the individual tends to increase the individual's motivation and compliance. The intervention proceeds in the following fashion.

First, the clinician instructs the patient in the determinants of the response of anxiety in that patient: (a) external triggering factors, such as specific individuals or stressful demands that can potentially elicit anxiety in the patient; (b) internal triggering factors, such as physiological responsivity and self-statements, that is, specific beliefs that can render the patient more vulnerable to anxiety or that can neutralize it; and (c) the patient's coping skills that neutralize or exacerbate the effects of these internal and external factors.

Second, the clinician instructs the patient in identifying the three sets of factors, and develops—with the patient—a checklist of the most likely factors for that patient. The clinician then asks the patient to describe a recent incidence of anxiety and assists the patient in identifying the three specific factors. In the example of performance anxiety, the patient (a) is assigned to give a quarterly business report at a board of directors meeting (external trigger); (b) has experienced moderate physiological reactivity during earlier public presentations: "I feel completely inadequate giving a speech to my superiors." "I know I'm going to screw up, and I'll be so embarrassed" (internal triggers); and (c) prefaces the presentation by asking the group's indulgence, saying that she is a better accountant than a public speaker (coping skills), and experiences feelings of inadequacy, dry mouth, sweaty palms, and heart palpitations while giving the presentation. Alternatively, an anxiety survey can be used, and if there are more than one anxiety responses, an anxiety hierarchy survey can be used.

Third, the clinician tells the patient to write down each incident in which she had experienced anxiety, the three factors, and what she did when experiencing that emotion (i.e., she quickly excused herself after giving the report, experienced some relief, and concluded that she had failed again). The patient then self-monitors these factors and responses between sessions by using the checklist/form.

Fourth, during subsequent sessions the clinician and the patient review the checklist. They analyze the factors, looking for commonalities and identifying coping skill deficits (i.e., she is likely to experience performance anxiety when addressing superiors, although she has no problem giving presentations to peers or inferiors).

Fifth, the clinician works with the patient to consider options when she is faced with external triggers (i.e., submitting a written rather than verbal report or having a colleague give the presentation, while she is present to field questions on the report).

Sixth, the clinician works with the patient to specify a plan for reducing the various internal triggering factors, that is, reducing physiological reactivity by controlled breathing or other relaxation exercises, and specifying more adaptive self-statements, that is, "My worth as a person and as an employee doesn't depend on how well I can give speeches. This is only one small part of my job"; "I know this material cold—certainly better than anyone on board. I can get through this 5-minute talk and maybe even enjoy it."

Seventh, the clinician trains the patient in learning relaxation skills, such as controlled breathing 10 minutes prior to giving a presentation, and other coping skills as an alternative to the anxiety and self-deprecatory responses. Treatment progress is evaluated on the basis of the patient's increasing capacity to face internal and external triggering factors with more adaptive coping behaviors. The patient's self-report of the absence of, or a significant reduction in, anxiety in such circumstances indicates that the treatment has been effective.

Resources

Suinn, R. (1977). *Manual: Anxiety management training.* Denver, CO: Rocky Mountain Behavioral Science Institute.

Suinn, R. & Deffenbacher, J. (1982). The self-control of anxiety. In P. Karoly & F. Kanfer (Eds.), *The psychology of self-management: From theory to practice* (pp. 132–141). New York: Pergamon.

Assertiveness Training

The purpose of assertiveness training is to increase an individual's capacity for expressing thoughts, feelings, and beliefs in a direct, honest, and appropriate manner without violating the rights of others. More specifically, it involves the capacity to say "no," to make requests, to express positive and negative feelings, and to initiate, continue, and terminate conversations. Lack of assertive behavior is usually related to specific skills deficits, but it is sometimes related to interfering emotional reactions and thoughts. Assertiveness training proceeds in the following fashion.

First, the clinician performs a careful assessment to identify the following: situations of concern to the patient; current assertiveness skills; personal and environmental obstacles that need to be addressed, such as difficult significant others or limited social contexts; and personal and environmental resources that can be drawn on.

Second, the clinician formulates an intervention plan. If appropriate behaviors are available but not performed because of anxiety, the focus may be on enhancing anxiety management skills. Discrimination training is required when skills are available but are not performed at appropriate times. If skill deficits are present, skill training is indicated.

Third, the intervention is introduced. For skill training, the clinician teaches the patient specific skills via modeling, behavioral rehearsal, feedback, and homework. Modeling effective behavior in specific situations is accomplished by using one or more of the following methods: *in vivo* demonstration of the behavior by the clinician, written scripts, videotapes, audiotapes, or films. In behavior rehearsal, the patient is provided opportunities to practice the given skill in the clinical setting.

Fourth, the clinician provides positive feedback following each rehearsal in which effective verbal and nonverbal reactions are noted and specific changes that could be made to enhance performance are identified. Homework assignments involve tasks that the patient agrees to carry out in real-life contexts.

Fifth, the length of assertion training depends on the domain of social behaviors that must be developed and on the severity of countervailing personal and environmental obstacles. If the response repertoire is narrow, such as refusal of requests, and the obstacles minor, only a few sessions may be required. If the behavior deficits are extensive, additional time may be required, even though only one or two kinds of social situations are focused on during intervention. Assertiveness training can occur in individual sessions or group therapy, as well as in other small contexts, such as support groups and workshops. Sank and Shaffer (1984) provided a detailed four-session assertiveness training module for use in a structured group therapy context.

Resources

Alberti, R. (1978). *Assertiveness: Applications and issues.* San Luis Obispo, CA: Impact Publications.

Sank, L. & Shaffer, C. (1984). *A therapist's manual for cognitive behavior therapy in groups.* New York: Plenum.

Cognitive Awareness Training

The purpose of cognitive awareness training is to reduce narcissistic injury, projective identification, and cognitive distortions. Increased recognition and awareness of distorted thinking and unrealistic expectations can attenuate resulting distress and acting-out behaviors. As such, this intervention is particularly useful in the treatment of individuals with personality disorders. Although this intervention is clinician initiated, it is essentially a self-management intervention that the individual must practice sufficiently to achieve some level of mastery. The intervention proceeds in the following fashion.

First, the clinician assesses the nature of the patient's cognitive distress, since the intervention is applied somewhat differently for narcissistic injury and projective identification than it is for cognitive distortions.

Second, assuming that the distress is attributed to narcissistic injury or projective identification, the clinician focuses cognitive awareness training on the social interactions that trigger dysfunctional conflicts. The goal is to understand the relationship between the other's anger-provoking behavior and the individual's own frustrated expectations. This involves specifying what it was about the other's behavior that was frustrating or hurtful and identifying what expectations were frustrated by the other's behavior. While using this technique, it is essential that the clinician help the individual to distinguish the reasonable aspects of the individual's expectations from the unreasonable aspect(s). Failure to recognize this expectation will be experienced by the individual as a narcissistic injury.

Third, assuming that the distress is attributed to cognitive distortion, the clinician focuses cognitive awareness training on the patient's thoughts and images associated with the onset and escalation of conflict. The clinician inquires about the individual's inner experience when anger begins welling up: What were the individual's thoughts, self-talk, and images of the other person as the argument began to escalate? By monitoring these cognitions, the individual can bring into conscious awareness many irrational thoughts and perceptions that had previously been either out of awareness or vague.

Resource

Novaco, R. (1978). Anger and coping with stress: Cognitive behavioral interventions. In J. Foreyth & D. Rathjen (Eds.), *Cognitive behavior therapy* (pp. 217–243). New York: Plenum.

Distress Tolerance Skill Training

Distress tolerance is the capacity to perceive one's environment without demanding it be different, to experience one's current emotional state without trying to change it, and to observe one's thought patterns and action patterns without attempting to stop them. Thus, it is the ability to tolerate difficult situations and accept them. Typically, lower-functioning individuals with borderline and histrionic personality disorders have difficulty tolerating distress. Distress tolerance training attempts to help the patient develop skills and strategies to tolerate and survive crises and to accept life as it is in the moment. Among individuals with mood lability and impulsivity, the ability to tolerate distress is a prerequisite for other therapeutic changes. This intervention is usually introduced and demonstrated by the clinician. It is then practiced and applied by the individual. As such, it is a self-management intervention. Initially, the clinician may have to cue the individual to apply the technique within and between treatment sessions. The intervention proceeds in the following fashion.

First, the clinician assesses the patient's ability to distract himself or herself from painful emotional thoughts and feelings, and to soothe himself or herself in the face of worry, loneliness, and distress. Skill deficits in either or both areas are noted.

Second, on the basis of this assessment, the clinician instructs the patient in one or both of the following essential skills and strategies: self-distraction and self-soothing methods. If there is a basic skill deficit with regard to self-distraction, it becomes the focus of treatment. Self-distraction techniques include thought-stopping, shifting attention by, say, making a phone call; watching television; listening to music; jogging; comparing oneself with others who are less well off; and experiencing intense sensations, for example, placing a hand in ice water or flicking a thick rubber band on one's wrist to produce a painful but harmless sensation intense enough to derail the thought and impulse for wrist-slitting or other self-harmful behaviors.

Third, if there is a basic skill deficit in self-soothing, it becomes the focus of treatment. Self-soothing techniques include controlled breathing exercises—in which air is drawn in slowly and deeply and then exhaled slowly and completely—savoring a favorite food or snack, or listening to or humming a soothing melody. Acceptance skills include radical acceptance—complete acceptance from deep within, turning the mind toward acceptance—choosing to accept reality as it is, and willingness vs. willfulness.

Resources

Linehan, M. (1993a). *Cognitive-behavioral treatment of borderline personality disorder*. New York: Guilford.

Linehan, M. (1993b). *Skill training manual for treating borderline personality disorder*. New York: Guilford.

Emotion Regulation Skill Training

Patients who habitually exhibit emotional lability may benefit from learning to regulate their emotions. Emotion regulation skills can be extremely difficult to teach because emotionally labile patients often believe that if they could only "change their attitudes," they could change their feelings. Labile patients often come from environments where others exhibits cognitive control of their emotions and show little tolerance of the patients' inability to exhibit similar control. Subsequently, labile patients often resist controlling their emotions because such control implies that others are right and they are wrong for feeling the way they do. Much of the labile patient's emotional distress is a result of such secondary responses, such as intense shame, anxiety, or rage, to primary emotions. Often, the primary emotions are adaptive and appropriate to the context. The reduction of the secondary distress requires exposure to the primary emotions in a nonjudgmental atmosphere. Accordingly, mindfulness to one's own emotional responses is essentially an exposure technique. This intervention typically proceeds in the following fashion.

First, the clinician assesses the patient's overall skill in emotion regulation and then the subskills of identifying and labeling affects, modulating affects, and mindfulness.

Second, the clinician formulates a plan for reversing the skill deficit(s). Skill training can occur in either an individual- or group-treatment context. Although the skills of emotion regulation can be learned in an individual-treatment context, the group context facilitates these efforts to a greater extent. Skill training groups can provide a measure of social support and peer feedback that individual treatment cannot.

Third, the clinician, whether in an individual context or a skill-group context, teaches, models, and coaches the patients in the given subskill of emotional regulation. The first step in regulating emotions is learning to identify and label emotions. Identification of an emotional response involves the ability to observe one's own responses as well as to describe accurately the context in which the emotion occurs. Identification is greatly aided if one can observe and describe the event prompting the emotion, interpret the event that prompts the emotion, differentiate the phenomonological experience, including physical sensations of the emotion, and describe its effects on one's own functioning.

Similarly, emotional lability can be attenuated by controlling the events that trigger the emotions or by reducing the individual's vulnerability to lability. Patients are more susceptible to emotional lability when they are under physical or environmental stress. Accordingly, patients should be assisted in reducing such stressors by achieving a more balanced lifestyle that includes appropriate nutrition, sufficient sleep, adequate exercise, avoidance of substance abuse, and increased self-efficacy. Although these targets seem straightforward, making headway on them with labile patients can be exhausting for both patients and clinicians. Work on any of these targets requires an active stance from the patients and persistence with the therapy until positive effects begin to accrue.

Increasing the number of positive events in one's life is one approach to increasing positive emotions. Initially, this involves increasing daily positive experiences. Subsequently, it means making life changes so that positive events will occur more often. In addition to increasing positive events, it is also useful to work on being mindful of positive experiences when they do occur and unmindful of worries that the positive experience will end. Mindfulness to current emotions means experiencing emotions without judging them or trying to inhibit them, block them, or distract oneself from them. The assumption is that exposure to painful or distressing emotions, without association to negative consequences, will extinguish their ability to stimulate secondary negative emotions. When a patient is already feeling "bad," judging negative emotions as "bad" leads to feelings of guilt, anger, or anxiety, which further increases distress intolerance. Frequently, patients can tolerate a painful affect if they can refrain from feeling guilty or anxious about feeling bad in the first place.

Fourth, the clinician works together with the patient to enable him or her to practice a given skill both within and outside the treatment context. Within the treatment context, the use of role play can be particularly valuable in reinforcing the patient's newly acquired skill. Particular situations and relationships can be targeted for practice outside the treatment context.

Resources

Linehan, M. (1993a). *Cognitive-behavioral treatment of borderline personality disorder.* New York: Guilford.

Linehan, M. (1993b). *Skill training manual for treating borderline personality disorder.* New York: Guilford.

Empathy Training

Empathy training is a technique for more directly enhancing the patient's empathic abilities. In empathy training, the patient is asked to think about and then communicate his or her understanding of the feelings and point of view of the other. These understandings are then checked out with the other individual, and inaccuracies are corrected. Particular attention is given to the patient's understanding of what he or she has done or said that has aroused hurt feelings in the other and what the other wishes had happened instead of what did happen. The technique of empathy training is a powerful tool for interrupting projective identification and splitting. It often leads to greatly increased awareness of the feelings and needs of the other. This, in turn, greatly facilitates constructive negotiation and problem-solving. Although there are various approaches to empathy training, the relationship enhancement approach has been demonstrated to be effective in individuals with personality disorders, including those with narcissistic personality disorder. The effect is seen in a relatively short time—in three to four sessions—particularly if empathy training takes place in the context of couples sessions. The intervention proceeds in the following fashion.

First, the clinician assesses the nature and extent of the patient's capacity to manifest the three skills of empathy: active listening, accurately interpreting interpersonal cues, and responding empathically.

Second, assuming an empathy deficit (i.e., in one or more of the three skills of empathy), the clinician begins the training by modeling the three skills of empathy. After continual modeling by the clinician, the patient begins to develop empathic understanding and responding.

Third, the clinician begins to coach the patient on the given skill(s), beginning with nonrelationship issues and then moving to positive feelings and before progressing to dealing with interpersonal conflicts. The clinician teaches the patient to access the underlying vulnerability and the healthy needs that underlie the narcissistic defense. This is done through the dual process of empathic listening and coaching on skilled expression of one's authentic feelings and point of view. The patient initially tends to both experience and express vulnerability in the form of anger, criticism, and blame. Empathic listening becomes a way of calming the patient's reflexive reactions and of creating a pause between the emotions and the reflexive, harmful behaviors that have resulted from those emotions.

Fourth, empathy training also assists patients in monitoring their emotional reactivity. Patients typically experience a supportive feeling that comes from listening empathically and responding within the guidelines for effective expression. They also begin to discover that when emotions are accurately observed and expressed subjectively, with increasing consciousness of how meanings affect feelings, these emotions shift or even vanish quite rapidly. What often perpetuates anger, for example, is the patient's lack of full attention to it and to the meanings and desires it reveals. When this attention neither inhibits nor defends the emotion, but instead maintains a compassionate and curious observer stance, changes in feelings, meanings, and actions can occur quickly.

Resources

Guerney, B. (1977). *Relationship enhancement: Skills programs for therapy, problem prevention, and enrichment.* San Francisco: Jossey-Bass.

Guerney, B. (1988). *Relationship enhancement manual.* State College, PA: IDEALS.

Impulse Control Training

Impulse control training is an intervention with a goal to reduce involuntary urges to act. This intervention is usually introduced and demonstrated by the clinician. It is then practiced and applied by the individual. As a result of this intervention, the individual increases self-control. This intervention involves three phases, assessment, training, and application, and proceeds in the following fashion.

First, the clinician assesses the pattern of the patient's thoughts and feelings that leads up to self-destructive or maladaptive impulsive behavior. Once this pattern is understood, it is possible for the patient to find other ways to accomplish the desired results that have fewer negative effects and are more likely to be adaptive.

Second, the clinician and the patient together examine the patient's thoughts and feelings that lead up to self-destructive or maladaptive impulse behaviors. For example, the patient is encouraged to keep a log of thoughts and feelings associated with each impulsive behavior.

Third, the clinician teaches the patient to form competing responses to impulses, by first inducing an urge to act impulsively and then helping the patient implement strategies to delay acting on that impulse for progressively longer periods of time; these strategies can be cognitive (i.e., counting to 10 before acting or speaking when upset) or muscle relaxation (i.e., progressive relaxation). The most common competing responses are systematic distractions that are either internal or external. Internal distractions are thoughts that are incompatible with the impulses. For example, the patient's self-talk becomes: "This is actually funny, and I'm going to smile instead of fuming." External distractions include a change in the environment that refocuses the patient's attention. For instance, the patient is prompted to leave the room when somebody is shouting at him, whereas in the past, he would have had the impulse to hit that person.

Fourth, the clinician helps the patient practice the skill and supplies feedback until the patient achieves a reasonable level of mastery. The clinician teaches the patient to apply internal and external distractions to neutralize maladaptive impulses. For example, when around a parent who is drinking heavily and is hostile, the patient avoids getting drawn into a fight by conjuring up in his mind an amusing image of Charlie Chaplin walking with a drunken limp or by saying he has to leave to meet a friend.

Finally, because self-destructive impulsive behavior can have serious consequences, it is essential for the clinician to develop a clear understanding of a patient's motivation by examining the thoughts and feelings leading up to the self-destructive impulses or behavior, and then by asking directly, "What were you trying to accomplish through this action?"

Suicide attempts, self-mutilation, and other self-destructive acts can be the result of many different motives: desire to punish others at whom the client is angry, desire to punish oneself to obtain relief from guilt, desire to distract oneself from even more aversive obsessions, and so forth. Once the motivation is understood, it is possible for the patient to find other ways to accomplish the desired result with fewer untoward effects and that are more likely to be adaptive. For example, it may be possible to substitute a minimally self-destructive behavior, such as marking oneself with a pen, for a more self-destructive act, such as wrist-slashing. The less destructive act can later be replaced by a more adaptive alternative. Not surprisingly, if there is high risk of the patient's performing seriously self-destructive acts and the above-described interventions do not prove effective in the limited time available, hospitalization may be needed to allow sufficient time for effective intervention.

Resources

Linehan, M. (1993). *Skill training manual for treating borderline personality disorder.* New York: Guilford.
Turkat, I. (1990). *The personality disorders: A psychological approach to clinical management.* New York: Pergamon Press.

Interpersonal Skills Training

Interpersonal skills refer to a broad range of skills in relating socially as well as intimately with others. These include distress tolerance, emotional regulation, impulse control, active listening, assertiveness, problem-solving, friendship skills, negotiation, and conflict resolution. Lower functioning individuals with personality disorders may have significant skill deficits, while higher functioning individuals with personality disorders tend to have better developed conversational skills. However, being effective interpersonally requires much more than the ability to produce automatic responses to routine situations. It also requires skills in producing novel responses or a combination of responses as a situation demands. Interpersonal effectiveness is the capacity to respond appropriately and assertively, to negotiate reasonably, and to cope effectively with interpersonal conflict. Effectiveness means obtaining the changes one wants, while maintaining the relationship and one's self-respect. And even if higher-functioning borderline patients possess adequate interpersonal skills, problems arise in the application of these skills in difficult situations. They may be able to describe effective behavioral sequences when discussing another person encountering a problematic situation but may be totally unable to carry out a similar behavioral sequence in their own situation. Usually, the problem is that both belief patterns and uncontrollable affective responses inhibit the application of social skills. These patients often prematurely terminate relationships, or their skill deficits in distress tolerance make it difficult to tolerate the fears, anxieties, or frustrations that are typical in conflictual situations. Similarly, problems in impulse control and emotional regulation lead to inability to decrease chronic anger or frustration. Furthermore, skill deficit problem-solving skills make it difficult to turn potential relationship conflicts into positive encounters. In short, interpersonal competence requires most of the skills described in this chapter as well as others. The intervention proceeds in the following fashion.

First, the clinician must assess the patient's current relational skills and skill deficits. The skills to be assessed include distress tolerance, emotional regulation, impulse control, assertiveness, problem-solving, active listening, friendship skills, negotiation, and conflict resolution. Specific skill deficits are noted.

Second, the clinician formulates a plan for dealing with the noted skill deficits. If there are global deficits, it might require referral to group therapy focused on social skills training. Such groups are invaluable in providing social support while patients are learning personal and interpersonal skills.

Third, skill training begins either in an individual- or group-treatment context. Usually, the sequence involves modeling of a given skill and then coaching to achieve increasing levels of mastery. Interventions that involve several modes of practice or enactment seem to be the most efficacious and time efficient. Video demonstration of the skills, role-play practice, and homework exercises are integral features of such an approach. When a patient who has been referred to a skills training group is also in individual treatment, the clinician assesses and monitors progress.

Fourth, the clinician works together with the patient to arrange for the patient to practice a given skill outside the treatment context. This usually includes initiating conversations with strangers, making friends, or making and going on dates. Assessment of the skill level is followed by additional modeling and coaching.

Resources

Liberman, R., De Risis, W., & Mueser, K. (1989). *Social skills training for psychiatric patients.* New York: Pergamon.

Linehan, M. (1993a). *Cognitive-behavioral treatment of borderline personality disorder.* New York: Guilford.

Linehan, M. (1993b). *Skill training manual for treating borderline personality disorder.* New York: Guilford.

Zimbardo, P. (1977). *Shyness.* New York: Jove.

Limit-Setting

Limit-setting is an intervention designed to help patients recognize aspects of themselves that they defend by resorting to a destructive, outer-directed activity or diversion. Individuals with personality disorders often have difficulty maintaining boundaries, as well as appreciating and anticipating the consequences, especially the negative consequences, of their actions. Limit-setting is a therapeutic intervention that is quite useful outside of treatment settings as well. The intervention proceeds in the following fashion.

First, the clinician observes or anticipates one of the following patient behaviors: treatment-interfering behaviors, such as coming late for sessions, missing a session, unnecessarily delaying or failing to make payments; harmful behavior to self or others, including parasuicidal behaviors; inappropriate verbal behavior (e.g., abusive language); dominating treatment sessions by excessive or rambling speech; attempts to communicate with the clinician outside the treatment context (i.e., unnecessary phone calls); inappropriate actions (e.g., hitting or unwanted touching, breaking or stealing items); or failure to complete assigned therapeutic tasks (i.e., homework). Here is an example from a real case: An obviously well-off patient complained of financial hardship and requested a special reduced fee and payment schedule.

Second, the clinician begins by setting the limit. The limit is specified with such phrases as "if ..., then ...." It is crucial that the clinician state the limit in a neutral, noncritical tone and nonjudgmental language. In the example above, rather than making special concessions to the patient, the standard fee arrangements were clearly explained. The patient was told that if treatment at this clinic was too expensive, the clinician would be sorry but would assist the patient in finding lower-cost treatment elsewhere.

Third, the clinician explains the rationale for the limit. In the example, it was further explained that allowing the patient to accumulate a huge bill would not be in the patient's best interests.

Fourth, the clinician specifies or negotiates with the patient the consequences for breaching the limit. In the example, that clinician told the patient that falling behind in payments by two sessions, according to clinic policy, meant that the patient had to wait until the balance was current before additional sessions would be scheduled.

Fifth, the clinician responds to any breeches of the set limits. Patients can and do test the set limits—whether for conscious or unconscious reasons—more commonly in the early phase of treatment, so such testing should be expected. The clinician should be prepared to respond by confronting or interpreting the testing; enforcing consequences and discussing the impact of the breech on the treatment; or predicting that such testing may reoccur. For example, in the above case, the patient did test the agreement once; the clinician expressed concern but upheld the limit. Thereafter, the patient kept up with the payments and the treatment continued.

Resource

Green, S. (1988). *Limit setting in clinical practice*. Washington, DC: American Psychiatric Press.

Mindfulness Training

There are at least two types of mindfulness training that have been found useful in treating individuals with personality disorders. The first one to be articulated, dialectual behavior therapy (DBT), involves six skills, and the other, mindfulness-based cognitive therapy (MBCT), involves four skills. The skill sets for both of these approaches are briefly described.

Dialectical Behavior Therapy

Mindfulness is the first, and most important, of four core skill sets that make up the psychoeducational component of DBT. These skills are usually taught in a group format by someone other than the patient's therapist. A recent adaptation of DBT for private practice allows patients to learn the skills in a one-to-one or group setting (Marra, 2005). Linehan (1993) divides mindfulness skills into two categories: "what" skills and "how" skills. The "what" skills include the following: Observe—just notice without getting caught in the experience; describe—put words on the experience; and participate—become one with your experience. The "how" skills include the following: Nonjudgmental—see, but do not evaluate; one-mindful—do one thing at a time; effective—do what needs to be done in each situation. The reader will note that unlike mindfulness in MBCT, DBT does not include any formal meditation. That is because Linehan contends that sitting meditation exercises are too demanding for individuals with severe personality disorders, such as borderline personality disorder. Following is a brief description of each of the six mindfulness skills in DBT.

Observing

Goal: The goal is to sense or experience something without describing or labeling the experience. It is noticing or attending to something without getting caught up in the experience and without reacting to it.

Activities for Skill Practice: Encourage patients to have a "Teflon mind" so that experiences, feelings, and thoughts that enter the mind slip right out. Develop exercises wherein patients can practice observing. For example, have them close their eyes and watch their thoughts coming and going like clouds in the sky. Have them notice each feeling, rising and falling, like waves in the ocean. Or have them take a walk and attend to every sensation they feel through their senses—what they feel as they step on the walkway or on small pebbles on a path, what scents they smell, what hues of colors they see, what sounds they hear, such as sounds of insects, animals, and the wind.

Describing

Goal: The goal is to use words or thoughts to label what has been observed. Describing involves reporting facts without making judgments or evaluations, for example, "It tasted sour" instead of "I didn't like the taste" and "He told me what happened" instead of "He's not very honest."

Activities for Skill Practice: Design exercises where patients can have an experience and provide a running commentary. For example, when a feeling, inner sensation, or thought arises, they might say out loud to a person they are paired up with: "I'm feeling anxious right now"... or ... " my stomach muscles are tightening" ... or ... "The thought 'I just can't do this exercise' has come into my mind." For homework, assign them a diary or journal exercise: Have them describe in writing whatever is happening; putting a name on their feelings, that is, calling a thought just a thought, a feeling just a feeling, without getting caught up in content.

The conveyor belt exercise: Have the patients imagine that their thoughts and feelings are coming down a conveyor belt. Ask the patients to sort them into categories. For example, there is a box for thoughts of any kind, a box for sensations in the body, and a box for urges to do something (e.g., stopping). Then, ask them to rate and log their efforts at developing this skill on a 1–10 scale, and review the log periodically.

Participating

Goal: The goal is to enter wholly into an activity, meaning that patients throw themselves 100% into something. It means becoming one with their experiences, completely forgetting themselves. It is spontaneous behavior to a certain extent, but it is done from a mindful perspective.

Activities for Skill Practice: Design activities in which patients can get fully involved in the moment, while letting go of ruminating. For example, have the patients actively practice a social skill in which they have a deficit; for example, have the individual who is shy and avoidant around others practice making small talk, talking about the weather or an upcoming social or sports event. The patient practices on the new skill through the entire course so that it can be done without any self-consciousness. Have the patients rate and log their efforts at developing this skill on a 1–10 scale, and review the log periodically.

Nonjudgmental

Goal: The goal is to take a nonjudgmental stance when observing, describing, and participating. Judging involves labeling or evaluation of something as good or bad, valuable or not, worthwhile or worthless. There is a difference between a judgment and a statement of fact. A statement of fact may seem to be a judgment because the fact is simultaneously being judged. For example, "I am fat" may simply be a statement of fact. But if one adds (in thoughts, implication, or tone of voice) that the idea of being fat is bad or unattractive, then a judgment is added.. The motto or mantra for this week should be: "Observe, but don't judge."

Activities for Skill Practice: Design exercises for a class format so that patients can focus on the "what" instead of the "good" or "bad" or the "should" or "should not." You might have them listen to clips of dialogue from a popular TV show or movie and have them point out a judgmental stance vs. a nonjudgmental stance. It is useful to give them home assignments in which they can note, in their diary or journal, situations in which they did practice or could have practiced a nonjudgmental stance. Have them rate and log their efforts at developing this skill on a 1–10 scale, and review the log periodically.

One-Mindful

Goal: The goal is to focus only on one activity or thing at a given moment—to be aware of what you are doing. This means bringing one's whole self into the task or activity. A motto or mantra for the course could be: "Do one thing at a time." When eating—eat. When walking—walk. When bathing—bathe. When working—work. When in a group or in a one-on-one conversation, focus attention only on the person speaking. When thinking—think. When worrying—worry. Do each thing with all of your attention. If other actions, thoughts, or strong feelings distract you, let go. Let go of distractions and get further in touch with your true self. The opposite of it is mindlessness, that is, automatic behaviors without awareness, and distracted behavior, that is, doing one thing while thinking about or attending to another and doing something again, and again, and again.

Activities for Skill Practice: Design exercises for a class format and for home assignments so that patients can practice focused attention or concentration. If they find they are doing two things at once, they must stop and go back to doing one thing at a time. Point out that focusing on one thing in the moment does not mean that they cannot do complex tasks requiring many simultaneous activities. But it does require that whatever one does, one should attend fully to it, that is, focus attention only on one activity or thing at a time, thus bringing one's whole self into the task or activity. Have them rate and log their efforts at developing this skill on a 1–10 scale, and review the log periodically.

Effective

Goal: The goal is to focus on being effective, that is, focusing on what works and doing what needs to be done in each situation. It means limiting the use of evaluative comments, such as "fair" and "unfair," "right" and "wrong," or "should" and "should not." As Marsha Linehan puts it: "Don't cut off your nose to spite your face."

Activities for Skill Practice: Plan exercises in which patients can act as skillfully as they can and meet the needs of the situation they are in. A useful home assignment is to have the patients keep a log or diary of the instances in the past week in which they attempted to keep sight of their objective in specific situations and to do what was necessary to achieve them. The goal is to accomplish an objective without vengeance, useless anger, or self-righteousness. Have them rate and log their efforts at developing this skill on a 1–10 scale, and review the log periodically.

Mindfulness-Based Cognitive Therapy Approach

MBCT is another strategy for incorporating mindfulness into psychotherapy. It utilizes a skill-training group format to teach four sets of mindfulness skills in order to increase patients' moment-to-moment awareness and to approach situations with an attitude of being nonjudgmental and of acceptance. It involves intensive training both in a class format, facilitated by an instructor rather than a therapist, and home practice. The four sets of meditative practices or skills are described below.

Body Scan

This skill guides patients to shift attention to various areas of the body to directly explore physical sensations, without having to change them or achieve any special state.

Stretch and Breath

This skill involves a sequence of five simple standing stretches to concentrate on body sensations during each movement, with focus on sensations of the breath.

Yoga

This skill involves simple stretches starting from a prone posture, to allow patients to explore sensations of the body in movement and stillness and to explore the how the body has limits that can be respected without judgment and self-criticism.

Sitting Meditation

This skill guides patients to focus, in turns, on the breath, the body, the sounds, the thoughts, and the emotions. Patients learn to view their own thoughts and emotions from a new perspective, relating to them as they relate to sounds, discovering that thoughts often come and go as leaves on a stream or as white clouds passing across a blue sky.

Resources

Kabat-Zinn J. (1994.). *Wherever you go, there you are: Mindfulness meditation in everyday life.* New York: Hyperion.

Linehan, M (1993a). *Skills training manual for treating borderline personality disorder.* New York, Guilford.

Linehan, M (1993b). *Cognitive behavioral treatment of borderline personality disorder.* New York, Guilford.

Marra, T. (2005). *Dialectic behavior therapy in private practice: A practical and comprehensive guide.* Oakland, CA: New Harbinger Publications.

Segal Z, Williams J., & Teasdale J. (2002). *Mindfulness-based cognitive therapy for depression: A new approach to preventing relapse.* New York: Guilford Press.

Problem-Solving Skills Training

Problem-solving skills training is a treatment intervention strategy through which individuals learn to use an effective set of skills to cope with distressing or troublesome personal and interpersonal situations. The goals of this form of social skills training is to assist individuals in identifying problems that cause their distress, to teach them a systematic method of solving problems, and to equip them with a method for approaching future problems. Problem-solving training is often a brief method of intervention that can be used in individual-, couples-, and group-treatment contexts. This is a clinician-initiated intervention than requires some training and practice on the part of the individual to master this set of skills. This intervention proceeds in the following fashion.

First, the clinician assesses the patient's capacity to solve problems in terms of the five skills involved in problem-solving: problem identification, goal-setting, generating alternative courses of action, decision-making, and implementation of the decided course of action.

Second, the clinician explores, with the patient, the origin and nature of a specific problematic situation (i.e., problem identification). For instance, the patient notes that she usually runs out of money about 1 week before receiving her monthly paycheck because of impulse buying during the first 3 weeks of the month.

Third, the clinician helps the patient assess the problem, identify causative factors, and set realistic goals. In the above example, impulse buying is identified as the cause, and the goal set is to budget money to last the entire month, and to save 10% of the salary in a bank account.

Fourth, the clinician helps the patient generate alternative courses of action. In the above example, one alternative is to develop a 30-day budget, a second is to ask to be paid biweekly, and the third is to have an automatic salary deposit in a bank account.

Fifth, the clinician helps the patient choose a course of action with regard to its short- and long-range consequences. In this example, the patient decides that setting up a budget is the most realistic short- as well as long-term course of action.

Sixth, the clinician offers information and supports the patient's efforts to implement the course of action. In this case, the patient agrees to meet with a financial planner to set up monthly and annual budget plans and also opens a savings account.

Resources

Hawton, K. & Kirk, J. (1989). Problem-solving. In K. Hawton, P. Salkovskis, J. Kirk, & D. Clark (Eds.), *Cognitive behavior therapy for psychiatric problems*. Oxford, England: Oxford University Press.

Self-Management Skills

Self-management skills are needed to learn, maintain, and generalize new behaviors and to inhibit or extinguish undesirable behaviors and behavioral changes. In its widest sense, self-management means efforts to control, manage, or otherwise change one's own behavior, thoughts, or emotional responses to events. Thus, the skills of distress tolerance, emotion regulation, impulse control, and anger management can be considered self-management skills. More specifically, self-management skills refer to the behavior capabilities that an individual needs to have to acquire further skills. To the extent that patients are deficient in self-management skills, their ability to acquire other skills is seriously compromised. Patients often need some knowledge of the principles of behavior change to effectively learn self-management skills. For instance, a patient's belief that individuals change complex behavior patterns in a heroic show of willpower sets the stage for an accelerating cycle of failure and self-condemnation. The failure to master a goal becomes additional proof that explanations of failure, such as laziness, lack of motivation, or lack of will power, are true. The clinician must confront and replace these notions of how individuals change. In short, the principles of learning and behavior control, as well as knowledge about how these principles apply in each individual's case, are important targets in teaching self-management skills. Learning these targeted concepts often involves changes in a patient's belief system. The intervention typically proceeds in the following manner.

First, the clinician assesses the patient's overall level of self-management, as well as specific subskills of goal-setting, self-monitoring, environment control, toleration of limited progress, and relapse prevention, and notes any skill deficits.

Second, the clinician formulates a plan for dealing with the skill deficits noted. If there are global deficits, referral to a group focused on social skills training might be required. Such groups are invaluable in providing social support while patients are learning personal and interpersonal skills.

Third, skill training begins either in an individual- or group-treatment context. Usually, the sequence involves the clinician modeling a given skill and then coaching the patient to achieve increasing levels of mastery. Interventions that involve several modes of practice or enactment seem to be the most efficacious and time efficient. Video demonstration of the skills, role-play practice, and homework exercises are integral features of such an approach. When a patient who has been referred to a skills-training group is also in individual treatment, the clinician continues to assess and monitor progress.

Patients need to learn how to formulate positive goals in place of negative goals, to assess both positive and negative goals realistically, and to examine their life patterns from the point of view of values clarification. Patients typically believe that nothing short of perfection is an acceptable outcome. Behavior change goals are often sweeping in context and clearly exceed the skills the patients may possess. Clinicians will need to teach patients such skills as self-monitoring and environment-monitoring, setting up and evaluating baselines, and evaluating empirical data to determine relationships between antecedent and consequent events and the patients' own responses. These skills are very similar to the hypothesis-testing skills taught in cognitive therapy.

The belief that a patient can overcome any set of environmental stimuli is based on the assumption that it is possible to function independently of one's environment. Given this belief, it is not surprising that some patients have skill deficits when it comes to using their environments as a means of controlling their own behavior. Nevertheless, some patients are more responsive to transitory environmental cues than are others. As a result, the capability to manage environmental surroundings effectively can be particularly crucial. Such techniques as stimulus narrowing, that is, reducing the number of distracting events in the immediate environment, and stimulus avoidance, that is, avoiding events that trigger problematic behaviors, can be targeted to counteract the belief that willpower alone is sufficient.

Some patients respond to a relapse or small failure as an indication that they are total failures and may as well give up. Accordingly, they will develop a self-management plan and then unrealistically expect perfection in adhering to the plan. The focus of relapse prevention is attitude change. It then becomes essential to teach patients to plan realistically for possible relapse, to develop strategies for accepting the possibility of a slip, and to alleviate the negative effects of relapse.

Because some patients have limited tolerance for feeling bad, they have difficulties carrying out behavior change action plans that require perseverance. Rather, they will often seek a quick fix that involves setting unreasonably short time limits for relatively complex changes. In other words, they expect instantaneous progress. If it does not occur, they believe they have failed. Therefore, emphasizing the gradual nature of behavior change and tolerance of concomitant negative affect should be a major focus of the clinician's effort.

Fourth, the clinician works together with the patient to arrange for the patient to practice a given skill or a set of skills outside the treatment context. This usually includes initiating conversations with strangers, making friends, making and going on dates. Assessment of the skill level is followed by additional modeling and coaching.

Resources

Linehan, M. (1993a). *Cognitive-behavioral treatment of borderline personality disorder.* New York: Guilford.

Linehan, M. (1993b). *Skill training manual for treating borderline personality disorder.* New York: Guilford.

Sensitivity Reduction Training

Sensitivity reduction training is an intervention to neutralize and delimit an individual's vulnerability to criticism, misperception, and suspiciousness. Individuals who habitually misperceive and negatively distort social cues are prone to defensive and acting-out behaviors. This intervention teaches individuals to more accurately and more effectively attend to, process, and respond to social cues. This is a clinician-initiated intervention wherein the clinician enables the patient to learn and practice more accurate use of social information. This intervention proceeds in the following fashion.

First, the clinician recognizes that these oversensitivity reactions involve errors and distortions in the course of information-processing. Information-processing can be thought of in terms of four components: attending, information-processing, responding, and feedback. Subsequently, this intervention is directed at these four components.

Second, the clinician assesses how the individual attends to the full range of social cues. This can be done by reviewing important social interactions of the individual, and critically assessing how the individual attends to pertinent social cues. For instance, an individual reports that as he enters a social gathering, a small group of people look at him and smile, and then he hears a whispered comment, after which everyone laughs. If the individual selectively attends only to the whispered comment and disregards the other two cues—smiling and laughter—he could misperceive the situation and respond defensively. If the individual is not identifying and attending to such pertinent cues, the clinician focuses training in this area.

Third, the clinician then assesses the accuracy of the individual's interpretation of this social information. Selective attention and misperception can cause the information to be processed as threatening. Teaching the individual to interpret social cues more accurately is essential. This training can be accomplished with role-playing, videotaped feedback, and instruction.

Fourth, the clinician assesses how the patient responds to cues. Responding refers to the individual's response to the social cues of others, ranging from spoken words, to paralanguage, to overt actions. Responses can range from appropriate and prosocial to inappropriate and harmful. To the extent that the individual is able to accurately attend to and process social cues, he or she is more likely to appropriately respond to them. Training is directed at appropriate responding. Although the focus of training is often on verbal responding, at times, the individual's tone of voice, facial expression, or hand gesturing may need to be changed to make the response less menacing.

Fifth, the clinician assesses how the patient uses the consequences of his or her social behavior and the extent to which it is appropriate or maladaptive. Even negative feedback can be useful information, and the individual needs to learn to use it constructively. Furthermore, with improvement in social behavior, positive consequences should accrue to the individual.

Resource

Turkat, I. (1990). *The personality disorders: A psychological approach to clinical management.* New York: Pergamon Press.

Symptom Management Training

Symptom management training is an intervention strategy for controlling the distressing manifestations (i.e., symptoms) of psychiatric disorders. Although symptoms are of varying types and levels of intensity and duration, patients tend to report them without such differentiation. Unless the clinician clarifies the type, intensity, and duration of symptoms, referrals or needless changes in treatments, such as altered medication dosage or added medications, can result in significant untoward effects on the treatment process. Individuals with personality disorders are more likely to experience low-grade, subclinical symptoms (i.e., persistent symptoms) than acute symptoms. Yet, they are likely to demand increased dosage or changes in medication, not realizing that persistent symptoms are rarely responsive to medication. Accordingly, this intervention often requires the use of psychosocial and psychoeducational methods. Symptom management training involves learning such skills as self-monitoring, medication compliance, and relapse prevention. It can be taught in individual- or group-treatment settings. It is a clinician-initiated intervention that involves collaboration to assess, teach/learn, and practice the requisite skills. This intervention proceeds in the following fashion.

First, the clinician assesses the type and nature of symptoms experienced by the patient. Symptoms are of three types: (a) persistent symptoms (i.e., chronic, low-grade symptoms not alleviated by medication), (b) warning symptoms (i.e., symptoms gradually increasing in intensity that precedes an acute episode), and (c) acute symptoms (i.e., the full-blown incapacitating symptoms that often signal acute decompensation). The nature of symptoms includes both their intensity and duration.

Second, the clinician works with the patient to increase awareness and understanding of the types and nature of his or her symptoms and the skills necessary to effectively manage those symptoms. The patient is taught the self-monitoring skill of identifying the type of symptom and intensity (i.e., rates and logs on a 5-point scale: 1 = mild, 5 = very severe), and duration (i.e., logs the amount of time in minutes and number of times the symptom types occur each day for 1 week).

Third, an intervention is planned and tailored to the particular type and expression of symptoms experienced by the individual. Accordingly, acute symptoms are usually treated with medication or a combination of medication and individual or group psychosocial or psychoeducational treatment. Psychoeducational methods include learning activities and formats, such as videotapes, role-playing, and homework assignments. Because warning symptoms can result from insufficient medication levels, it is useful to raise medication levels or consider additional medication. Because warning symptoms can also result from stopping or decreasing medication, it is essential to find out about medication noncompliance, which may necessitate checking with a caregiver or significant other. In contrast, persistent symptoms seldom suggest insufficient medication levels or noncompliance. Thus, they do not require changing the dosage or drug regimen but rather the psychoeducational methods, such as distraction techniques. For example, individuals with low-level but chronic dysphoria might achieve considerable relief by distracting themselves from the low energy and blue mood, for example, by listening to uplifting or energetic music or by watching a funny movie.

Fourth, the patient practices the interventions (i.e., rating and logging symptoms) and distraction techniques within a given time frame and reports the results at the next meeting with the clinician.

Resource

Liberman, R. (1988). *Social and independent living skills: Symptom management module: Trainers manual*. Los Angeles, CA: Rehabilitation Research.

Thought-Stopping

Thought-stopping is a self-control intervention to block or eliminate ruminative or intrusive thought patterns that are unproductive or anxiety-producing. It may also have the effect of increasing the patient's sense of control and reducing distress. This intervention is usually introduced and demonstrated by the clinician. It is then practiced and applied by the individual. The intervention proceeds in the following fashion.

First, the clinician instructs the client on the distinction between normal thoughts and obsessional/intrusive thoughts. They reach an agreement to try to reduce the duration of the intrusive thoughts, thus making these thoughts more "normal" and increasing the client's sense of control.

Second, the clinician and the client draw up a list of three obsessional thoughts and several specific triggering scenarios. Then, they make a list of up to three alternative thoughts (i.e., interesting or relaxing thoughts). For example, image of a pleasant scene from a movie, lying on a sandy beach, or taking a walk through the woods. Each obsessional thought is rated for the discomfort it produces on a scale of 1–10 (1 = lowest, 10 = highest).

Third, the clinician demonstrates how to block obsessional thoughts and substitute them with alternative thoughts. The clinician directs the individual to close the eyes and relax and to raise a hand when an obsessional thought is first experienced. For example, the clinician may say: "Sit back and relax, and let your eyes close. I'll mention a specific triggering scene to you, and then you will describe your experiencing an obsessional thought. As soon as you begin to think the thought, raise your hand, even if I'm still describing the scene." The clinician then describes a typical triggering scene, and as soon as the individual raises a hand, the clinician says, "Stop!" loudly. The clinician asks the client whether the obsessional thought was blocked and whether the individual was able to imagine an alternative scene in some detail. The discomfort arising from the obsessional thought is then rated on the 1–10 scale.

Fourth, the clinician then leads the client in practicing thought-stopping with different triggering scenes and alternative thoughts, and the discomfort ratings are recorded. Practice continues until the individual can sufficiently block and replace the obsessional thoughts.

Fifth, the procedure is modified so that following the clinician's description of the triggering scene and the patient's obsessional thought, the patient says, "Stop!" and describes the alternative scene. Practice continues until the individual can sufficiently block and replace the obsessional thought.

Sixth, the clinician gives an intrasession assignment (homework) to the client for 15 minutes of practice a day at those times when the client is not distressed by intrusive thoughts. A log is kept with ratings of 1–10 for the distress and vividness evoked by the intrusive thought.

Finally, after a week of practice, the clinician prescribes the intervention to be used to dismiss mild to moderately distressing thoughts as they occur. The client is instructed that as the sense of control increases, the thoughts, when they do occur, will become less distressing (on the 1–10 scale) until the individual experiences little or no concern about them.

Resource

Hawton, K., Salkovskis, P., Kirk, J., & Clark, D. (Eds.). (1989). *Cognitive behavior therapy for psychiatric problems.* Oxford, England: Oxford University Press.

☐ Summary

Character has been rediscovered as a basic component of personality and as a key factor in the effective treatment of personality disorders. To the extent that an individual's temperament dimensions or styles are dysregulated, the individual will experience distress or be distressing to others. Higher functioning individuals socialize and learn self-management and relational skills to regulate such style dimensions as impulsivity, labile affects, and aggressivity during the course of normal development in childhood and adolescence. A hallmark of the early onset of personality disorders is deficits in some or many of these coping skills. Both structured psychosocial interventions and medication can be useful in regulating or modulating these style dimensions. This chapter has detailed 15 structured treatment intervention strategies that are useful in modulating affective, behavioral, relational, and cognitive styles.

II
Part

CBT Strategies for Specific Personality Disorders

The second part of this book focuses on specific treatment strategies for six common personality disorders that are considered reasonably amenable to treatment. There are two parts to this introductory section: an overview of Chapters 4–9 and a set of general guidelines for treating more severe or impaired individuals. The following is the common outline for these chapters:

I.   Clinical Conceptualization of the Specific Personality Disorder
II. DSM-IV Description and Criteria
III. Effective Treatment Strategies
    1.   Engagement Strategies
       Initial Session Behavior
       Facilitating Collaboratioin
       Transference/Countertransference
    2.   Pattern Analysis Strategies
       Optimal Criteria
       Schema/Character
       Style/Temperament
    3.   Pattern Change Strategies
       Schema/Character Change
       Style/Temperament Change
       Medication

Group/Family/Couple Therapy
Combined/Integrative Therapy
4. Pattern Maintenance/Termination Strategies
Termination Issues
Relapse Prevention
IV. Summary
V. Case Example

☐ An Overview of Chapters 4–9

The first section: Clinical Conceptualization of the Specific Personality Disorder lists the clinical features and formulations for each disorder. Readers wanting further information are referred to the *Handbook of Diagnosis and Treatment of DSM-IV-TR Personality Disorders, Second Edition* (Sperry, 2003).

The second section: DSM-IV Description and Criteria presents the DSM-IV description and criteria for the particular disorder.

The third section describes the treatment process and effective strategies for treating each of the personality disorders considered amenable to treatment. Engagement, pattern identification, pattern change, and pattern maintenance refer to the stages of the treatment process from which specific effective strategies have been derived to guide treatment.

The subsection on Engagement describes relationship factors that are likely to be encountered with individuals manifesting a particular disorder. Specific behaviors that are likely to be manifest in the initial session are described. Specific challenges that the clinician must face in facilitating a working alliance or therapeutic collaboration are noted, as well as the most common transferences and countertransferences.

The subsection on Pattern Analysis Strategies describes optimal criteria, schemas, and style/skills dimensions for each disorder. The optimal DSM-IV single criterion for each disorder is given. Obviously, the diagnosis of personality disorders would be easier if clinicians had only one criterion to remember for each personality disorder. *Schemas* refer to the patient's core beliefs about the self and the world. Schemas reflect the characterological dimension of the disorder. *Style* refers to the temperament or style dimension of the personality disorder, whereas *skills* refers to the type and level of self-regulation skills and social skills as well as the skill deficits most characteristic of a particular personality disorder.

The subsection on Pattern Change Strategies describes several therapeutic interventions and methods for changing the schemas or modifying the characterological dimensions of the particular disorder. It also provides a number of treatment methods for modifying the style or tempera-ment dimensions that are under- or overmodulated for a given disorder. Typically, treatment is initially directed at modulating or regulating dysregulated dimensions of temperament that increase the patient's read-iness and availability to engage in therapeutic change directed at the char-acter dimension of the disorder. Finally, other modalities that are useful and necessary for treatment effectiveness are briefly described.

The subsection on Pattern Maintenance and Termination Strategies offers specific suggestions and directions on terminating the treatment process and preventing relapse. Although premature termination is common among individuals with personality disorders, it is less common when treatment is tailored. Nevertheless, planned termination of treatment is particularly difficult with certain personality disorders. When compared with Axis I or symptom disorders, a tailored relapse prevention plan is an absolutely essential treatment strategy with Axis II or personality disorders.

The Case Example section presents the many ideas and strategies previ-ously described in the context of a clinical case. An in-depth case example illustrates how engagement strategies, pattern analysis strategies, pattern change strategies, and pattern maintenance and termination strategies were used in an actual case. It goes without saying that to ensure confi-dentiality, actual names have not been used.

☐ Guidelines for Modifying Treatment Strategy

Throughout Chapters 4–9, several specific treatment strategies will be suggested and described. Many of these strategies are illustrated with specific case material. The challenge of anyone teaching or writing about psychiatric treatment is to articulate general and specific principles and methods so that these principles and methods can be reasonably applicable to a variety of patients. As the cases of Keri and Cindy (described earlier) demonstrate, individuals with personality disorders can present with widely different levels of symptom severity and functional impairment. The clinician's task is to choose, combine, and tailor therapeutic interven-tions to optimize the treatment process and outcome. Unfortunately, texts cannot effectively teach this skill of combining and tailoring treatment strategies. At best, they can only offer general guidelines for working with the more symptomatic and impaired individuals with personality disorders. Here are four such guidelines that might be useful.

First, specify the type and degree of symptoms severity and impairment of functioning. Severity and impairment can be focal or global. Furthermore, both severity and impairment change: There is either a movement toward improvement—which may or may not be related to treatment, or—what is not uncommon among patients with personality disorders—there may be a pattern of waxing and waning of severity or impairment or of both. Therefore, it is useful to assess the type and degree of both. A strong case can be made for adopting a standardized or self-developed assessment or rating system and using it regularly to treat patients with personality disorders. As health care continues to demand greater accountability in the form of treatment outcome data, this kind of routine rating of a patient's symptomatic presentation and functional level will become commonplace.

Symptoms should be assessed or rated in terms of subtype and degree. Symptom subtypes include such standard categories as those found in standardized instruments—for example, the SCL–90R (Derogatis, 1983), and Compass–OP (Sperry, Brill, Howard, & Grisson, 1996)—which include adjustment, anxiety, depression, bipolar symptoms, obsessive-compulsive symptoms, phobia, and psychosis. Symptoms can also be addressed in terms of intensity and duration, as being either acute, warning, or persistent symptoms (Sperry, 1995).

Level of functioning or impairment can be specified by such subtypes as those used in the Social Security Disability Guidelines or the Compass-OP. These include family, health, intimate relationships, self-management, social relationships, and occupational relationships (work, school, home). A rating system developed by Kennedy (1992) elaborates the GAF scale of Axis V of DSM-IV. It consists of four categories: social skills, dangerousness, occupational, and substance abuse, and an overall rating of psychological impairment.

Second, on the basis of an assessment of severity and impairment, establish a problem list. The problem list should be focused, specific, and workable. Symptoms and functional areas are viewed as treatment targets. The more the patient is symptomatic or experiencing impairment, the more structured the treatment should become. As such, treatment functions as a "holding environment" that is itself therapeutic.

Third, on the basis of the treatment list, focus treatment accordingly. A basic premise of this book is that focused treatment tends to be more effective with symptomatic or lower-functioning individuals with personality disorders than is generic treatment. A related premise is that as tailored and integrative modalities become increasingly necessary, the level of treatability is lowered. Accordingly, treatment with difficult patients should focus on alleviating a specific symptom or a specific area of functioning. For symptom management, it may mean introducing medication, increasing dosage, or changing to or adding another medication. Or it may mean using a specific behavioral intervention as the main intervention or as an adjunct to medication.

Decreasing functional impairment almost certainly requires combined treatment. Usually, this means changing to a more behavioral focus, that is, behavioral rehearsal, social skills training, and so on. It may also mean adding modalities based on the cognitive and emotional styles and the treatment expectations of the patient. Treatment delivered in combination can have an additive, and sometimes synergystic, effect. Traditional modalities, such as group, family, or couple sessions, may be useful, but so may referral to a support group, such as Alcoholics Anonymous, Recovery, Inc., or groups sponsored by the National Depressive and Manic Depressive Association. It may just as likely mean "environmental engineering" (i.e., encouraging a patient to leave an abusive relationship or move out of a living situation that fosters substance abuse or dependence).

Fourth, continue monitoring severity and impairment during the course of treatment. Ongoing data collection can prove extremely useful when working with individuals with severe disorders. Being able to view graphic representations of the trends of symptoms and functioning over the course of several sessions can be quite revealing for both patient and clinician. Patterns might be detected that otherwise could be missed. For example, increased symptomatology may be found to be related to previously unrecognized circumstances, thoughts, or relationships. Or one particular area of functional impairment, such as work, may continue to lag behind other areas and may never have been seriously addressed in sessions. Charting out the changes in both the subtypes and degrees of symptoms, as well as functional subtypes and degrees, may be a useful prognostic guide. Little or no change after several sessions may indicate that the goals of treatment, treatment strategy, and the patient's motivation for change need to be reviewed. These are some general clinical guidelines to keep in mind while reading and applying the specific guidelines presented in the following chapters.

CHAPTER

Avoidant Personality Disorder

Avoidant personalities are aloof, ill-at-ease, awkward, and hypersensitive individuals with low self-esteem. Although they are desperate for interpersonal involvement, they avoid personal contact with others because of their heightened fear of social disapproval and rejection. Although the treatment of individuals with avoidant personalities involves a number of unique therapeutic challenges, these patients can be effectively treated. As in the rest of this book, the chapter describes specific engagement, pattern analysis, pattern change, pattern maintenance, and pattern termination strategies for effectively managing and treating this disorder. In addition to individual psychotherapeutic strategies and tactics, group, couple, family, medication, integrative, and combined treatment strategies are detailed. A detailed case example illustrates the treatment process. Before turning to treatment strategies, the DSM-IV description and criteria are briefly presented.

Clinical Conceptualization of Avoidant Personality Disorder

Triggering Event(s)	Demands for close interpersonal relating and/or social and public appearances
Behavioral Style	Shy, mistrustful, aloof; apprehensive; socially awkward; controlled, underactive behavior; feelings of emptiness and depersonalization

Interpersonal Style	Guardedly "tests" others; rejection-sensitive and self-protectant; desires acceptance but maintains distance; has basic interpersonal skills, but fears using them
Cognitive Style	Perpetual vigilance; thoughts easily distracted by their hypersensitivity
Feeling Style	Shy and apprehensive
Attachment Style	Preoccupied and fearful
Temperament	Irritable
Parental Injunction	"We don't accept you, and probably nobody else will either."
Self View	"I'm inadequate and frightened of rejection."; chronically tense, fatigued, self-conscious; devalues achievement, self-critical
World View	"Life is unfair, people reject and criticize me, but I want someone to like me. Therefore, I'll be vigilant, demand reassurance, and, if all else fails, fantasize and daydream."
Maladaptive Schemas	Defectiveness; social isolation; approval-seeking, self-sacrifice
Optimal DSM-IV-TR Criteria	Avoids occupational activities that involve significant interpersonal contact, fearing criticism, disapproval, or rejection

☐ DSM-IV Description and Criteria

DSM-IV offers the following description and criteria for avoidant personality disorder (Table 4.1):

TABLE 4.1. DSM-IV Description and Criteria for Avoidant Personality Disorder

301.82 Avoidant Personality Disorder

A pervasive pattern of social inhibition, feelings of inadequacy, and hypersensitivity to negative evaluation, beginning by early adulthood and present in a variety of contexts, as indicated by at least four of the following:

(1) Avoids occupational activities that involve significant interpersonal contact because of fears of criticism, disapproval, or rejection

(2) Is unwilling to get involved with people unless certain of being liked

(3) Shows restraint within intimate relationships because of the fear of being shamed or ridiculed

(4) Is preoccupied with being criticized or rejected in social situations

(5) Is inhibited in new interpersonal situations because of feelings of inadequacy

(6) Views self as socially inept, personally unappealing, or inferior to others

(7) Is unusually reluctant to take personal risks or to engage in any new activities because they may prove embarrassing

---

Reprinted with permission from the *Diagnostic and Statistical Manual of Mental Disorders, Fourth Edition—Text Revision*. Copyright 2000, American Psychiatric Association.

☐ Engagement Strategies

Early Session Behavior

In the initial session, these patients are likely to be somewhat guarded and disengaged. Initially, their communication style tends to be monotonic, monosyllabic, and perhaps even circumstantial. Some will appear suspicious or quite anxious, but all are hypersensitive to rejection and criticism. Accordingly, they will observe the clinician closely for any indication of acceptance or rejection. Such reluctance and guardedness should be approached with empathy and reassurance. The clinician would do well to avoid confrontation, which these patients will interpret as criticism. Rather, the clinician's judicious use of empathic responding encourages sharing of past pain and anticipatory fears. When these patients feel that clinicians understand their hypersensitivity and will protect them, they become considerably more willing to trust and cooperate with treatment. After the patient begins to feel safe and accepted, the atmosphere of the interview changes dramatically. When sufficient rapport has been established, the patients are more comfortable in describing their fears of being embarrassed and criticized, as well as their sensitivity to being misunderstood. They may experience these fears of being embarrassed as silly but troubling. However, when clinicians retreat from an empathic and accepting stance, these individuals are likely to feel ridiculed and will withdraw again (Othmer & Othmer, 2002).

Facilitating Collaboration

Although the process of achieving collaboration with the avoidant patient tends to be both difficult and protracted, it is well worth the effort. Basic to the difficulty is the avoidant patient's tendency to "test" the clinician and the treatment process and the tendency toward premature termination. Because of their underlying sensitivity to criticism and their mistrust of people, these patients have become masters of testing their psychological environment to ascertain which individuals will be positive or at least neutral toward them and which ones are likely to criticize, tease, or emotionally challenge them. Usually, there may be a very small number of persons—usually a family member and a friend or colleague—whom they feel somewhat comfortable to be with and trust to some degree. However, they tend to be rather uncomfortable and distrusting of most individuals, including new clinicians. Subsequently, they will test new clinicians in early sessions by changing appointment dates and times, canceling at the last minute, coming late for sessions, or failing to do homework. The testing continues until they become convinced that the clinician's initial noncritical and nonjudgmental behavior is more than a social veneer that falls away when challenged. Beneath this testing is the belief that people really are basically uncaring and critical. When the clinician is able to remain supportive, caring, and uncritical in the initial sessions in the face of this testing, the avoidant patient becomes more amenable to establishing a tentative bond and trust with the clinician. Only then does collaboration become possible. And when the clinician "fails" these tests, the clinician should not be surprised by premature termination. If there is even the slightest hint that a patient is rejection-sensitive or mistrustful, the clinician would do well to anticipate that the patient will engage in testing behaviors and to respond accordingly, particularly with unconditional regard (Sperry, 2003).

Transference and Countertransference

The most common transference of the avoidant patient is testing the clinician's capacity to be nonjudgmental and caring. As noted in the section above, this transference is very common in the initial sessions. Accepting and sometimes interpreting—particularly through a predictive intepretation—the patient's testing behavior can be useful. Once the clinician passes the various tests, the avoidant patient tends to become increasingly trusting of the clinician. Needless to say, the clinician's stance of unconditional regard is so attractive to these patients that the clinician may be perceived by them as their confidant and most trusted friend. Accordingly, the clinician's task is to resist the exclusivity of this role and work toward broadening the patient's social support system. Later on in the treatment process, overdependence on the clinician is commonly noted. The avoidant patient may also endeavor to have the clinician assume responsibility for many or all of his or her personal decisions. The clinician's challenge is to gently but firmly set limits on the patient's dependency (Gabbard, 2005).

Common countertransferences are the clinician's feelings of frustration at the patient's testing behavior. There is also a brittle quality to these patients that may arouse the clinician's rescue fantasies. In the era of managed care, it is not uncommon for these countertransferences to be provoked in situations when clinical protocols emphasize patient engagement and require setting treatment goals in the very first session. In these situations, the patient's brittleness and proclivity to premature termination clearly must be given greater consideration than the protocol. As the avoidant patient becomes more involved in the collaborative treatment process, the clinician may fall prey to unrealistic expectations of the patient with regard to increased social involvement (Gabbard, 2005). The clinician may erroneously assume that because the patient has been able to establish such a trusting relationship with him or her, it can be replicated with others as well. Awareness and control of these feelings and urges, rather than acting on them, is necessary for the treatment process to be effective.

□ Pattern Analysis Strategies

Pattern analysis in the case of individuals with avoidant personality disorder involves accurate diagnostic and clinical evaluations of schemas, styles, and triggering stressors, as well as level of functioning and readiness for therapeutic change. Knowledge of the optimal criterion specified by DSM-IV and of the maladaptive pattern of the individual with avoidant personality disorder, is not only useful in specifying diagnosis but also in planning treatment that is tailored to the histrionic patient's unique style, needs, and circumstances. The optimal criterion specified for the avoidant personality disorder is avoidance of occupational activities that involve significant interpersonal contact because of fear of criticism, disapproval, or rejection (Allnutt & Links, 1996). Planned treatment goals as well as interventions should should take into consideration this fear of rejection and anticipatory avoidance.

Pattern refers to the predictable and consistent style and manner in which avoidant individuals think, feel, act, cope, and defend themselves. Pattern analysis involves both the triggers and the response—the "what" as well as an explanatory "why" about the pattern of a given avoidant patient. Obviously, such a clinical formulation will depend on the particular schemas and temperamental styles unique to a given individual rather than the more general ones that will be noted here.

Triggers

Generally speaking, the "triggers" or "triggering" situations for avoidant patients are stressors related to close relationships and public appearance (Othmer & Othmer, 2002). This means that when individuals with avoidant disorder are doing anything, discussing, or even thinking about the demands of relationships or being in public and they become distressed, their disordered or maladaptive pattern is likely to be triggered and their characteristic symptomatic affects, behaviors, and cognitions will be experienced or exhibited. Rather than face the demands of others and risking humiliation and rejection, avoidant individuals prefer to place themselves in safe, rejection-free environments. Usually, this means being alone or in a low-demand social environment.

Schemas

The underlying schemas in the avoidant personality involve a self-view of social inadequacy and unlikability, and a view of the world as unfair, critical, and demeaning, alongside a demand that others like and accept the avoidant individual (Beck, Freeman, Davis, & Associates, 2004; Sperry & Mosak, 1996). Not surprisingly, the avoidant patient's dysfunctional strategy is to avoid valuative situations as well as unpleasant feelings or thoughts. Common maladaptive schemas observed in these individuals include the defectiveness/shame schema and the undesirability/alienation schema. The defectiveness/shame schema refers to the core set of beliefs that one is inwardly defective and flawed, and thus basically unlovable and unacceptable. The undesirability/alienation schema refers to the core set of beliefs that one is outwardly different from others or is undesirable to others (Bricker, Young, & Flanagan, 1993).

Style/Temperament

There are three style, temperament, and skill dimensions: affective, behavioral-interpersonal, and cognitive. Individuals with avoidant personality disorder have affective styles characterized as shy, tense, apprehensive, and highly vulnerable to rejection and humiliation. Their behavioral, interpersonal style is characterized by social withdrawal, shyness, and underassertive communication. Their cognitive style is one of hypervigilance and self-doubt as they scan their emotional environment searching for clues to either unconditional acceptance or potential rejection (Sperry, 2003).

☐ Pattern Change Strategies

Generally speaking, the overall goals of treatment for individuals with avoidant personality disorder are to increase their capacity to tolerate feedback from others and become more selectively trusting of others. That means that instead of automatically assuming that others intend to criticize, reject, or humiliate them, or reflexively "testing" the trustworthiness of others, avoidant individuals will be able to take some measured risks in relating to others. This might mean assertively communicating their needs and wants, or it might mean taking the risk of requesting some feedback from others who previously have been supportive of them.

Avoidant patients already know how to relate to a small and select number of individuals, often relatives. If the clinician simply becomes one of them, the patient's basic pattern of avoidance may remain unchanged. It is only when these patients learn to recognize the impact of their pattern on others and take risks in new relationships that they can change.

Although individual therapy can help avoidant patients recognize and analyze their pattern of avoidance and withdrawal, couples therapy and group therapy enable both clinician and patient to observe the impact of this pattern on others and for the patient to risk new behaviors. If the patient is married or in a long-term relationship, triangular patterns are often present. For instance, the avoidant patient may be married to a spouse who travels extensively and makes few, if any, emotional demands on their avoidant partner, providing the avoidant partner the opportunity for a secret extramarital affair. This triangular pattern provides not only some degree of intimacy but also protection from public humiliation while also ensuring interpersonal distance.

Schema Change

The schemas of avoidant patients include themes of defectiveness, inadequacy, and unlikability. These schemas are supported by injunctive beliefs, such as "don't show your feelings," "don't get close to others," "don't get intimate," and "don't be disloyal to your family" (Beck, Freeman, & Associates, 1990). Schema change from a cognitive therapy perspective has the clinician and patient working collaboratively to understand the developmental roots of the maladaptive schemas. Then, these schemas are tested through predictive experiments, guided observation, and reenactment of early schema-related incidents. Finally, these patients are directed to begin to notice and remember counterschema data about themselves and their social experiences.

CBASP Strategies

Although cognitive behavior analysis system of psychotherapy (CBASP) was originally developed by McCullough (2002) for the treatment of chronic depression, it has been extended to the treatment of avoidant personality disorder as well (Driscoll, Cukrowicz, Reardon, & Joiner, 2004). The basic premise of CBASP is that by evaluating the patient's problematic thoughts and behaviors, the clinician can help the patient discover why he or she did not obtain a desired outcome. The main intervention of this approach is situational analysis, which has been shown to be clinically effective in identifying and correcting maladaptive pattens of thinking and behavior characteristic of avoidant personality disorder (Driscoll, et al., 2004). Situational analysis is a process that is recorded by the client on the Coping Survey Questionnaire, usually before a session and then reviewed with the therapist during the session. It helps articulate six elements of a problematic situation and the client's interpretations and behaviors.

Generally speaking, clients with avoidant personality disorder are considered to be excellent candidates for CBASP. Nevertheless, it has been noted that they tend to underestimate and underreport positive social experiences while discounting their influence in successful social situations. Because of their basic social avoidance, a central therapeutic strategy in early sessions is in-session role-playing combined with *in vivo* exposure homework assignments. These individuals are often pessimistic, perfectionistic, hypersensitive to rejection, and hypervigilant to threat cures, and so they are prone to all-or-nothing thinking, magnification, overgeneralization, and mind-reading. Accordingly, clinicians should anticipate that these cognitive distortions will be regularly encountered when assisting these clients in evaluating and revising inaccurate interpretations during the remediation phase of treatment (Driscoll, et al., 2004).

In addition, cognitive behavior group therapy is recommended as an adjunct to individual CBASP for the purpose of enhancing client motivation, self-determination, and acceptance. Group sessions that are sufficiently structured can increase client social competence while reducing social anxiety. Such sessions typically involve in-session exposure exercises, progressive *in vivo* exposure assignments, as well as traditional cognitive restructuring exercises. In these group sessions, clients are asked to identify their desired outcomes for in-session role plays and in vivo homework situations. Clinical experience shows that having these clients specify how modifying distorted interpretations and changing behaviors will help them achieve their desired outcomes enhances their self-determination, mindfulness, and acceptance in anxiety-provoking situations. The interested reader will find an extended transcription of the use of CBASP to treat such patients (Driscoll, et al., 2004).

Style-Skill Change

Because avoidant patients avoid thinking about matters that cause unpleasant emotions, they may report that their minds "go blank," or they may shift topics when they experience more than mild emotions during sessions. Increasing emotional tolerance is an early treatment goal. This can be accomplished by affect regulation training, in which patients are helped to become aware of and "stay with" their distressing thoughts and fantasies. Repeated experiences of "staying with" strange emotions engender emotional tolerance and reduce their hypersensitivity while modifying maladaptive beliefs about experiencing uncomfortable emotions.

Avoidant patients tend to exhibit a cognitive style of hypervigilance that results in cognitive avoidance, just as in their avoidance of unpleasant thoughts. Unpleasant thoughts include those from early childhood as well as current concerns, such as job and family responsibilities and especially treatment-related issues, such as intersession assignments and activities. They may even report that they are unaware of any thoughts during anxiety-producing situations, particularly interpersonal situations. Instead, they describe their internal experiences in terms of fleeting, negatively tinged sensations or images. In such instances, the clinician should encourage the patients to provide verbatim accounts of what was said and done. Prompting this endeavor will assist the patient in identifying such cognition. In time, the patient will become more able and willing to "stay with" experiences rather than "shutting down." Sensitivity reduction training can also be useful in reducing hypervigilance.

Avoidant patients have social skill deficits because of their relational style and their impoverished social experience. These can range from a few circumscribed social deficits to multiple deficits encompassing most social interactions. Alden (1992) listed several types of deficits: (a) behavioral avoidance, wherein patients turn down invitations, cancel appointments, or avoid answering the phone; (b) inhibition, whereby these patients avoid eye contact, initiate few conversations, and talk less than others; (c) surface agreement and compliance, wherein they are likely to voice agreement and comply with the requests of others, even when they do not endorse the plan or intend to follow through; (d) assumption of a moderate position, that is, they avoid taking a stand or expressing their own opinion in issues; (e) and absence of self-disclosure, that is, because of their belief that they are defective, they are extremely anxious about revealing personal information and do not reciprocate the self-disclosures of others.

Assertive communication training can be used to teach patients to think and speak more assertively and with a "nonavoidant voice." Interpersonal skills training can be useful in reversing some of these skill deficits, as well as modifying these patients' shy, inhibited style. In the psychotherapeutic setting, patients may need to be encouraged to act "as if" they are confident, assertive, and likable.

Medication Strategies

Stylistic or temperament treatment targets for this disorder are anxiety or fearfulness, shyness, and interpersonal sensitivity. The first consideration should be given to a medication evaluation for an co-morbid Axis I disorder. With avoidant personality disorder, an anxiety or depressive disorder is often present. Because social anxiety disorder has been shown to overlap considerably with avoidant personality disorder, a medication trial can be routinely considered, particularly if response to skills training is limited (Reich, 2002). Where there is shyness or prominent anxiety without impulsivity, it is reasonable to begin treatment with a selective serotonin reuptake inhibitor (SSRI). If there is no response, switching to another SSRI is indicated. If there is a partial response, a long-acting benzodiazepine or clonazepam can be added or even used as the sole medication following multiple SSRI trials (Reich, 2005).

Group Treatment Strategies

Patients with avoidant personality disorder typically fear group therapy in the same way they fear other novel and socially demanding situations. As a result of taking a measured risk of self-disclosure and receiving feedback from other group members, avoidant individuals can greatly modify their social sensitivity. For this reason, group therapy is particularly effective for avoidant patients who can be persuaded to undergo this mode of treatment. Empathetic group therapy can assist these individuals in overcoming social anxieties and developing interpersonal trust and rapport.

Because avoidant individuals tend to avoid activities that involve significant interpersonal contact for fear of being exposed or ridiculed, it should not be surprising that it takes longer for them to adapt to a group setting and actively participate in treatment. Accordingly, combining cognitive therapy and social skills training in a group-therapy context can be quite effective in identifying underlying fears, increasing awareness of the anxiety related to fears, and shifting attentional focus from fear-related thinking to behavioral action. The group therapist's role in pacing the avoidant patient's disclosure and engagement within the group can be very important. Structured activities can help the avoidant individuals to organize how they think and act so that they are more efficient both inside and outside the therapy context. For example, interpersonal skills training that focuses on the process of friendship formation is particularly well suited for group treatment contexts (Sperry, 2003).

Marital and Family Therapy Strategies

Although there is value in recognizing how their current dysfunctional patterns originally developed, the real measure of treatment success with avoidant individuals is improvement in interpersonal functioning. Because avoidant patients may provide clinicians with vague descriptions of their interpersonal experiences, it may be necessary to query relatives and significant others to fill in the important gaps of information. Family treatment may be indicated to establish a family structure that allows more room for interpersonal exploration outside the tightly closed family circle. Furthermore, couples therapy is indicated for avoidant individuals in marriages or long-term relationships where intimacy problems are prominent, that is, where interpersonal distance characterizes the avoidant partner's relational style and is the source of conflict (Sperry, 1995).

Combined and Integrative Treatment Strategies

Clinical experience suggests that avoidant individuals are often unable to focus on the patient–clinician relationship to the degree necessary to use traditional psychodynamic approaches. Likewise, these patients may have difficulty fully using cognitive-behavioral interventions in the interpersonal context of therapy. Therefore, an integrative treatment strategy may be more appropriate. Alden (1992) described an integration of the cognitive and psychodynamic-interpersonal approaches that has been developed specifically for the treatment of avoidant personality dynamics. This approach focuses on modifying the cognitive-interpersonal patterns of the avoidant personality, which is characterized by dysfunctional beliefs of being different or defective and these defects and feelings being obvious to others who will respond with disgust, disapproval, or dismissal.

Alden (1992) described four steps in the integrative approach. The first step is recognition of treatment process issues. The clinician must quickly recognize that these patients tend to withhold or understate information that is clinically relevant. It should be anticipated that these patients will respond to direct questions with "I don't know" or "I'm not sure" answers.

In the early phase of treatment, such noncommital and evasive responses characterizes their thought processes and also prevents them from encoding details about social encounters. Rather then interpreting "resistance" or focusing on global and vague interpersonal beliefs and behaviors as treatment targets, the clinician can simply recognize that this communication style reflects the patient's inability to process positive information, maintain attentiveness, and change firmly established negative beliefs and schemas.

The second step in the treatment focuses on increasing the awareness of cognitive-interpersonal patterns. There are four components to an interpersonal pattern: (a) beliefs and expectancy of the other person; (b) the behavior that arises from these beliefs; (c) the other person's reaction; and (d) the conclusion drawn from the experience. The patient's task is to engage in a process of self-observation and analysis of the relational patterns, whereas the clinician's task is to draw attention to the beliefs that underlie the patient's self-protective behaviors.

In the third step, as the patients come to recognize and understand their cognitive-interpersonal patterns and styles, the clinician can increase their motivation to try new behaviors by helping them recognize that old and new views of self are in conflict and that such conflict can be reconciled. Assisting patients in integrating their current beliefs with their earlier interpersonal experiences helps them understand that their social fears and expectations resulted from both their experience of how they were parented and their temperament. As they continue to recognize and understand their cognitive-interpersonal patterns, these individuals begin to try different strategies, either on their own or with the clinician's prompting.

The fourth step involves behavioral experimentation and cognitive evaluation. Friendship formation and assertive communication are the two basic interpersonal skills that avoidant patients must develop. Role-playing and directed assignments are particularly useful in developing assertive communication skills (Sperry, 1995).

A basic premise of this book is that although a single treatment modality, such as psychotherapy, may well be effective for the highest-functioning individual with a personality disorder, that modality is less effective in moderate-functioning individuals and largely ineffective in the more severely dysfunctional individuals. Most often, lower-functioning patients tend to be more responsive to combined treatment modalities. Even though avoidant patients initially are reluctant to engage in group therapy, moderate- and lower-functioning avoidant patients tend to make considerable progress when involved in both individual therapy and group therapy concurrently. When this is not possible, time-limited skill-oriented group training sessions or a support group may be sufficient. Because their pattern of avoidance and social inhibition makes entry into and continuation with therapeutic groups distressing, individual sessions can be focused on transitioning these patients into the group. Finally, medication may be necessary in the early stages of treatment and can be particularly useful in reducing distress and self-protective behavior during the transition into concurrent group treatment.

☐ Pattern Maintenance and Termination Strategies

Termination Issues

Termination of treatment can be particularly problematic for avoidant patients. Although these patients were prone to premature termination in the initial phase of treatment, once they become engaged in the treatment process they often find it difficult to face planned termination. For this reason, it is essential that the treatment plan includes provision for weaning therapy in the final phase. Avoidant patients typically need prompting and encouragement to test out their fears about reducing the frequency of sessions. Occasionally, some avoidant patients are ready and willing to terminate the treatment process but may fear hurting the clinician's feelings by suggesting or readily agreeing that they are ready for termination.

Spacing out sessions allows patients to deal with and discuss their fear of termination, particularly regarding rejection. It also allows them the opportunity to engage in new social and interpersonal experiences between sessions and deal with the risks attendant to such experiences. If they had been on medication and involved in weekly individual or group therapy, they might have scheduled medication monitoring appointments at 3- to 6-month intervals already. If they had not been receiving medication or had already been weaned from medication, they might have booster sessions scheduled at 3-, 6-, or 12-month intervals.

Finally, it is helpful if clinicians and avoidant patients collaboratively develop a plan of self-therapy and self-management following termination. It is recommended that these patients set aside an hour a week to engage in activities that continue the progress made during formal treatment. They could try to identify any situations they might have avoided that week and analyze the obstacles and interfering thoughts encountered. Or they might look ahead at the coming week and predict which situations could be troublesome and plan ways to cope with possible avoidance behaviors. The goal of such efforts is, of course, to maintain treatment gains and maintain the newly acquired pattern.

Relapse Prevention Strategies

Another essential aspect of the treatment plan and process is relapse prevention. Because avoidant patients can easily revert to their previous avoidant pattern, it is necessary to predict and plan for relapse. The final phase of treatment should largely focus on relapse prevention. An important goal of relapse prevention is predicting likely difficulties in the time period immediately following termination. The patient needs to be able to analyze specific external situations, such as new individuals and unfamiliar places, as well as internal states, such as specific avoidant beliefs, fears, and other vulnerabilities that increase the likelihood of their responding with avoidant behavior in the face of predictable triggers. Once these stressors have been identified, patients can develop a contingency plan to deal with them. Clinicians may find it useful to have avoidant patients think about and talk through the following questions: What can I do if I find myself resorting to avoidant patterns? What should I do if I start believing in my old avoidant beliefs more than my new beliefs? What should I do if I relapse?

A belief that is particularly troubling for avoidant patients is: "If others really knew me, they would reject me." This belief is typically activated when avoidant patients begin developing new relationships or when they attempt to self-disclose at a deeper level with individuals they already know. In such instances, it can be helpful for patients to face these fears and to review what actually happened in past instances when they were able to self-disclose. Finally, a relapse prevention plan will specify specific outcome goals and activities for the posttermination period: Usually, these goals involve establishing new friendships, deepening existing relationships, acting more assertively, tackling previously avoided social tasks, and trying new experiences, such as volunteering or attending a workshop alone.

☐ Case Example

Cindy K. is a moderately obese, 41-year-old, never-married, white, female administrative assistant, who presented with a 3-week onset of sad mood, loss of appetite, insomnia, and increasing social isolation. She had not showed up for work for 4 days, which prompted the clinical intervention. Cutbacks at her office had led to a transfer from the accounting department—a small and close-knit group—where she had worked for 11 years, to a similar position in a much larger, more diverse department at another location.

Engagement Process

She had missed the first appointment for the initial evaluation and came late for the second appointment with the explanation that she could not find the clinic. She indicated she had come only at the insistence of the director of human resources and did not believe she needed treatment. Self-disclosure was clearly difficult for her. She did, however, view her job transfer as a significant loss, and she thought that it might have triggered her depressive symptoms and isolative behavior. There was no indication that she was a danger to herself, and it appeared that outpatient treatment was possible. Because the clinician anticipated that she would "test" and provoke him into criticizing her for changing or canceling appointments or coming late and that setting up a follow-up appointment would probably be difficult, the clinician had made a predictive interpretation to that effect near the end of the session. Needless to say, the appointment for her next appointment was made with ease, and Cindy did arrive on time for it.

Pattern Analysis

Cindy reported no personal or family psychiatric history or alcohol and substance abuse history. However, she described intense feelings of humiliation and rejection following the birth of her younger brother, after having been very much spoiled by her parents when she was an only child. She came to believe that the opinions of others were all that counted. She had been teased and ridiculed by her peers for her personal appearance, especially her obesity. There were also strong parental injunctions against discussing important matters with "outsiders." It appeared that she distanced and isolated herself from others, anticipating and fearing their disapproval and criticism. She viewed others as critical and harsh and was convinced she was viewed by others as inadequate. Therefore, she was slow to warm up and trust others, and "tested" others' trustability by being late for, canceling, or missing agreed-on engagements. She also spent much of her free time reading romance novels and watching TV rather than going out. Lack of social skills in relating to new or less-known individuals and a limited social network further contributed to an isolated lifestyle and reinforced her beliefs about self, the world, and others. With the exception of social relations, she functioned above average in all life tasks. She agreed she was severely depressed and wanted to cooperate in a combined treatment with medication, started and monitored on an outpatient basis, and time-limited psychotherapy. She was not particularly psychologically minded and had significant skill deficits in assertive communication, trust, and relational skills. However, she had maintained smoking cessation for

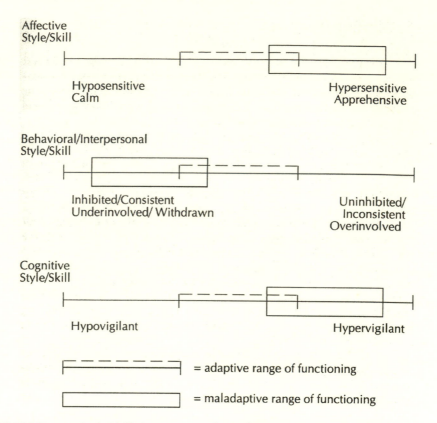

FIGURE 4.1. Style/skill dimensions of avoidant personality disorder.

2 years after completing a program. Her support system included some contact with an older female friend and a pet collie.

Developmental history data suggested that Cindy had internalized the schemas of defectiveness/shame and social undesirability/alienation, which are associated with the avoidant personality. Her apprehensive affects, hypervigilance, shyness, and deficits in assertiveness and other interpersonal skills were also indicative of the avoidant personality. Her history and mental status exam were not only consistent with a diagnosis of single-episode major depressive disorder but also met the criteria for avoidant personality disorder. Figure 4.1 summarizes these style features.

Pattern Change

The treatment plan for Cindy was developed on the basis of her presentation as well as her pattern and prognostic factors. Combined treatment with an antidepressant and psychotherapy would focus on alleviating symptoms, returning to work, establishing a supportive social network, and increasing interpersonal skills, which were established as the initial treatment outcome goals. The treatment and the strategic goals were developed to facilitate these therapeutic outcomes by maximizing therapeutic leverage while minimizing the influence of previous perpetuants and other forms of resistance to change.

Treatment consisted of a trial of an antidepressant, which also had sedative properties and, it was hoped, would cure her insomnia as well as her depression. Twenty-minute weekly outpatient sessions with the psychiatrist focused on symptom reduction and returning to work. This required initiation of some collaboration with her supervisor with regard to work and peer support. The supervisor agreed that Cindy needed familiar, trusting social support and moved one of Cindy's co-workers in the previous office to Cindy's new office. An initial treatment agreement was established for six 45-minute sessions combining medication and interpersonal therapy. The clinician and Cindy also discussed that skill-oriented group therapy was probably the treatment of choice for her to increase trustability and decrease her social isolation. Aware that Cindy's pattern of avoidance would make her entry into and continuation with the group difficult, they planned for the individual sessions to serve as a transition into group therapy; later, shorter individual sessions would focus on medication management, probably on a monthly basis and then on a bimonthly basis.

Knowing Cindy's pattern, the clinician anticipated that she would test the clinician's and group therapist's trustability and criticalness. Throughout treatment, both clinicians continued to be mindful of the therapeutic leverage—Cindy's strengths and her previous success with smoking cessation—as well as the perpetuants that would likely hamper treatment.

The initial treatment plan for her involved the combined modalities of medication and a short course in interpersonal psychotherapy for depression, with gradual transition into a time-limited group therapy focused on interpersonal skill development. As her depressive symptoms decreased and a maintenance medication schedule was established, the clinician began preparing her for transition to group therapy. Because of Cindy's fear of and ambivalence about the group process, the clinician suggested, and Cindy agreed, that it might be helpful for Cindy to meet with the group therapist who was to lead the interpersonal skills group she was slated to join. During the fifth session of Cindy's individual therapy, the clinician briefly introduced the group therapist to Cindy, and the three of them discussed and agreed on a three-way treatment. They agreed that Cindy would continue with individual weekly appointments concurrent with the weekly group sessions. And if things proceeded well enough, sessions with the prescribing clinician would be reduced to monthly medication checks.

After a discussion, the group therapist and the clinician concluded that there was little likelihood that projective identification and splitting would be issues with Cindy. Instead, difficulty maintaining active group participation and follow-up on "homework" between group sessions were predicted to be problem areas. The clinician agreed to encourage and support Cindy's group involvement in concurrent individual sessions with her. Furthermore, the group therapist and the clinician planned on conferring again after the third group session regarding Cindy's transition from weekly to monthly sessions with the clinician.

Pattern Maintenance and Termination

Treatment proceeded with few surprises. Cindy's depressive symptoms were reduced within 5 weeks, and she continued on a maintenance dose for a period of 1 year. Medication monitoring sessions were reduced to monthly visits for the first 4 months and bimonthly afterward. Progress in group sessions was evidenced in Cindy's increased confidence in social situations, especially in her job setting. After 6 months of weekly group sessions, she felt ready to terminate treatment, but she continued with bimonthly sessions with the prescribing clinician. She continued to maintain some interpersonal reserve, but she was able to socialize regularly with two other female co-workers. Her job performance gradually returned to baseline.

☐ Summary

Effective treatment of individuals with avoidant personality disorder requires that these patients become sufficiently committed to a treatment process that is tailored and focused on modifying their maladaptive avoidant pattern. Because these patients tend to have considerable difficulty engaging in and profiting from traditional psychotherapy, an integrative-combined approach that focuses on characterological, temperament, and skill dimensions is usually essential for effective treatment outcomes. The case example illustrates the common challenges that these patients present and the kind of clinician flexibility and competence as well as treatment resources required. Table 4.2 summarizes the treatment intervention strategies most likely to be effective in treating this disorder.

TABLE 4.2.   Treatment Strategies for Avoidant Personality Disorder

Phase	Issues	Strategy/Tactics
Engagement	Premature termination; "Testing" behavior: canceling appointments/ difficulty scheduling; Distrusting clinician's caring and fear of rejection; Difficulty with self-disclosure	Anticipate patient's trust "testing"
Transference	"Testing"; Overdependence	Accept and interpret "testing" behaviors; Set limits on dependency
Countertransference	Frustration and helplessness; Unrealistic treatment expectations	Monitor
Pattern Analysis	Triggers: Close relationships and public appearance	
Pattern Change	Treatment Goals: Better toleration of feedback; Becoming more selectively trusting	
Schemas	Defectiveness/shame; Social undesirability/ alienation	Schema change strategy; Interpretation strategy
Style/Skills		
a. Affective Style	Hypersensitive and apprehensive	Affect regulation
b. Behavioral/ Interpersonal Style	Avoidance/withdrawal behavior; Shyness and under-assertiveness	Interpersonality skills training; Assertive communication training
c. Cognitive Style	Hypervigilance	Sensitivity reduction training
Maintenance/Termination	Homework avoidance; Anxiety and ambivalence about termination	Daily log/diary; Space out sessions; Booster sessions

Borderline Personality Disorder

Borderline personalities tend to be emotionally labile and impulsive individuals who exhibit a pattern of intense and chaotic relationships. Their personal lives are characteristically unfocused and unstable and are marked by frequent disappointments and rejections. Not surprisingly, the treatment of borderline personalities involves a number of unique therapeutic challenges. Although many clinicians remain skeptical about the treatability of this disorder, there is increasing hopefulness that these individuals can and do respond to effective treatment strategies. This chapter describes specific engagement, pattern analysis, pattern change, and pattern maintenance, and termination strategies for effectively managing and treating this disorder. In addition to individual psychotherapeutic strategies and tactics, group, marital, family, medication, and integrative and combined treatment strategies are briefly noted. An extensive case example illustrates the treatment process. Before turning to treatment strategies, the DSM-IV description and criteria are briefly presented.

Clinical Conceptualization of Borderline Personality Disorder

Triggering Event(s)	Expectation of meeting personal goals and/or maintaining close relations
Behavioral Style	"Hemophiliacs" of emotion; resentful, impulsive, acting-out behavior; helpless, dysphoric, empty, "void"; irregular circadian rhythms (sleep–wake, etc.)

Interpersonal Style	Paradoxical—idealizing and clinging versus devaluing and oppositional; rejection sensitivity—abandonment depression; separation anxiety as prime motivator; role reversal
Cognitive Style	Inflexible—rigid abstracting—grandiosity and idealization, splitting; reasons by analogy: does not learn from experience; external loss of control—blaming; poorly developed evocative memory
Feeling Style	Extreme liability of mood and affect
Attachment Style	Disorganized
Temperament	*Dependent type:* passive infantile pattern—low autonomic nervous system reactivity
	Passive Aggressive type: "difficult" infantile pattern—affect irritability
Parental Injunction	"If you grow up, bad things will happen to me (parent)."; overprotective, demanding, or inconsistent parenting
Self View	"I don't know who I am or where I'm going."; identity problems involving gender, career, loyalties, and values; self-esteem fluctuates with current emotion
World View	"People are great; no, they're not." "Having goals is good; no, it's not." "If life doesn't go my way, I can't tolerate it." "Don't commit to anything."
Maladaptive Schemas	Abandonment; Defectiveness; abuse/mistrust; emotional deprivation; social isolation; insufficient self-control
Optimal DSM-IV-TR Criteria	Frantic efforts to avoid real or imagined abandonment

☐ DSM-IV Description and Criteria

DSM-IV offers the following description and criteria for borderline personality disorder (BPD) (Table 5.1).

TABLE 5.1. DSM-IV Description and Criteria for Borderline Personality Disorder

301.83 Borderline Personality Disorder

A pervasive pattern of instability in interpersonal relationships, self-image and affects, and marked impulsivity beginning by early adulthood and present in a variety of contexts, as indicated by five (or more) of the following:

(1) Frantic efforts to avoid real or imagined abandonment. (Note: Do not include suicidal or self-mutilating behavior covered in Criterion 5.)

(2) a pattern of unstable and intense interpersonal relationships characterized by alternating between extremes of idealization and devaluation

(3) identity disturbance: markedly and persistently unstable self-image or sense of self

(4) impulsivity in at least two areas that are potentially self-damaging (e.g., spending, sex, substance abuse, reckless driving, binge-eating). (Note: Do not include suicidal or self-mutilating behavior covered in Criterion 5.)

(5) recurrent suicidal behavior, gestures, or threats, or self-mutilating behavior

(6) affective instability due to a marked reactivity of mood (e.g., intense episodic dysphoria, irritability, or anxiety usually lasting a few hours and only rarely more than a few days)

(7) chronic feelings of emptiness

(8) inappropriate, intense anger or difficulty controlling anger (e.g., frequent displays of temper, constant anger, recurrent physical fights)

(9) transient, stress-related paranoid ideation or severe dissociative symptoms

---

Reprinted with the permission from the *Diagnostic and Statistical Manual of Mental Disorders, Fourth Edition--Text Revision*. Copyright 2000, American Psychiatric Association.

☐ Engagement Strategies

Early Session Behavior

Due to the instability and ambivalence of individuals with BPD, interviewing them presents clinicians with a special challenge. Lability or instability is present not only in their moods and cognitions but also in their rapport with the clinician. Instability involving rapport can be handled by empathically focusing on it. This can be accomplished by focusing the discussion, tracking the discussion, and curbing outbursts and diversions. With this patient, open-ended questioning is preferable to closed-ended and pointed questioning.

Furthermore, instability can be handled by focusing on its pathological part that needs to be explored. Because instability affects rapport, the clinician should continually acknowledge its presence and effect. As a result of these strategies, patients with BPD become less defensive and more willing to disclose, which leads to increased rapport (Othmer & Othmer, 2002).

In a manner similar to the way in which they relate to others, these patients will also direct their angry and rageful affects toward their clinicians. Experienced clinicians expect patients with BPD to relate in this manner right at the outset of treatment. Nevertheless, this manner of relating does heighten tension in the therapeutic relationship. Managing this tension and providing the resources to keep the therapeutic relationship at an active working level is a constant challenge in the treatment of these patients (Sperry, 1995).

Dealing with ambivalence requires confronting the patients' contradictory statements while displaying an understanding of their ambivalent feelings. They may enthusiastically describe a new relationship one moment and then devalue it the very next moment when they recall something unpleasant about that relationship. Generally speaking, therapeutic confrontation can effectively neutralize the patients' splitting and projective identification, just as it moderates over-idealization and devaluation. Therapeutic confrontation also helps them realize that their ambivalence is the result of a perceived lack of support and understanding from others. Finally, therapeutic confrontation permits the patients to realize—however painfully—the extent to which they have allowed others to profoundly influence their sense of well-being (Waldinger, 1987).

Therapeutic confrontation is probably not indicated when there is evidence of childhood sexual and physical abuse in the patient with BPD, at least in the early phases of treatment. There is growing literature on how treatment is modified when such abuse issues are present (Gunderson & Chu, 1993). In fact, some would contend that interpretation of aggressive themes and transference interpretations must be made carefully, if at all, and that the clinician must validate the role of bad parenting in the patient's past as a motivating force for that aggression (Buie & Adler, 1983).

Family members are often incorporated into the treatment process, with the expectation that the patient's self-harmful behavior can be reduced and that compliance with medication or other aspects of treatment will be improved. Clinicians should anticipate the emotional response of family members toward the patient whenever they are involved in the treatment process, particularly during family treatment sessions. Family members may be intrusive and overcontrolling at certain times or rejecting and hostile at other times. This vacillating pattern can significantly complicate the treatment process, making family sessions difficult, if not impossible, to handle. Unless this pattern is therapeutically confronted, family communications will not improve. Nor is it likely that compliance will increase or that self-harmful behavior will be reduced. More on involving family members in treatment is described in a subsequent section (see Marital and Family Strategies).

Facilitating Collaboration

By definition, individuals with BPD find it difficult to cooperate and collaborate, much less take responsibility for their own behaviors. This is particularly true for those patients who typically enter treatment for the express purpose of feeling better rather than making changes in their lives. They want to have their abandonment feelings disappear, their worries soothed, and their problems of daily living resolved. Their secret desire is that someone all-powerful and all-nurturing will "make up" for their chaotic and rejection-ravaged life so far. In short, they believe that it is someone else's responsibility to make everything better for them; it is certainly not their responsibility because they did not create their problem-strewn lives. In the therapeutic setting, that "someone" is the clinician.

Limit-setting and treatment-contracting are two other powerful strategies for achieving engagement. Usually, these strategies are used with lower-functioning patients with BPD who are parasuicidal or act out in various other ways (Linehan, 1993a). Establishing a written contract to avert suicidal behaviors is one of the most common strategies. Contracts can be used to facilitate treatment adherence, such as attendance for aftercare programs, reducing fighting or compulsive behaviors, or increasing medication compliance.

Clinicians should consider the "no treatment option" whenever evaluating treatment requests involving a an individual with BPD. In this option, patients with a long history of treatment failure are not automatically offered psychotherapy or even medication management when it is requested or demanded (Francis, Clarkin, & Perry, 1984). When there is a high likelihood of a patient repeating the failure pattern, and when no noticeable change in readiness for treatment is observed, the clinician has two options. The first is to offer to reevaluate the patient at a later time when the patient is more ready for treatment. The second is to offer an extended treatment evaluation in three to four sessions, during which the clinician will evaluate the patient's readiness for treatment on the basis of response to prescribed intersession tasks. Compliance with the tasks demonstrates some measure of willingness for collaboration and self-responsibility and leads to an extension of the treatment contract for an additional set of sessions. This strategy reinforces the patient's success with treatment sessions, rather than reinforcing the patient's failure as in previous treatment episodes. Examples of intersession tasks include keeping a log of symptoms or target behaviors, accomplishing specific tasks, such as attending two 12-step meetings, and finding a 12-step sponsor within a given time frame.

Another common engagement strategy is establishment of a holding environment, which can refer to the clinician's containment function or to a treatment philosophy in an inpatient or partial hospitalization program. The holding or containing function refers to the clinician's capacity to receive and "hold" the patients' projections without absorbing them or acting on them. Furthermore, the clinician is able to mediate these projections back to patients so that they may integrate these parts of themselves that previously were not tolerable, such as anger and rage. Kernberg (1984) described how a holding environment could serve as the operational philosophy in an inpatient unit or partial hospital program for the treatment of patients with BPD.

Transference and Countertransference

Given that interpersonal relationships tend to be inordinately troublesome for patients with BPD, matters involving transference and countertransference should be of considerable concern to the clinician. Transference in these patients runs the gamut from helplessness and merger fantasy to scornfulness. Dependency transferences may be the most common. In dependency transference, the patient relies on the clinician to make decisions and otherwise take responsibility for their well-being. As noted earlier, this underlying attitude considerably limits treatment progress.

Common clinician countertransferences include anger, guilt, antagonism, fear, rejection, feelings of manipulation, and rescue fantasies. Clinicians can easily become angry because of the patient's demandingness, overdependency, or acting-out behavior. Obviously, clinicians need to monitor their thoughts and reactions to these patients who are incredibly sensitized to the paralanguage of others. For instance, the clinician can respond to the patient's hostility by saying, "I'm getting the impression you're trying to make me angry at you instead of letting me help you. Let's see if we can understand what's happening." Because of the patient's rejection sensitivity and tendency to feel blamed, it is therapeutically valuable to emphasize the interpersonal nature of the verbal interaction. In addition, clinicians may have to set limits on the patient's hostility so as to hold their own countertransference in check: "I'm not sure we're going to accomplish anything if you continue screaming. It's important that you work on controlling your anger so you can express it in a less provocative way."

☐ Pattern Analysis Strategies

Pattern analysis in individuals with BPD involves an accurate diagnostic and clinical evaluation of schemas, styles, and triggering stressors, as well as their level of functioning and readiness for therapeutic change. Knowledge of the optimal DSM-IV diagnostic criterion along with the maladaptive pattern of the individual with BPD is not only useful in specifying diagnosis but also in planning treatment that is tailored to the patient's unique style, needs, and circumstances. The optimal criterion specified for borderline personality disorder is "frantic efforts to avoid real or imagined abandonment" (Allnutt & Links, 1996). Individuals with BPD often respond to abandonment with angry outbursts as well as splitting and projective identification. Self-destructive impulsive behaviors, such as wrist-slashing, overdosing, promiscuity, and substance abuse, are common. Fear of abandonment also amplifies ambivalence about relationships, which further interferes with establishing and maintaining stable, enduring relationships. This means that treatment planning must, of necessity, target these overmodulations of affective style, behavioral style, and cognitive style for intervention.

Pattern refers to the predictable and consistent style and manner in which a patient thinks, feels, acts, copes, and defends the self. Pattern analysis involves both the triggers and the responses—the "what"—as well as a clinical formulation or explanatory statement—the "why"— about the pattern of a given patient with BPD. Obviously, such a clinical formulation specifies the particular schemas and temperamental styles unique to a given individual rather than the more general ones that will be noted here.

Generally speaking, the "triggers" or "triggering situations" for patients are stressors related to close personal relationships and personal goals. This means that when these individuals are engaging in certain behaviors, discussing or even thinking about certain relationships, or achieving certain personal goals, they become distressed; their disordered or maladaptive pattern is likely to be triggered, and their characteristic symptomatic affects, behaviors, and cognitions are likely to be experienced or exhibited. Individuals with BPD perceive these triggers in a typical ambivalent fashion. For instance, the stress of a close relationship may trigger the thought, "People are great; no, they are not," while the stress of a personal goal triggers the thought: "Goals are good; no, they are not" (Othmer & Othmer, 2002). Whether the individual's full maladaptive pattern, particularly the acting-out behavior, ensues is dependent on various situational factors.

Schemas

Generally speaking, the underlying schemas of individuals with BPD involve a self view based on uncertainty about self-identity, gender, career, and their very worth. Their world view is equally uncertain as they are ambivalent about others' loyalty to them, the stability of the world, and the likelihood that they can make a commitment to anything or anyone (Sperry & Mosak, 1996). Among the most frequently encountered schemas in these patients are unlovability/defectiveness, abandonment/ loss, and dependency/incompetence (Layden et al., 1993; Young, 1994). The unlovability/defectiveness schema refers to the core belief that one is internally flawed and that if others recognize this, they will withdraw from the relationship. The abandonment/loss schema is central to this personality disorder and refers to the expectation that one will imminently lose any and every close relationship. The dependency/incompetence schema refers to the core belief that one is incapable of handling daily responsibilities competently and independently and so must rely on the clinician to make decisions and initiate new tasks.

Style/Temperament

There are three style/temperament dimensions that may need to be addressed in formulating the treatment for borderline personality disorder: affective, behavioral-interpersonal, and cognitive. Needless to say, these styles exacerbate and are exacerbated by their schemas. Borderline individuals are prone to overmodulated thinking, such as splitting and projective identification. They are also characteristically impulsive, and their affects, particularly moods, tend to be overmodulated (Mara, 2005). This impulsive style can further exacerbate their proclivity to self-destructive behavior, including self-mutilation. Relationally, because of their history of impulsivity and overmodulated affects, these individuals tend to exhibit limited interpersonal skills, which further exacerbates their schemas of abandonment, unlovability, and incompetence.

☐ Pattern Change Strategies

Generally speaking, the overall goal of treatment is to achieve some measure of stability and cohesiveness. Accomplishing this goal requires a fourfold strategy: (a) reduce symptoms of the Axis I disorder; (b) remodulate problematic temperament/style features, such as impulsivity, distress intolerance, and parasuicidality; (c) increase the patient's levels of life functioning; and (d) modify character/schema features. This section describes six different strategies for pattern change: style modulation, medication, schema modification, group treatment modalities, marital and family therapy modalities, and combined/integrative modalities.

Schema Therapy

In schema therapy, individuals with BPD are viewed as having been vulnerable children who were lonely and mistreated and behave inappropriately as adults because they are desperate. Having lacked a healthy adult role model that they could internalize in their early years, they now lack the internal resources to sustain themselves when they are lonely as adults. To compound their difficulty, the only people they may be able to turn to are those who would hurt and abuse them. Accordingly, these clients often need much more than what their therapists can or should attempt to provide. Furthermore, they often expect the therapist to function as their parents. Young, Klosko, and Weishaar (2003) advocated providing "limited parenting" as a realistic and therapeutic alternative to that expectation.

Clients with BPD present a unique challenge to therapists who endeavor to focus treatment around schema change. The main challenge is that these clients can rapidly shift from one extreme emotional state to another. Schemas, which are presumed to be reflect traits rather than states, cannot explain this rapid shifting. Efforts to assess schemas can be confusing, since these clients seem to have so many maladaptive schemas. For instance, it is not unusual for clients with BPD to endorse nearly all the maladaptive schemas on the Young Schema Questionnaire (Young & Brown, 2001). As noted in Chapter 2, Young and his colleagues adopted the construct of a schema model to represent this rapid shifting. A schema model involves "those schemas or coping responses—adaptive or maladaptive—that are currently active for an individual" (Klosko & Young, 2004, p. 276).

Schema therapy with BPD is an intensive and extensive treatment process. It consists of three stages:

- The bonding and emotional regulation stage, in which the goals are to facilitate the reparenting bond and negotiate limits, as well as contain and regulate affects.
- The schema model change stage, in which the goals are to build the client's healthy adult model—modeled on their therapist—to care for the Abandoned Child, to expunge the Punitive Parent, and to teach the Angry and Impulsive Child appropriate ways to express emotions and needs.
- The autonomy stage, in which the goal is to foster healthy relationships outside of therapy and generalize from the therapy relationship to those with appropriate significant others outside the treatment context (Klosko & Young, 2004).

Each stage of treatment consists of experiential, cognitive, and behavioral interventions. For example, in Stage 1, interventions include dialectical behavior therapy (DBT) methods, such as mindfulness meditation, which fosters calming and affect regulation (Linehan, 1993); assertiveness training; and more cognitive-focused techniques, such as flash cards and the schema diary, which are utilized between sessions. Flash cards are small cards that clients carry around and read whenever they encounter an upsetting situation. The therapist and the client work to compose messages on different cards for different trigger situations. The schema diary is a log kept by clients, which helps them think through a problem and generate a healthy response. (Young, et al., 2003).

Dialectical Behavior Therapy

Linehan and colleagues view BPD as reflecting a pervasive pattern of affective, behavioral, and cognitive instability and dysregulation. The defining feature of DBT is its emphasis on dialectics, the reconciliation of opposites. The basic dialectic for therapists using DBT is accepting clients just as they are—their behaviors, thoughts, and affects in the moment—while simultaneously encouraging them to change. Accordingly, DBT treatment requires "moment to moment changes in the use of supportive acceptance versus confrontation and change strategies. This emphasis on acceptance as a balance to change flows directly from the integration of a perspective drawn from Eastern (Zen) practice with Western Psychological practice" (Linehan, 1993, p. 19).

Linehan (1993) specified four primary modes of treatment in DBT: individual therapy; group-based skills training, telephone contact, and therapist consultation. Group therapy and other modes of treatment may be added at the discretion of the therapist.

The individual therapist is the primary therapist, and the main work of therapy is carried out in the individual therapy sessions. Individual therapy is conceptualized as having three stages: beginning, middle, and end (Marra, 2005). Essential components of individual therapy from a DBT perspective include: dialectical analysis and coaching clients to think dialectically about their own situation; validation of the client's feelings, thoughts, and experiences; balancing emotion-focused and solution-focused coping; prompting improved shifting of attention from internal to external cues; teaching new psychological coping skills; and nonpejorative interpretation of the client's behavior and affect.

Telephone contact with the therapist after hours is offered, not as psychotherapy but rather to help and support in clients to find alternatives to self-injury and for relationship repair when the client believes the relationship with the therapist has been damaged and wants to rectify it prior to the next session.

Clinicians using DBT are encouraged to participate regularly in therapist consultation groups. These groups provide both emotional support for therapists dealing with difficult clients as well as ongoing training in DBT methods.

Following an initial period of pretreatment involving assessment, commitment, and orientation to therapy, DBT consists of three stages of treatment.

- The first stage focuses on reducing parasuicidal and suicidal behaviors, therapy-interfering behaviors, and behaviors that comprise quality of life. It also focuses on developing the necessary skills to resolve these problems. Skills training is usually carried out in a group context, ideally by someone other than the individual therapist. In the skills training groups, clients are taught skills considered relevant to the particular problems of the individuals with BPD. There are four groups of skills: core mindfulness skills, interpersonal effectiveness skills, emotion modulation skills, and distress tolerance skills.
- The second stage deals primarily with difficult problems of living, including treatment of posttraumatic-stress-related issues that may be present. Much of this work is done in individual sessions.
- The focus of the third stage is on self-esteem and individual treatment goals.

The targeted behaviors of each stage are brought under control before moving on to the next phase. In particular, post-traumatic stress–related problems, such as those related to childhood sexual abuse, are not dealt with directly until Stage 1 has been successfully completed. Therapy at each stage is focused on the specific targets for that stage, which are arranged in a definite hierarchy of relative importance. These include decreasing suicidal behaviors, decreasing therapy-interfering behaviors, decreasing behaviors that interfere with the quality of life, increasing behavioral skills, decreasing behaviors related to posttraumatic stress, improving self-esteem, and individual targets negotiated with the client.

The core strategies in DBT are "validation" and "problem–solving." Attempts to facilitate change are surrounded by interventions that validate clients' behaviors and responses in relation to the client's current life situation and that demonstrate an understanding of their difficulties and suffering. Problem-solving focuses on the establishment of necessary skills. Other treatment modalities include contingency management, cognitive therapy, exposure-based therapies, and medication. Because parasuicidal, suicidal, and other forms of acting-out behaviors are common among individuals with BPD, contingency management is commonly employed in each stage of treatment.

The provision of DBT is easier to accomplish in an inpatient, partial hospitalization, or residential treatment setting than in private practice. The reason is that, as described by Linehan (1993a), DBT is better implemented with a treatment team, in which one therapist provides psychosocial skill training, another provides individual therapy, some others provide a consultation function, and the therapists have access to a consultation group for support.

Marra (2005) offered suggestions for adapting DBT for private practice settings. While he recommended that skills training be provided by another therapist, he also offered guidelines for situations when that is not possible. Nevertheless, he encouraged therapists in private practice using DBT to have regular contact with a psychotherapy consultant as a substitute for involvement in a therapist consultation group. The purpose of such consultation is to discuss diagnosis, treatment plans, and specific interventions with another professional who can offer a fresh perspective, confront the therapist's interpretation of data and situations, and warn of potential boundary violations.

CBASP Strategies

Cognitive behavior analysis system of psychotherapy (CBASP) was originally developed by McCullough (2002) for the treatment of chronic depression, but it has been extended to the treatment of BPD. On the basis of his experience treating clients with BPD, McCullough (2002) was not convinced that CBASP itself could be effective in treating patients with severe BPD, especially those with co-morbid chronic depression, while some others believe that CBASP can be used as the main treatment for BPD (Driscoll, Cukrowicz, Reardon, & Joiner, 2004).

The basic premise of CBASP is that the therapist can help clients discover why they did not obtain a desired outcome by evaluating their problematic thoughts and behaviors. The main intervention of this approach is situational analysis, which has been shown to be clinically effective in identifying and correcting maladaptive patterns of thinking and behavior characteristic of BPD Situational analysis is a process that is recorded by the client on the Coping Survey Questionnaire usually before a session and then reviewed with the therapist during the session. It helps the therapist articulate the elements of a problematic situation and the patient's interpretations and behaviors.

Clinicians using CBASP note that patients with BPD often have interpretations of interpersonal encounters that reflect early maladaptive schemas of loss, guilt, and mistrust (Driscoll, et al., 2004). Accordingly, when using CBASP, clinicians should attend to these schema-related interpretations and challenge whether they helped or hindered the patient's progress in achieving a desired outcome. This form of challenging tends to be experienced by patients as less judgmental, and thus less likely to elicit negative reactions, compared with more direct challenges of schema-related cognitions and beliefs. Similar to the DBT approach, the CBASP approach to challenging interpretations can validate the patients' experiences of how they express their thoughts during problematic situations, as well as encourage them to consider revising their disruptive interpretations.

The CBASP strategy can also be quite useful in analyzing crises that occur between sessions. In these circumstances, the clinician focuses attention on the interpretations the patients had during the crises and the specific behaviors involved. This strategy helps patients understand how various behaviors and interpretations can escalate a crisis. It also identifies targets for change. When dealing with the more dysregulated patients with BPD, the clinician should probably focus more attention on overt behaviors initially, whereas more focus on interpretations is possible with the less dysregulated individuals earlier in the treatment process (Driscoll, et al., 2004).

Another application of CBASP is helping individuals with BPD understand conflicts with clinicians that occur during a treatment session. In these circumstances, the goal is to highlight the disruptive interpretations, behaviors, and desired outcomes during the conflict with the clinician. Because this process requires patients to deal with strong emotions arising from the conflict, it is recommended for use in later phases of treatment. The interested reader is directed to a transcription of a session in which CBASP was utilized (Driscoll, et al., 2004).

Style Change Strategies

For all practical purposes, style modulation strategies include medication and social skills training. Either alone or in combination with rational psychopharmacotherapy, social skills training is an effective strategy for remodulating disordered style dimensions. The goal of this strategy is to achieve sufficient affective, behavioral, and cognitive stability so that the patient will be sufficiently ready and amenable to work on more traditional therapeutic issues.

Needless to say, many individuals with BPD have unmodulated styles because they never adequately learned sufficient self-control skills during their formative years. Thus, it becomes necessary for them to reverse these specific skill deficits in the context of treatment. Within either an individual- or group-treatment context, these skills are learned and practiced. Six different types of skill training are particularly useful for the kind of unmodulated styles most commonly seen in patients with BPD. Emotion awareness training and emotion regulation training target overmodulated affects. Impulse control training targets impulse dyscontrol. Self-management training is particularly useful in stemming self-destructive behaviors, such as self-mutilation and multiple forms of parasuicidality. Interpersonal skills training is targeted for a wide range of interpersonal skill deficits, including effective communication and making and keeping friends. Cognitive awareness training targets the propensity for splitting and projective identification. Finally, distress tolerance training targets distressing thoughts in the patient—that he or she can no longer cope with further stressors without incurring disastrous consequences.

Not surprisingly, the course of treatment for patients with BPD—particularly for those with lower functioning—can easily become crisis oriented because of their chaotic pattern. Not only can level of readiness change from session to session, but continuity of therapeutic focus can seldom be maintained through all the sessions, particularly in the early stages of treatment. For this reason, it is useful to assess the patient's level of readiness and to specify related and relevant treatment objectives at each session. One way of assessing the patient's readiness at each session is in terms of treatment or intervention targets. This scheme is more sensitive than the stages of readiness for change described in Chapter 1 and is considerably modified from the hierarchy of treatment targets described by Linehan (1993). She described five sets of progressive treatment targets: (a) parasuicidal behaviors; (b) behaviors interfering with the conduct of treatment, such as missing sessions or medication noncompliance; (c) escape behaviors that interfere with making or maintaining changes outside of treatment, such as substance abuse or illegal actions; (d) acquisition of skills that are necessary to function more effectively in and outside of treatment; and (e) achievement of the patient's personal goals.

Clearly, patients who are parasuicidal or continually acting out during treatment are not as ready to work on schema change as are patients who are sufficiently engaged in treatment and have the requisite skills to collaborate in processing regressive issues, such as emotional or sexual abuse. Table 5.2 lists four sets of treatment targets that can serve as both an assessment tool and a treatment menu in the early course of treatment. The suggested treatment strategy for using these targets is to assess the patient's current level of treatment readiness and then focus on that level as long as necessary before proceeding to the next level. Thus, if the patient reports or admits to any suicidal ideation, no other "higher" level issues, such as the patient's social security disability application or lost welfare check, can be discussed until the "lower," or more basic, treatment issue is reasonably resolved.

TABLE 5.2.   Intervention Targets Based on Levels of Treatment Readiness

1.   Parasuicidal Behavior
   - Suicidal plans
   - Suicidal gestures (wrist-slashing, drug overdose, etc.)
   - Intense/frequent suicidal ideation
   - Self-mutilation (specify)
   - Other self injurious behavior (specify)
   - Substance dependence/chronic eating disorder
   - Engaging in any activities AMA

2.   Treatment Threatening Behavior
   - Unwillingness to acknowledge and accept psychiatric illness
   - History of treatment noncompliance/adherence to medications, appointments, staffing
   - Noncompliance with sessions, medications, or assigned homework
   - Boundary problems: excessive phone calls, overdependence on or overdemanding of clinician
   - Demanding focus of treatment be on highly regressive topics before the patient is "ready"
   - Coming late for sessions
   - Not following up on agreed plans, volunteer work, etc.

3.   Escape Behaviors
   - Substance abuse beyond occasional social drinking
   - Antisocial behavior: stealing, prostitution, drugs, child abuse
   - Binging, purging, fasting
   - Other addictive/impulsive behavior
   - Being inattentive, "spaced out," and internally preoccupied in treatment programs, volunteer work, etc.
   - Teasing, rough-housing, nontherapeutically challenging other patients or staff
   - Isolating self from others in treatment program, family, group home, etc. and sitting alone listening to music with earphones, etc.

4.   Skills
   +Symptoms Management Skills: Acute Symptoms = Abrupt Onset of Clinical Sx:
   - Auditory hallucinations or other hallucinations
   - Delusions: persecution, grandiose, somatic
   - Mania: flight of ideas, high energy, little sleep
   - Depression: sadness, despair, crying spells, anhedonia, disturbed sleep
   - Intense and/or frequent suicidal/homicidal ideation
   - Intense anxiety/panic/compulsive behavior
   - Strong desire for substance use/abuse

TABLE 5.2. Intervention Targets Based on Levels of Treatment Readiness (Continued)

+Symptoms Management Skills: Persistent Symptoms = Chronic, Subclinical Symptoms: Goal = to distract/divert/control through coping skills

- Chronic low intensity auditory hallucinations or delusional thoughts
- Compulsive rituals which can be diverted
- Low-grade apprehensiveness, hypersensitivity, occasional panic
- Vague or infrequent suicidal ideation
- Rejection sensitivity and emptiness feelings
- Low-grade sadness/helplessness
- Persistent, negative self-talk
- Persistent negative thoughts about life and future
- Continuous urge for substance abuse/including caffeine, nicotine, sugar, etc.

+Warning Signs/Symptoms of Relapse = Subclinical Symptoms with Increasing Intensity

- Sleep problems, appetite change, weight change, anhedonia
- Trouble concentrating or making decisions
- Social withdrawal and isolation
- Vague feelings of unrealness or increasing sense of inner emptiness
- Tenseness or nervousness
- Cravings for substances
- Feeling too much energy, too talkative, racing thoughts
- Suspiciousness/fear of others
- Irritability, argumentativeness, or temper
- Moodiness, discouragement, lowered energy
- Vague thoughts of self-harm or hurting others
- Feelings of worthlessness

+Skills: Self-Management Skills

- Personal hygiene and grooming
- Obtaining, handling, and maintaining housing
- Using transportation system
- Food preparation skills
- Job finding/interview skills
- Job maintaining skills
- Obtaining and managing money
- Self-responsibility for actions

TABLE 5.2.   Intervention Targets Based on Levels of Treatment Readiness (Continued)

+Skills: Relational Skills

- Friendship and intimacy promoting behaviors
- Assertiveness in communication
- Negotiation
- Problem-solving
- Conflict resolution
- Identification and expression of feelings
- Modulation of impulses
- Modulation of cognitions
- Modulation of affects
- Capacity to cooperate and collaborate with others
- Empathy

+Skills: Treatment Management Skills

- Knowledge of medications, side effects, and compliance strategies
- Ability to collaborate with treatment team and clinician
- Recognizing and coping with persistent symptoms
- Recognizing and managing warning symptoms

Medication Strategies

Stylistic or temperament treatment targets for this disorder usually are affective instability, interpersonal sensitivity, impulsivity, aggressivity, transient psychotic episodes, and self-harming behavior. Lithium and carbamezapine have been effective for affective instability, while serotonergic agents have been effective for impulsivity and aggressivity. Serotonergic agents, such as fluoxetine and sertraline, are effective for reducing interpersonal sensitivity and reactivity (Reich, 2002). In patients with rejection sensitivity, and a history of good treatment compliance, a trial of a monoamine oxidase inhibitor (MAOI) can be considered if all other approaches have failed. Serotonergic agents have some efficacy in lower-functioning histrionic patients who exhibit impulsivity and affective instability (Reich, 2002). Transient psychotic episodes, including mild thought disorders and dissociation, are best addressed with atypical antipsychotics instead of traditional neuroleptics, which have the risk of tardive dyskinesia. Finally, for self-harming behavior, SSRIs have been shown to be helpful. If they are not, an adjunctive trial of naltrexone can be considered, if necessary (Reich, 2005).

There are some potential complications or disadvantages with pharmacotherapy in the treatment of patients with BPD. First is the matter of noncompliance, related to either side effects or secondary gain. Medications can be used by patients as leverage to control the prescribing clinician or other caregivers. Demands for frequent changes in dosage or type of medication, overdosing, and failure to take the medication prescribed are all means of transference acting-out. Second, these patients may appear to others to have improved due to the medication, but the patients may report that they feel worse, or vice versa. Gunderson (1989) suggested that this apparent contradiction may ensue when the patient believes that symptomatic improvement will result in undesirable consequences, such as loss or abandonment of dependent gratifications.

Schema Change Strategies

Once the patient with BPD has achieved a sufficient measure of stability, it is then possible to address the more traditional therapeutic issues. As noted earlier, schemas of abandonment/loss, unlovability/defectiveness, and dependence/incompetence are often seen in these patients. There are two general approaches to modifying such schemas. The more traditional one is the psychodynamic approach, in which the strategy is clarification, confrontation, interpretation, and working through. According to Masterson and Klein (1990), therapeutic confrontation is the most effective psychodynamic tactic for working with patients with BPD.

The other basic approach to modifying schemas is the cognitive therapy strategy. Layden et al. (1993) described the use of memory reconstruction, schema identification, imagery exercises, and the use of physical cues for modifying borderline schemas. Five extended case examples illustrate the cognitive therapy strategy of schema modification. Turner (1992) described an interesting integrative approach, which he called dynamic-cognitive behavior therapy of borderline personality disorder. In this approach, schemas are modified with both dynamic and cognitive therapy methods.

Group Treatment Strategies

The general consensus is that group therapy can be extremely effective in treating patients with BPD. Group therapy has a number of advantages over individual therapy. Particularly noteworthy is that group tends to "dilute" intense transferences that otherwise would be directed toward the individual clinician. Instead, such affects as rage are diluted and directed toward other group members. These patients find it easier to accept feedback and confrontation from group peers than from the individual clinician. Groups also provide opportunities to understand and master such borderline defenses as splitting and projective identification.

There are some disadvantages and difficulties in treating patients with BPD in groups. First, because of their propensity for acting out, these patients can be quite disruptive in traditional therapy groups consisting of high-functioning individuals. Second, they may feel deprived due to the competition of other group members for the group leader's nurturance. Third, these patients may become easy scapegoats because of their primitive manner of expression. And they may maintain a certain distance in the group because of their private attachment to their individual psychotherapist. For this reason, patients with BPD seem to fare better in homogeneous groups consisting of all or mostly others with the same personality disorder.

Behaviorally oriented groups for patients with BPD focus less on intra-psychic and interpersonal dynamics and more on disordered patterns and symptomatic behavior. Accordingly, they are particularly suited for helping these patients acquire the specific skills necessary to control their affects, reduce their cognitive distortions and projective identifications, and find alternatives to self-destructive behaviors. Linehan (1993) provided a manual-guided strategy for the treatment of self-destructive behavior and impulsivity. Group sessions use didactic instruction, skills training, and behavioral rehearsal techniques. Some of these social skills training interventions, such as distress tolerance training and interpersonal skills training, were described in Chapter 3 of this book. These twice weekly sessions for 1 year are complemented by weekly individual counseling.

Research supports the clinical observation that these intervention strategies are remarkably effective (Linehan et al., 1991). Parasuicidal female patients with BPD were randomly assigned to dialectical behavior therapy groups or to traditional community treatment. Those in the behavioral therapy groups had fewer incidents of parasuicidal behavior and had significantly fewer inpatient psychiatric days compared with those in traditional treatment. They were also more likely to remain in individual therapy (Linehan et al., 1991).

Marital and Family Therapy Strategies

Parents and siblings of patients with BPD are found to have a high incidence of affective disorders, alcoholism, antisocial personality disorder, and borderline personality disorder or traits. Usually, the parent–child relationship in such families is characterized by both neglect and over-protectiveness. These families are also noted to display increased impulsivity, affective instability, as well as significant problems with individuation, boundary violations, and enmeshment. Thus, involving the patient's family or partner can be useful in decreasing enmeshment, respecting boundaries, and facilitating individuation. Family therapy can also improve overall family functioning and communication and provide education about the nature of the disorder while supporting compliance with medication or other treatment modalities. Family therapy can be useful—and, in some instances, necessary—in maintaining patients with BPD in outpatient psychotherapy. This is particularly the case when these patients remain financially or emotionally dependent on family members. To the extent that family members are motivated and have some capability of modulating affects and controlling projections, they may be a helpful adjunct to the overall treatment plan. Glick, Clarkin, and Goldsmith (1993) suggested that a mixture of systems—psychodynamic, behavioral, and psychoeducational family therapy intervention—is preferable to a single approach to family therapy.

Following are three specific family approaches for working with patients with BPD in the context of their families.

1. A *psychodynamically oriented approach* with five specific treatment goals: (a) increasing the family's ability to reduce the systemic splitting process; (b) increasing family members' capacities for owning split-off objects and moving toward interacting with others as a "whole person"; (c) reducing oppositional and stereotypic behavior of all family members; (d) "resetting" external boundaries for both unclear and intergenerational systems and internal boundaries for spousal, parent–child, and sibling subtypes; and (e) permitting a clearer alliance between the parents and limiting the reciprocal intrusiveness of children and parents. Five treatment strategies for accomplishing these goals in an outpatient family treatment setting are (a) developing and maintaining a therapeutic structure; (b) reality testing in the family; (c) interactional disengagement; (d) intervening in the intergenerational system; and (e) solidification of the marital alliance and sibling subsystems. (Everett, Halperin, Volgy, and Wissler, 1989).

   Solomon (1998) and Lachkar (1998) also described psychodynamically based treatments for troubled relations when one of the partners meets the criteria for borderline personality disorder, while the other meets criteria for narcissistic personality disorder. Both of these approaches emphasize the self-psychology perspective but recognize that systemic dynamics need to be considered.

2. A *structural family approach* is particularly useful for couples when the partner with BPD is overly involved in the relationship, while the other is distant and disengaged. Such issues as inclusion and rejection, nurturance and neglect, and symbiosis and abandonment become the basis for structurally rebalancing the couple subsystem within the larger family system (Sperry, 1995).
3. *Relationship enhancement therapy* is a potent psychoeducational intervention that has also been shown to be particularly useful in couples relationships when one partner has borderline pathology. Because patients with BPD have major deficits in self-differentiation and communication, the focus of relationship enhancement on skill-building seems promising, particularly for mildly to moderately dysfunctional patients with BPD. The clinician functions largely as a coach to develop the necessary relational skills in the course of 2-hour conjoint sessions (Waldo & Harman, 1993, 1998).

A history of child abuse can complicate efforts to use family modalities, especially if family members were party to the trauma. If the abuse had been particularly malevolent, family involvement probably should not be encouraged. However, if the trauma had been less malevolent, family sessions may eventually be possible (Perry et al., 1990).

Combined and Integrative Treatment Strategy

There is growing consensus that combined treatment is essential for effective outcomes for the individual with BPD (Koenigsberg, 1993). This consensus arises from recognition of the severity of this condition and its apparent treatment resistance. Clinical experience suggests that there are clear differences between the prognosis and treatability of high-functioning patients (i.e., GAF over 65) and low-functioning patients (i.e., GAF below 45). Use of long-term psychoanalytically oriented psychotherapy may be possible with the highest-functioning patients, but it is likely to be too regressive for lower-functioning patients. In line with the basic premise of this book, the lower the patient's functioning, motivation, and readiness for treatment, the greater is the likelihood that treatment approaches must be integrated and combined for effective outcomes.

Combined treatment is indicated for those patients with BPD with severe symptoms, when symptom relief has been slow with psychosocial treatment; for those with overmodulated affects; for those with impulsive aggressivity; and for those with transient psychotic regression. These patients should have combined treatment with medication and individual therapy. Similarly, patients with significant interpersonal disturbance and identity issues should be considered for combined medication, individual, and group treatment modalities. Furthermore, to increase medication compliance and to more accurately assess the effects of medication, conjoint treatment, comprising family sessions or sessions with a significant other, roommate, or job supervisor, should also be considered.

Contraindications to combined treatment include a variety of patient presentations. Patients who are at high risk for overdose and cannot be controlled with limit-setting are probably not candidates for combined treatment. Group treatment, including partial hospitalization, may be an alternative. Patients who may be responsive to medication but have a history of negative therapeutic reactions probably should not be offered individual psychotherapy. Similarly, patients who use medication to precipitate crises in therapy or with whom medication becomes the central focus of therapy probably should not be offered combined treatment (Koenigsberg, 1993).

Combining medication with individual therapy is the most common integrative modality. Klein (1989) skillfully described the integration of pharmacotherapy within an individual psychotherapy context. He provided three guidelines for the effective use of medication: (a) careful attention to diagnostic precision, (b) evaluation of objective signs rather than subjective symptoms when determining when and which medication to use, and (c) controlled awareness of the risks to therapeutic medication. There are several case examples that illustrate these guidelines.

A variety of transference phenomena can complicate efforts at combined treatment for patients with BPD. Patients with a history of transference enactments should probably be offered a trial of medication prior to the introduction of intensive individual psychotherapy to avoid or reduce such enactments. Otherwise, the clinician should consider using a structured medication management protocol in an individual format. Furthermore, issues of splitting are common in these patients, especially when medication is monitored by one clinician and psychotherapy is provided by another. However, splitting can also manifest when the prescribing clinician provides formal psychotherapy as well. In the case of two clinicians being involved in the treatment, when both clinicians are able to integrate the psychological and biological perspectives and regularly collaborate with one another to present a "united front," splitting can be reduced or eliminated (Woodward, Duckworth, & Guthiel, 1993). In the case of a single clinician, splitting is only possible when the clinician has a split view (i.e., biological vs. psychological) of treatment.

The task differential between medication prescribing and practicing psychotherapy can further complicate matters. Psychotherapy favors spontaneous discourse and activity on the part of the patient, whereas medication monitoring is much more directive and requires considerable clinician activity. Because patients with BPD may find it disruptive and difficult to move between these two tasks, it can be useful to set aside a few minutes at the beginning of a session to review medication effects and arrange for prescription and then shift to the more obvious psycho-therapeutic mode of discourse (Koenigsberg, 1993).

Medication compliance is often a problem in combined treatment for patients with BPD, especially when medication is perceived by the patient as a chemical means by which the clinician can exert control over the patient's mind and will. Thus, the patient can view medication compli-ance as acquiescing to the control of the clinician and noncompliance as taking back that control. For this reason, it is important for the clinician to elicit the specific fantasies the patient has about medication and its effects, as well as the meaning of medicating the patient for the clinician in the countertransference (Koenigsberg, 1991). The interested reader is referred to Koenigsberg (1991; 1993) for a more detailed discussion of the issues in combined treatment for patients with BPD.

Finally, combined treatment for lower-functioning patients with BPD can be accomplished in a community-based setting. Usually, several treatment modalities will have to be combined. These often include indi-vidual therapy, group therapy, medication, drug and alcohol rehabilita-tion services, psychosocial rehabilitation, crisis intervention, and crisis housing. These modalities are often provided concurrently and usually are coordinated by a case manager (refer to Nehls & Diamond, 1993, for a detailed description of this strategy).

☐ Pattern Maintenance and Termination Strategies

Termination Issues

Termination can be extremely difficult and distressing for patients with BPD. Because abandonment is an essential dynamic in borderline pathol-ogy, modifying the abandonment schema has to be the central focus of treatment. For this reason, it is essential that the treatment plan include provision for dealing with past interpersonal losses. Saying good-bye and grieving are skills most patients with BPD have never developed, and so therapy becomes the place where the development of these skills and the corrective emotional experience usually begin. Treatment must also deal with the anticipated loss of the current clinician in the final phase of treat-ment. Losses need to be reframed as "necessary losses" and abandonment as "memories" that are treasured and not forgotten. Necessary losses are viewed as developmental opportunities to trade a secure, predictable experience and set of feelings for newer growth opportunities that can only occur when an earlier experience is relinquished, but never really forgotten. In short, necessary losses and past memories are prerequisites for personal growth and development.

The issue of loss is still germane to the treatment of the lower-functioning, more severely disordered patients with BPD, who will require continued medication long after formal psychotherapy is completed. Even though the patient may have quarterly medication monitoring sessions, the intensity of daily or weekly meetings with one or more clinicians no longer exists, and so it is perceived as a loss. Usually, the hypersensitivity that many of these individuals experience with the anticipation of loss can be, in part, desensitized by weaning sessions. In longer-term therapies, this may mean reducing the frequency of sessions from daily to weekly to biweekly to monthly and then to even quarterly over the last year of a 2- to 3-year course of treatment or for the last half or third of therapy in 1- to 2-year treatment courses. When only 12 to 20 sessions per year can be scheduled, it may be possible to meet weekly for 5–10 sessions and then spread the remaining sessions out on a biweekly basis and then monthly basis for the remainder. Spacing out sessions allows patients to "contain" their abandonment fears. It also allows them the opportunity to use transitional objects and develop a sense of self-constancy between sessions, something they never would have believed was possible.

Finally, it is helpful for clinicians and patients to collaboratively develop a plan of self-therapy and self-management following termination. It is recommended that these patients set aside an hour a week to engage in activities that continue the progress made in formal treatment. They might keep a diary or work on selected exercises. They could observe, monitor, and analyze obstacles and thoughts that interfere. Or they might look ahead at the coming week and predict which situations could be troublesome and plan ways to cope with feelings of loss or impulses to act out. The goal of such efforts is, of course, to maintain treatment gains and maintain the newly acquired pattern.

Relapse Prevention Strategies

Another essential aspect of the treatment plan and process is relapse prevention. Because patients with BPD can easily revert to their maladaptive patterns, it is necessary to predict and plan for relapse. The final phase of treatment should largely focus on relapse prevention. An important goal of relapse prevention is predicting likely difficulties in the time period immediately following termination. Patients need to be able to analyze specific external situations, such as new individuals and unfamiliar places, as well as internal states, such as specific, predictable avoidant beliefs and fears and other vulnerabilities that increase the likelihood of responding with avoidant behavior. Once predicted, patients can develop a contingency plan to deal with these stressors. Clinicians may find it useful to have patients think about and talk through the following questions: What can I do if I find myself resorting to my previous pattern? What should I do if I start believing in my old beliefs more than in my new beliefs? What should I do if I relapse?

A belief that is particularly troubling for these patients is, "I'll be alone forever. Everyone that I really need abandons me." This belief is easily activated and individuals with BPD need to dispute it whenever it comes to mind. Furthermore, they need to anticipate the situations and circumstances wherein this belief is likely to arise and plan for dealing with it.

☐ Case Example

Tammy R., a 25-year-old, single, white woman, presented with a 6-year history of inpatient and outpatient psychiatric treatment. Two weeks after she got married, she had experienced suicidal ideation and abandonment feelings that led to the first of six hospitalizations. This hospitalization appeared to have been precipitated by her husband leaving her to go to an out-of-town meeting. Since then, she had been in continuous treatment of one sort or another with four different therapists and three different psychiatrists. Her most recent therapist of 2 years had focused on a number of regressive issues, including early childhood emotional abuse, which probably accounted for the four hospitalizations during that time.

At the time of the current evaluation, Tammy complained of vague, occasional suicidal ideation, dysphoria, initial insomnia, and confusion about life and career goals. She was notably deficient in the skills of symptom management, interpersonal effectiveness, and self-management of affect regulation and impulse control. The skill deficit in affect regulation and impulse control were noted in her mood lability, as well as chronic dysphoria and parasuicidality, which involved impulsive wrist-slashing, binge-drinking, and overdosing on prescribed medications. She regularly used projective identification and splitting. Records showed that the patient had been functioning with a Global Assessment Functioning (GAF) level in the mid-60s prior to her first admission but over the past 2½ years had fluctuated between 30 and 52. Currently, she was receiving Social Security Disability and was living alone in an apartment. She reported receiving regular morning phone calls from her mother asking her "if I made it through the night without hurting myself."

Tammy's developmental history included a chaotic family environment with an alcoholic father, who reportedly left when the patient was 5 years old, and a mother who appeared to be inconsistent but overly enmeshed with the patient even at the time of the evaluation. The patient had been an honor student in high school, had had particular difficulty maintaining friendships with female peers, and described a series of ill-fated relationships with boyfriends. She had married right after high school, and this relationship had lasted 18 months before her husband left her "because of my crazy, clinging behavior." After high school, she had worked as a restaurant cashier while attending college. During the past 6 years, she had accumulated over 90 semester hours but had changed majors so frequently that it might require as much as another 2 years to complete degree requirements.

Tammy's medical history was noncontributory. She binged on wine and beer usually on weekend evenings when she was "lonely and mad that everyone else is going out and having fun." She had smoked marijuana in high school for a while but denied any current use of it or other substances, including various over-the-counter medications. She denied using tobacco and admitted that she consumed no more caffeine than the equivalent of two cups of coffee a day. She had had trials of several antidepressants and neuroleptics. At the time of the evaluation, she was being prescribed Mellaril 75 mg hs and Zoloft 50 mg qd. Medication compliance appeared to have been inconsistent, although compliance with therapy sessions—individual, twice weekly—had been relatively consistent. She indicated that she had been compliant with medication prior to her first overdose episode and thereafter had been ambivalent about filling prescriptions believing that if she had medications around her apartment she might be tempted to overdose again. At one point, family therapy had been suggested, but since her mother refused to participate, the matter was never broached again. The following treatment strategies were used with Tammy.

Engagement Process

Like many individuals with BPD, Tammy believed that the purpose of therapy was the therapist taking responsibility for making her feel better. However, because of her dependency needs, Tammy also felt she needed to please her therapist. Thus, she had good attendance for partial hospital programs and appeared to collaborate in the treatment, when, in fact, she did not. For example, she would "forget" to fill prescriptions and "misunderstand" how she was to keep a diary of her feelings, thoughts, and behaviors and had difficulty taking responsibility for herself.

With regard to her expectations of treatment outcomes, when queried, Tammy indicated that even though she had tried individual therapy in the past, it did not seem to have worked for her. She said that somehow the treatment "just got stuck" and she was not sure that it really would be any different this time. Still, she recognized that she needed help and that she did not believe she could make it without some kind of treatment.

Pattern Analysis

Tammy's pattern was characterized by abandonment, dependency schemas, and a dysregulated temperament. Her developmental history suggested that she wanted to be loved, taken care of, and directed. And although she had attempted to individuate from her family, she was doubtful of her ability to function independently. An underlying belief—a core schema—was that if she functioned autonomously, her mother, husband, or significant other would rebuke her and abandon her. She learned that to obtain love, she had be compliant and emotionally needy and that being self-reliant led to being reproached and abandoned. Although she wanted to be independent and make her own decisions, taking control of her life frightened her because she was unsure of what she would do with her life. Her struggle to decide on a college major reflected this conflict. Consequently, she vacillated between submission and depression. Unfortunately, neither her early environment nor later life fostered the development of the necessary self-regulation and relational skills. This, along with her maladaptive schemas of abandonment and dependency, led to her proneness to acting out and self-harm as well as to her submissiveness and depression. Finally, it appeared that actual or perceived rejection involving close relationships triggered this maladaptive pattern and her impulsive acting out. Diagnostically, she met the criteria for major depressive episode, recurrent and borderline personality disorder with dependent and histrionic features. Figure 5.1 summarizes these style features.

Pattern Change

Because Tammy had essentially failed to respond to weekly individual therapy sessions in the past, it was unlikely that she would respond now, even if therapy was specifically directed toward modifying her maladaptive schemas. Her impulsive acting-out suggested an unmodulated style/temperament, which needed to be addressed prior to address-

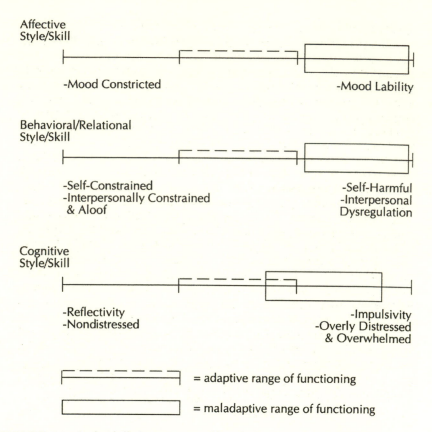

FIGURE 5.1. Style/skill dimensions of borderline personality disorder.

ing schema issues. Her negative set about past treatment outcomes and her low expectations of the efficacy of current psychopharmacotherapy and psychotherapy in an individual format were sufficient to warrant a change in modality. Clearly, a tailored, combined treatment was indicated.

Accordingly, she was referred to a partial hospital program and a focused treatment program for patients with severe personality disorders. The 5-day-a-week program attempted to achieve a holding environment in which participants could work at modulating troublesome affects, behaviors, and cognitions and reduce deficits in self-management and relational skills. The program consisted of daily symptom management, distress tolerance, and social skill training groups, as well as weekly medication and individual therapy sessions that focused only on her progress in the program and on issues and concerns that Tammy was unable to discuss in group sessions. Twice-weekly occupational therapy and preemployment training was also part of the program. Tammy quickly responded to the consistency and stability of the program structure. Her binge-drinking and fear of overdosing on prescribed medication subsided in the first 2 weeks. Therefore, plans for substance abuse counseling were shelved. After 6 months in the program, Tammy's GAF was 60. She then moved to a partial hospitalization and aftercare program for approximately 12 months. It consisted of a twice-weekly program for occupational training and a relapse-prevention group, as well as individual and group therapy sessions that focused on her abandonment and dependency schemas. During this time, three family evaluation sessions were held with Tammy and her mother to foster more functional boundaries between mother and daughter. Even though somewhat reluctant, Tammy's mother agreed that it would be more helpful for Tammy the adult to make phone contact with her just once a week instead of the mother's usual daily wake-up call. These efforts appeared to be successful.

Tammy's patterns were interpreted as learned patterns rather than immutable traits, and thus they could be changed through self-observation, cognitive restructuring, and skill training. Medication was considered an essential component of treatment because of Tammy's dysphoria and insomnia. The consensus was that combined medication and group treatment would probably replace the negative set she had toward medication. Therefore, she was placed in a medication group in the partial hospital program that emphasized symptom management training for persistent symptoms. For Tammy, these included chronic dysphoria and parasuicidality. Over time, Malarial (which had been prescribed for the insomnia) was replaced by Desyrel, and the selective serotonin reuptake inhibitor (SSRI), Zoloft, was increased to 100 mg. It was hoped that in addition to stabilizing mood, the increased dose of the SSRI would reduce impulsivity (Siever & Davis, 1991; Silk, 1996), but it did not. Thus, more reliance was placed on impulse control training in skill training groups. Later, medication was monitored in individual outpatient sessions.

Pattern Maintenance and Termination

Not surprisingly, termination issues for Tammy involved abandonment fears. After completing 18 months in the partial hospitalization and aftercare program, she continued with monthly individual sessions that included medication monitoring. It was anticipated that after 1 year, these monthly sessions would be decreased to quarterly sessions. Because much of her individual and group therapies were directed toward the abandonment schema and because the intensity of treatment had been reduced from daily to monthly sessions, Tammy would be reasonably desensitized to rejection/abandonment.

In establishing a plan for preventing relapse, it was necessary to target the situations and circumstances in the patient's pattern that triggered relapse. Tammy was most vulnerable to relapse on weekend nights when she felt lonely, angry, and abandoned and had access to alcohol. The plan Tammy developed in her relapse prevention group included arranging to have scheduled activities for weekends, even if it meant just going out to a movie by herself and not keeping alcohol in her apartment.

After 12 months, she was able to return to her college classes full time, work part time at a low-stress retail sales job, and continue in a twice-weekly relationship skills group and a monthly medication group. Seven months later, her GAF was estimated at 70 when she was "graduated" to monthly individual therapy sessions, which included medication monitoring. She graduated from college a year later and began working full time as an elementary school teacher. Although she dated occasionally, she had no plans for remarrying. She established gratifying friendships with two other teachers at her school and was able to set and maintain limits on phone calls from her mother. As noted above, she would probably continue on medication indefinitely, with quarterly follow-ups. Finally, no hospitalizations nor suicide gestures were reported since the tailored treatment began some 3 years ago.

☐ Summary

Effective treatment of patients with borderline personality disorder requires the establishment of a collaborative therapeutic relationship fostered by focal treatment interventions to modify the maladaptive pattern and to maintain the more adaptive pattern. Patients with BPD have considerable difficulty focusing on the patient–clinician relationship to the extent necessary to work within a traditional individual psychotherapeutic mode. Usually, it is not until these patients experience some degree of modulation of their affective, behavioral, and cognitive styles that they are amenable to modifying or changing their character structures. Thus, an integrative and combined approach, usually including medication, can be effective in treating even symptomatic, lower-functioning patients. Table 5.3 summarizes the treatment intervention strategies most likely to be effective in treating this disorder.

TABLE 5.3. Treatment Interventions for Borderline Personality Disorder

Phase	Issue	Strategy/Tactic
Engagement	'Patient's difficulty viewing clinician as helpful/ collaborative	Confrontation and limit-setting; Treatment contract and "holding environment"
Transference	Dependency, merger fantasy	Set limits, confront, interpret
Countertransference	Anger, rescue fantasies	Monitor
Pattern Analysis	Triggers: personal goals, close relations	
Pattern Change	Treatment Goal: increase stability and cohesiveness	
Schemas/Character	Abandonment/loss schema Unlovability/defective schema, Dependency/ incompetence schema	Interpretation strategy, Schema changing strategy
Style/Temperament		
a. Affective Style	Overmodulated affects	Emotional awareness and regulation training
	Impulse dyscontrol	Impulse control training
b. Behavioral/ Relational Style	Self-mutilation and parasuicidality	Self-management training
	Interpersonal deficits and vulnerability	Interpersonal skills training
c. Cognitive Style	Overmodulated thinking and projective identification	Cognitive awareness training
	Distress intolerance	Distress tolerance training
Maintenance/Termination	Abandonment fears, relapse proneness	

CHAPTER

Dependent Personality Disorder

Dependent personality disorder (DPD) is recognized by its pervasive pattern of dependency and submissive behavior. Even though it is considered more amenable to treatment than borderline or narcissistic personality disorders, effective treatment of DPD involves a number of unique therapeutic challenges. This chapter describes a number of specific strategies for effectively managing and treating this disorder with regard to engagement, pattern analysis, pattern change, and pattern maintenance. In addition to individual psychotherapeutic strategies and tactics, group, marital, family, medication, and integrative and combined treatment strategies are detailed. An extensive case example illustrates the treatment process. Before turning to treatment strategies, the DSM-IV description and criteria are briefly presented.

Clinical Conceptualization of Dependent Personality Disorder

Triggering Event(s)	Expectations of self-reliance and/or being alone
Behavioral Style	Docile, passive, nonassertive; lack of self-confidence
Interpersonal Style	Pleasing; self-sacrificing; clinging, compliant; expecting others to take responsibility
Cognitive Style	Suggestible: Pollyannaish about interpersonal relations; overprotective—the "too good parent"
Feeling Style	Pleasant, but anxious, timid, or sad when stressed

Temperament	Low energy level; fearful, sad or withdrawn during infancy; melancholic
Attachment Style	Preoccupied
Parental Injunction	"You can't do it by yourself."
Self View	"I'm nice, but inadequate (or fragile)"; self-doubting
World View	"Others are here to take care of me" (because I can't do it myself)
Maladaptive Schemas	Defectiveness; self-sacrifice; approval-seeking; self-sacrifice
Optimal DSM-IV-TR Criteria	Needs others to assume responsibility for most major areas of his or her life

☐ DSM-IV Description and Criteria

DSM-IV offers the following description and criteria of dependent personality disorder (Table 6.1):

TABLE 6.1. DSM-IV Description and Criteria for Dependent Personality Disorder

301.6 Dependent Personality Disorder

A pervasive and excessive need to be taken care of that leads to submissive and clinging behavior and fears of separation, beginning by early adulthood and present in a variety of contexts, as indicated by five (or more) of the following:

(1) Has difficulty making everyday decisions without an excessive amount of advice and reassurance from others

(2) needs others to assume responsibility for most major areas of his or her life

(3) has difficulty expressing disagreement with others because of fear of loss of support or approval. (*Note*: Do not include realistic fears of retribution.)

(4) has difficulty initiating projects or doing things on his or her own (because of a lack of self-confidence in judgment or abilities rather than to a lack of motivation or energy)

(5) goes to excessive lengths to obtain nurturance and support from others, to the point of volunteering to do things that are unpleasant

(6) feels uncomfortable or helpless when alone because of exaggerated fears of being unable to care for himself or herself

(7) urgently seeks another relationship as a source of care and support when a close relationship ends

(8) is unrealistically preoccupied with fears of being left to take care of himself or herself

---

Reprinted with permission from the *Diagnostic and Statistical Manual of Mental Disorders, Fourth Edition Text Revision*. Copyright 2000, American Psychiatric Association.

☐ Engagement Strategies

Early Session Behavior

In early sessions, especially the first, individuals with DPD typically wait for the clinician to begin the conversation. After the clinician inquires about the reason for coming to the sessions, these patients can present an adequate description of their current situations but, later, are likely to become silent. Predictable comments include, "I'm not sure what to say. I've never been in therapy before," or "Ask me something, then I'll know how to answer your question." When the clinician asks other questions, the cycle tends to be repeated.

Nevertheless, interviewing these individuals and establishing rapport can be relatively easy and enjoyable. After experiencing some initial anxiety, these patients can quickly establish a bond of trust with the clinician. For this reason, patients with dependent personalities are among the easiest of individuals with personality disorders to engage in the therapeutic process. When the clinician provides pleasant advice and support, as well as being empathic in the face of the patients' indecisiveness and failures, the interview will flow smoothly. Yet, as the clinician moves to explore the detriments of their submissiveness, these patients predictably become noticeably uncomfortable—particularly in the early phase of treatment. If the matter of dependency is not pursued with empathy, these individuals may move to another clinician. But if the subject is pursued empathically, these individuals are likely to cooperate and meet their clinician's expectations. The clinician can expect them to respond to questions and to clarify and elaborate. They can also tolerate abrupt transitions and will allow deep feelings to be probed. However, they do not easily tolerate confrontations and interpretations of their dependency needs and behaviors (Othmer & Othmer, 2002).

Facilitating Collaboration

Unlike in the treatments for most other personality disorders, collaboration can be achieved or at least approximated rather early in the treatment course in the case of dependent personality disorder. Largely because of their strong needs to please and be accepted by others (particularly authority figures), individuals with DPD are likely to be quite willing to respond positively to the expectations and demands of the clinician. Thus, they will, more likely than not, collaborate with psychotherapeutic and medication regimens if the clinician requests and expects collaboration. However, because they have an equally strong propensity to enlist others in taking care of them and making decisions for them, dependent patients may not really want to assume the degree of responsibility that real therapeutic collaboration requires. So, they may be passive and compliant and take prescribed medications as directed; but they may not actively follow through on other treatment matters that were "mutually agreed" on or initiate self-responsible behaviors unless reminded by the clinician. In other words, compliance is much easier than collaboration for dependent patients, and both patients and clinician may mistake compliance for collaboration. Clearly, the distinction between the two must be pointed out, and the transference issue underlying it must be dealt with (Sperry, 2003).

Transference and Countertransference

Predictable transference and countertransference problems are noted to arise in treating individuals with DPD. Perhaps the most common transference involves patients' efforts to engage clinicians in assuming responsibility for all of their personal decisions. Unfortunately, this transference can provoke a countertransference, in which clinicians succumb to the patients' efforts, either because the clinicians feel exasperated by the patients' frequent protestations of their inadequacies or because of the clinicians' wish to be idealized. These responses not only reinforce patients' overreliance on clinicians but also their belief that they really do not have to become independent or self-sufficient.

Another transference involves patients' failure to make progress in treatment while maintaining their attachment to clinicians. So, as noted above, they may passively respond to the clinical directive but not take initiative or become truly active in the treatment process (Gabbard, 2005). Unfortunately, as noted earlier, this compliant attitude may be mistaken for collaboration with treatment goals. The countertransference involved here is the clinician's failure to confront the lack of actual change and the unwitting reinforcement of the patient's refusal to be responsible and become more self-reliant.

A final transference involves the sheer number of requests for advice, nurturance, and guidance that these patients make early in the course of treatment. The clinician's efforts to modulate these requests—which are essentially demands—early in treatment to prevent the patient from becoming overly disappointed may result in premature termination of treatment. This transference invites the clinician's countertransference response of emotional withdrawal, which subsequently reinforces the patient's neurotic guilt about his or her neediness (Perry, 1995). Generally speaking, it is useful for the clinician to make aspects of the patient's dependent transference explicit. Although an open discussion of the patient's dependency needs may not always be appropriate very early in treatment, this discussion is both useful and necessary after a working relationship has been established. Timing of the feedback is important. Typically, such feedback is best communicated in the context of the specific situation wherein the patient's dependent behaviors have been problematic.

☐ Pattern Analysis Strategies

Pattern analysis of individuals with DPD involves an accurate diagnostic and clinical evaluation of schemas, styles, and triggering stressors, as well as their level of functioning and readiness for therapeutic change. Knowledge of the optimal DSM-IV diagnostic criterion along with the maladaptive pattern of the patient is not only useful in specifying diagnosis but also in planning treatment that is tailored to the patient's unique style, needs, and circumstances. The optimal criterion specified for DPD is that the patient needs others to assume responsibility for most major areas of his or her life (Allnutt & Links, 1996). This reliance on others serves to alleviate the anxiety around decision-making while maintaining a subservient posture in the relationship. With this criterion in mind, the clinician can plan and direct treatment to focus on the deficits in self-confidence as well as the overreliance on others.

Pattern refers to the predictable and consistent style and manner in which a patient thinks, feels, acts, copes, and defends the self. Pattern analysis involves both the triggers and response—the "what"—as well as a clinical formulation or explanatory statement—the "why"—about the pattern of a given patient. Obviously, such a clinical formulation will be based on the particular schemas and temperamental styles unique to a given individual rather than the more general ones that will be noted here.

Triggers

Generally speaking, the "triggers" or "triggering situations" for patients with DPD are stressors related to self-reliance and being alone. This means that when these individuals are engaging in behaviors, discussing or even thinking about being alone, or relying on their own resources and becoming distressed, their disordered or maladaptive patterns are likely to be triggered and their characteristic symptomatic affects, behaviors, and cognitions are likely to be experienced or exhibited. For instance, the thought "I hate to be alone" triggers anxious, panicky feelings and the likelihood of giving up their own aspirations and goals to cling to another for guidance (Othmer & Othmer, 2002).

Schemas

The underlying schemas of individuals with DPD generally involve a self-view of weakness, defectiveness, and inadequacy. Their world view is that others will protect and care for them (Sperry & Mosak, 1996). Among the most frequently encountered schemas in these patients are functional dependency/incompetence and failure to achieve. The dependency/incompetence schema refers to the core set of beliefs that one is incapable of handling daily responsibilities competently and independently and so must rely on others to make decisions and initiate new tasks. Failure to achieve refers to the core set of beliefs that one cannot perform as well as others, and so no attempt is made out of fear of failure (Bricker, Young, & Flanagan, 1993; Young, Kloako, & Weishaar, 2003).

Style/Temperament

There are three styles/temperaments that may need to be addressed in formulating treatment for DPD: affective, behavioral-interpersonal, and cognitive. Needless to say, these styles exacerbate and are exacerbated by their schemas. Dependent individuals are prone to overmodulated anxiety. Their cognitive style is one of uncritical cognitive appraisal and the naive perception of others' capacity and desire to care for them. Cloninger (2005) noted that their behavioral response style is characterized by harm avoidance. As such, they are considerably inhibited and are unlikely to show initiative or to function independently. Accordingly, they tend to be limited in assertiveness and deficient in problem-solving skills, such as planning, decision-making, and implementing decisions, and other self-management skills related to independent functioning. Relationally, they have been so consistently overreliant on others, and thus need to please others, that they have not developed adequate skills in assertive communication, negotiation, or conflict resolution (Sperry, 2003).

☐ Pattern Change Strategies

In general, the long-range goal of psychotherapy for a patient with DPD is to increase the individual's sense of independence and ability to function interdependently. At other times, the clinician may need to settle for a more modest goal, that is, helping the individual become a "healthier" dependent personality. Treatment strategies typically include challenging the individual's convictions or dysfunctional beliefs about personal inadequacy and teaching ways in which to increase the patient's assertiveness. A variety of intervention strategies are useful in achieving these goals.

After the maladaptive pattern has been identified and analyzed in terms of schemas and style and skill deficits, the therapeutic process involves helping the patient relinquish that pattern and replace it with a more adaptive pattern. Thus, the pattern change process involves modifying schemas, modulating style dysregulations, and reversing skill deficits. The process of modifying the maladaptive schemas of patients with DPD usually follows efforts to modify style and skill-deficit dimensions because schema change early in the course of treatment is often resisted by the patient.

Schema Change

The functional dependency/incompetence and failure to achieve schemas are supported by such injunctive beliefs as, "I'm helpless when I'm left alone"; "Somebody must be around at all times to help me do what I need to do or in case something goes wrong"; "I must not do anything that offends my supporters and helpers"; and, particularly, "I can't make decisions on my own" (Beck, Freeman, Davis, & Associates, 2004). In the schema change process, the clinician and patient work collaboratively to understand the developmental roots of the maladaptive schemas. Then, these schemas are tested through predictive experiments, guided observation, and reenactment of early schema-related incidents. Finally, dependent patients are directed to begin to notice and remember counter-schema data about themselves and their social experiences.

Style/Temperament Change

Unlike borderline personality disorder and narcissistic personality disorder, in which temperaments are markedly overmodulated in all three style dimensions—affective, behavioral/relational, and cognitive—

dependent personality disorder does not display as much dysregulation (Sperry, 2003). Nevertheless, skill-training interventions are quite effective in modulating styles and reversing skill deficits.

Anxiety dysregulation can be modulated with the graded exposure strategy that is a core feature of anxiety management training. Assertive communication training and problem-solving training are useful in reducing dependent patients' harm avoidance and inhibition and thereby increase their capacity to function more energetically and independently. This training also reduces their skill deficits in problem-solving, particularly decision-making. Cognitive awareness training and pinpointing and challenging automatic beliefs can be helpful in redirecting their cognitive style marked by naive, uncritical appraisal.

Medication Strategies

Stylistic or temperament treatment targets for this disorder usually are anxiety or fearfulness and sometimes interpersonal sensitivity. If no Axis I disorder coexists, medication has a limited role in the treatment of patients with dependent personalities. In fact, medications are contraindicated because anxiolytics—particularly benzodiazepenes, such as Xanax and Valium—are likely to be abused by these patients, and antidepressants are inappropriate for reactive symptoms. However, when there is prominent anxiety but no impulsivity, it is reasonable to begin treatment with a selective serotonin reuptake inhibitor (SSRI). If there is no response, switching to another SSRI is indicated (Reich, 2002). If there is a partial response, a long-acting benzodiazepine or clonazepam can be added or even used as the sole medication following a multiple-SSRI trial. If these fail, the use of beta blockers or atypical antipsychotics can be considered (Reich, 2005).

Group Treatment Strategies

Group treatment can be particularly effective in treating individuals with DPD. In deciding if group treatment should be extended, and if it is, two factors need to be considered. The first involves the patient's motivation and potential for growth. If they are reasonably high, a more interactional psychotherapy group may be indicated. This type of group provides a therapeutic milieu for exploring the inappropriateness of passive-dependent behavior and for experimenting with greater assertiveness (Yalom, 1985). On the other hand, if dependent traits reflect severe personality impairment and the absence of prosocial behavior (such as assertive communication, decision-making, and negotiation), an ongoing supportive problem-solving group or a social skills training group might be indicated. The second involves considering whether the group should be homogeneous, wherein dependency issues are shared by all group members, or heterogeneous, wherein group members have different personality styles or disorders. Clinical lore suggests that dependent patients tend to get "lost" in heterogeneous groups, whereas time-limited assertiveness training groups that are homogenous and have clearly defined goals have been shown to be very effective (Lazarus, 1981).

Marital and Family Therapy Strategies

There is very limited literature on family therapy interventions involving individuals with DPD. Clinical experience suggests that these individuals are brought to family therapy by their parents. These individuals are frequently older adolescents or young adults between the ages of 20 and 35 years who present with neurotic or psychotic symptoms. Changing enmeshed family relationships tends to provoke anxiety in all parties, and thus, there is considerable resistance from other family members when only one member of the family is in therapy (Harbir, 1981).

Similarly, there is relatively little literature on marital therapy for individuals with DPD. Clinical experience suggests that dependent partners can function adequately if their marital partners consistently meet their needs, but they often become symptomatic and impaired when their marital partners' support is withdrawn or withheld. Accordingly, it is useful to engage the cooperation of the marital partners in treatment because of the negative impact on the relationship as the dependent partners become less anxious and more independent, and because treatment progress results when the marital partners are also committed to the treatment goals (Sperry, 1995).

Nurse (1998) described the marital dynamics between a partner who meets the criteria for dependent personality disorder and a partner who meets criteria for narcissistic personality disorder. He also offered an interesting approach to planning treatment based on the Millon Multiaxial Clinical Inventory (MMCI-III). This approach to treatment emphasizes feedback of MMCI-III data to the couple, communication training, and homework assignments.

Barlow and Waddell (1985) described a 10-session couples group intervention for the treatment of agoraphobia, in which the symptomatic partner exhibits dependent personality features. This intervention encourages the nonsymptomatic partners to function in a coaching role, thus collaborating on treatment goals, which effectively discourages the role of reinforcing their partners' agoraphobia and dependency. Over the course of this group treatment, panic and agoraphobia symptoms remit, and the marital relationship shifts from dependency to interdependency.

Combined and Integrative Treatment Strategies

Barlow and Waddell's (1985) effort to combine behavior therapy in a group setting with dependent couples is one of many examples of combining modalities in treating individuals with DPD. However, there is relatively little research published on integrative treatment strategies for treating these patients. Nevertheless, there have been some case reports of anxiety-reducing strategies used in both dynamic and cognitive therapies (Sperry, 1995).

One such example was reported by Glantz and Goisman (1990), who described their effort to integrate relaxation techniques within psychodynamic psychotherapy for dependent patients. In the course of exploration psychotherapy, a controlled breathing and progressive muscle relaxation strategy was used to merge split self-representations. The strategy was introduced after signs of split self-representation had been identified. Patients practiced the strategy with the clinician and were also prescribed to practice it as homework. When they achieved an adequate level of relaxation in the session, they were asked to describe visual images of the conflicting self-representations. After clear images were elicited and discussed, the patients were instructed to merge the images. The results of this strategy were noteworthy in that most dependent patients responded with improved interpersonal relationships.

☐ Pattern Maintenance and Termination Strategies

Termination Issues

Termination can be very difficult for dependent patients because termination represents relinquishing an important, necessary relationship with a nurturing, caring figure. Recall that dependent patients erroneously view independence as being totally alone and without the support of anyone, while dependence means being totally cared for and supported. Not surprisingly, termination can particularly produce anxiety in these patients. Therefore, the clinician must endeavor to minimize the negative effects of termination, and present termination as a therapeutic intervention in and of itself.

Three therapeutic strategies can facilitate treatment termination with the dependent patient. First, termination will be made easier if the clinician makes it clear that termination does not mean a permanent break in the therapeutic relationship. However, the clinician should not send a mixed message, implying that the patient is ready to terminate but is not "really" terminating. Rather, the clinician must present the termination in a manner that emphasizes the patient's successful work during treatment (Bornstein, 1993; 1994).

Second, the clinician should offer the predictive interpretation that dependency needs may complicate the termination process. Conveying this prediction to the patient in a matter-of-fact, nonjudgmental fashion can preempt the patient's conscious or unconscious wish to subvert termination and continue therapy indefinitely and, at the same time, provide the patient with useful feedback regarding the ways in which dependency strivings can adversely affect other important interpersonal relationships.

Third, spacing out sessions allows patients to gradually become more independent of the clinician and the treatment process. In this process of becoming less reliant on the clinician's direct support during weekly sessions, they learn to rely more on their own resources as well as develop or maintain other support systems. As they become increasingly able to tolerate this separation, their maladaptive dependency pattern shifts to a more adaptive and healthier pattern of interdependence. A variant of spacing sessions is to set a specific termination date at the very outset of treatment. Mann (1973) described this option for higher-functioning individuals with relatively fewer focal issues, including dependency, for a 12-session dynamically oriented treatment he called "time-limited psychotherapy." With higher-functioning patients with DPD, it is possible to set a specific termination date and then focus treatment on increasing self-reliance; however, clinical experience indicates that considerably more than 12 sessions are needed.

If the patients continue to be prescribed medication, they might slowly shift to scheduled medication monitoring appointments at 3- to 6-month intervals. If they are currently not receiving medication or have already been weaned from medication, they might have booster sessions scheduled at 3-, 6-, or 12-month intervals.

Finally, it is helpful for clinicians and dependent patients to collaboratively develop a plan of self-therapy and self-management following termination. It is recommended that these patients set aside an hour a week to engage in activities that continue the progress made in formal treatment. They might work on selected exercises. They might look ahead at the coming week and predict which situations could be troublesome and plan ways to cope with dependent behaviors. The goal of such effort is, of course, to maintain treatment gains and maintain the newly acquired pattern.

Relapse Prevention Strategies

Another essential aspect of the treatment plan and process is relapse prevention. Because dependent patients can easily revert to their previous avoidant pattern, it is necessary to predict and plan for relapse. The final phase of treatment should largely focus on relapse prevention. An important goal of relapse prevention is predicting likely difficulties in the time period immediately following termination. The patient needs to be able to analyze specific external situations, such as new individuals and unfamiliar places, as well as internal states, such as specific avoidant beliefs, fears, and other vulnerabilities that increase the likelihood of responding with avoidant behavior in the face of predictable triggers. Once the avoidant behavior has been predicted, patients can develop a contingency plan to deal with these stressors. Clinicians may find it useful to have patients think and talk through the following questions: What can I do if I find myself resorting to dependent patterns? What should I do if I start believing in my old dependency beliefs more than in my new beliefs? What should I do if I relapse?

A belief that is particularly troubling for dependent patients is: "I can't stand being alone." This belief is typically activated when dependent patients face situations that require self-reliance or being alone. In such instances, it can be helpful for patients to imagine what their clinician would want them to think and do in such circumstances. With this imaginal strategy, patients will no longer feel totally alone or feel that they must be totally self-reliant.

☐ Case Example

Janet R., a 29-year-old mother of a 4-year-old daughter, experienced her first panic attack while on a business trip with her husband. Sweating, difficulty breathing, numbness and tingling of the extremities, and chest pain convinced her that she was having a heart attack. She was quickly transported to a local emergency room, where physical examination ruled out a myocardial infarction. After intramuscular Valium partially relieved her symptoms, Janet cut short her trip and returned home. In the subsequent week, her sleep improved and her anxiety subsided to some extent. But because she had been experiencing anxiety episodes of increasing severity and had begun to avoid crowded places and shopping malls in the past 2 years, she readily accepted her family physician's referral to a psychiatrist.

Engagement Process

Before ending their initial session, the psychiatrist asked Janet to keep a daily log of the sensations, events, thoughts, and feelings associated with each episode of anxiety and what she did about it. The expectation was that accomplishing this task would not only provide Janet a sense of control but also assess her readiness and capacity for treatment. One week later, she reported moderate improvement in symptoms: no panic attacks, decreased anticipatory anxiety, less fitful sleep, and better concentration.

Pattern Analysis

The psychiatric evaluation elicited a family history of anxiety, particularly, depression in her mother. Recent stressors for Janet included having few friends because they had just moved from another city, her daughter's starting kindergarten, and anticipatory anxiety about the above-mentioned recent business trip. She had been unable to tell her husband that she was frightened about accompanying him on the trip and had felt guilty when the trip had to be rescheduled because of her panic attack. Needless to say, she had considerable difficulty expressing negative feelings, particularly toward authority figures, including her husband. She met DSM-IV criteria for panic disorder with agoraphobia and dependent personality disorder.

Janet recalled being reprimanded as a child, whenever she directly expressed her feelings: From an early age, as the oldest child, she had assumed many parental duties because of her mother's long-term psychiatric hospitalizations. As a result, she had little opportunity to develop an identity distinct from that of looking after others. She believed she was inadequate as a parent, wife, and person. Similarly, she believed that she needed others not only to survive but also to be happy. In addition to the core schema of dependency/incompetence that is typical of dependent personality disorder, Janet also internalized the self-sacrifice schema. Furthermore, she used the defenses of denial and suppression to cope with anger. These defenses underlay her maladaptive pattern, which was to refrain from expressing her needs and avoid confronting others in order to garner their support, avoid their rejection, and

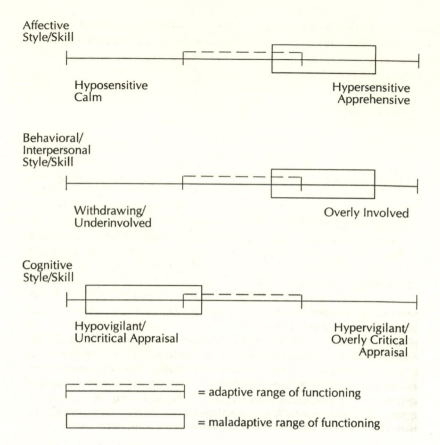

FIGURE 6.1. Style/skill dimensions of dependent personality disorder.

enlist them in making decisions for her. She had noticeable skill deficits in assertiveness and anxiety modulation. Figure 6.1 summarizes these style features.

Pattern Change

In the second session, the psychiatrist prescribed relaxation training to help Janet regulate her psychological and physiological arousals and an antidepressant to block panic attacks and her anticipatory anxiety. Between sessions, she had considerable difficulty with the controlled breathing exercises; whenever she tried to do deep breathing, she started hyperventilating. Fearful that she would have another panic attack, she abandoned the exercise. Subsequently, in the third session, adjunctive group treatment was discussed. With some hesitation, Janet agreed to participate in an eight-session anxiety modification group program in addition to biweekly individual sessions with the psychiatrist.

The group sessions emphasized relaxation and assertive communication. By the fourth session, she had few symptoms but was still fearful of a panic attack. She continued to depend on the antidepressant to "keep me safe and secure." Her response to the assertiveness training was equivocal. For example, she had been able to refuse a request to coordinate a school event, and yet she could not stand up to her husband and felt guilty when she thought about confronting him about his burdensome demands. Janet and her group therapist collaboratively developed a desensitization program for her phobic avoidance. Then, Janet developed a hierarchy of fear-provoking activities and situations, and used her new relaxation skills to avert anxiety in each activity and situation. She was able to begin shopping in relatively uncrowded stores and dine out during off-peak hours. During the last group session, Janet developed a relapse prevention plan.

Meanwhile, in individual sessions, the psychiatrist helped Janet explore her dependency/self-sacrificing schema. During the sixth session, Janet recognized the intensity of her anger and became more anxious for several weeks. But in the 11th session, she reported a new confidence from being able to cope principally by controlling her symptoms with relaxation rather than with medication alone. By now, the antidepressant dosage was changed from a daily dose to an as-needed or prn dose. In the 13th session, she indicated that she thought that treatment could now be stopped, citing expense and her new-found confidence as reasons. The psychiatrist hypothesized that she had been frightened by a glimpse of her anger at her parents and her husband, but she rejected this interpretation. She said that despite her husband's appreciation of her symptomatic improvement, he seemed annoyed by what he perceived as her growing reliance on treatment but that he refused a conjoint session to discuss the matter. The clinician acceded to her request to stop treatment; however, he emphasized his availability should she wish to explore further the psychological predisposition of her illness.

Two months later, Janet returned to treatment in dismay. Her anxiety had recurred following news of her sister's impending divorce. There had been continuous phone calls at all hours of the day and night. Janet had to frequently interrupt her daily responsibilities "to be available to my sister in her time of need." Janet's husband, who had been supportive up to this point, was now becoming exasperated. In 12 further individual sessions spread out over 5 months, Janet explored these conflicts and the underlying schemas of dependence/incompetence and self-sacrifice in a focal dynamic psychotherapy mode. Her objective was to understand that she was identifying with the psychiatrist's caregiving role to the detriment of both her sister and herself. Was this not a familiar pattern? And was this behavior not alienating her husband, the one person who was sensitive to her needs? The transference interpretation struck home. She advised her sister to seek psychiatric treatment. With her husband's help, she set limits on her sister's intrusion. Janet identified how her compliance with the clinician's statements had been, in fact, a defense against her rage when he did not gratify her dependency needs.

Pattern Maintenance and Termination

By the 25th individual session, Janet was relatively symptom-free. More important, she understood how to manage her emotions and personal relationships. The earlier conceived relapse prevention plan was reviewed and revised. Fully active again, Janet terminated treatment. Follow-up consisted of participation in an assertiveness training group, in which she functioned as the group facilitator. In the ensuing months, she rarely used the antidepressants she had been prescribed. One year later, Janet reported an increased capacity to deal with anxiety and with her concerns about self-sufficiency. She continued to practice assertive communication and relaxation. To her surprise, she noted the beneficial effects that her new insight and competence had on her husband and family members.

☐ Summary

Effective treatment of patients with dependent personality disorder requires the establishment of a trusting patient–clinician relationship fostered by focal treatment interventions to modify the maladaptive pattern and then maintain the new pattern. Higher-functioning dependent patients may be reasonably adaptive and functional at work and socially and thus may be able to profit from a single-modality treatment. However, many dependent patients have concurrent symptom disorders with their personality disorder and are much less adaptive and functional. These patients have considerable difficulty making progress in traditional individual psychotherapy. Thus, an integrative and combined approach, which may include medication, can be effective in treating the majority of these patients. Table 6.2 summarizes the treatment intervention strategies most likely to be effective in treating this disorder.

TABLE 6.2. Treatment Interventions for Dependent Personality Disorder

Phase	Issue	Strategy/Tactic
Engagement	Silent demand for clinician to make decisions and solve problems; Complies rather than collaborating	Allow measured amount of dependence at first; Gradually introduce collaboration theme; Distinguish collaboration from compliance
Transference	Clinging resistance; Multiple requests; Idealizes clinician	Set clear limits on clinician–patient relationship; Frustrate patient's dependency fantasies by refusing to collude
Countertransference	Rescue fantasies; Directive role; Failure to confront patient's limited progress	Monitor own thoughts/feelings regarding rescue/directive role; Confront patient's limited progress
Pattern Analysis	Triggers: Self-reliance and being alone	
Pattern Change	Treatment Goal: Autonomy with interdependency/ healthier dependence	
Schema/Character	Dependency/ Incompetence schema; Failure to achieve schema	Interpretation Strategy
Style/Temperament		
a. Cognitive Style	Naive, uncritical cognitive appraisal	Pinpoint/challenge automatic thoughts
b. Emotional Style	Anxiety dysregulation	Anxiety management training; Graded exposure
c. Behavioral/ Relational	Assertiveness training; Problem-solving training; Involve significant others in treatment process	
Maintenance/Termination	Fear of termination/ abandonment with paradoxical worsening of progress	Predictive interpretation; Weaning/spacing out sessions; Time-limited format with target termination date; Scheduled booster session

CHAPTER 7

Narcissistic Personality Disorder

Narcissistic personality disorder (NPD) has become increasingly recognizable as a diagnostic entity in the Western world. At the same time, the definition and determinants of this disorder have been carefully articulated. For instance, Masterson (1993), among others, differentiated two versions of the disorder: the "exhibitionistic" narcissistic personality disorder and the "closet" narcissistic personality disorder. The more common version, the exhibitionistic or grandiose form of this disorder, is specified in DSM-IV. The treatment of both versions of this disorder involves a number of unique therapeutic challenges. Nevertheless, individuals with NPD can be effectively treated. This chapter describes specific engagement, pattern analysis, pattern change, pattern maintenance, and termination strategies for effectively managing and treating the grandiose form of this disorder. In addition to individual psychotherapeutic strategies and tactics, group, marital, family, medication, and integrative and combined treatment strategies are detailed. An extensive case example illustrates the treatment process. Before turning to treatment strategies, the DSM-IV description and criteria are briefly presented.

Clinical Conceptualization of Narcissistic Personality Disorder

Triggering Event(s)   Evaluation of self
Behavioral Style: Conceited, boastful, snobbish; self-assured, self-centered, pompous; impatient, arrogant, thin-skinned

Interpersonal Style:	Disdainful, exploitative, irresponsible; socially facile but without empathy; use others to indulge themselves
Cognitive Style:	Cognitive expansiveness and exaggeration; focus on images and themes: take liberties with facts; persistent and inflexible
Feeling Style:	Self-confidence; narcissistic rage
Temperament:	Active and responsive; special talents, attractiveness, early language development
Attachment Style:	Fearful and dismissing
Parental Injunction:	"Grow up and be wonderful, for me."
Self View:	"I'm special and unique, and I'm entitled to extraordinary rights and privileges whether I've earned them or not."
World View:	"Life is a banquet table to be sampled at will. People owe me admiration and privilege. Therefore, I'll expect and demand this specialness."
Maladaptive Schemas	Entitlement; defectiveness; emotional deprivation; insufficient self-control; unrelenting standards
Optimal DSM-IV-TR Criteria	Has grandiose sense of self-importance

☐ DSM-IV Description and Criteria

According to DSM-IV, the narcissistic personality disorder is described as a pervasive pattern of grandiosity (in fantasy or behavior), need for admiration, and lack of empathy, beginning by early adulthood and present in a variety of contexts. It is indicated by at least five of the following nine criteria listed in Table 7.1.

TABLE 7.1. DSM-IV Description and Criteria for Narcissistic Personality Disorder

301.81 Narcissistic Personality Disorder

A pervasive pattern of grandiosity (in fantasy or behavior), need for admiration, and lack of empathy, beginning by early adulthood and present in a variety of contexts, as indicated by five (or more) of the following:

(1) Has a grandiose sense of self-importance (e.g., exaggerates achievements and talents, expects to be recognized as superior without commensurate achievements)

(2) is preoccupied with fantasies of unlimited success, power, brilliance, beauty, or ideal love

(3) believes that he or she is "special" and unique and can only be understood by, or should associate with, other special or high-status people (or institutions)

(4) requires excessive admiration

(5) has a sense of entitlement, that is, unreasonable expectations of especially favorable treatment or automatic compliance with his or her expectations

(6) is interpersonally exploitative, that is, takes advantage of others to achieve his or her own ends

(7) lacks empathy; is unwilling to recognize or identify with the feelings and needs of others

(8) is often envious of others or believes that others are envious of him or her

(9) shows arrogant, haughty behaviors or attitudes

Reprinted with permission from the *Diagnostic and Statistical Manual of Mental Disorders, Fourth Edition—Text Revision*. Copyright 2000, American Psychiatric Association.

☐ Engagement Strategies

Early Session Behavior

Effective interviewing of narcissistic individuals requires considerable ability to recognize, understand, and respond to their unique dynamics. Throughout the interview, they give the distinct impression that the interview has only one purpose: to underscore their self-promoted importance (Othmer & Othmer, 2002). These individuals often present themselves as self-assured, pretentious, and entitled to having their needs met, and they appear indifferent to the clinician's perspective. Typically, they are unwilling to conform to expectations associated with the "patient" role but have well-defined expectations for the clinician's role. They expect clinicians to mirror or reflect their specialness and will respond by idealizing them—at least temporarily—as wonderful clinicians and human beings. However, should a clinician confront their grandiosity early in the treatment process, they will inevitably respond with rage and possibly terminate treatment prematurely. Not surprisingly, narcissistic individuals prefer open-ended questions that permit them extended descriptions of their many talents, accomplishments, and future plans.

Narcissistic patients may present for treatment in pain following a narcissistic injury. They want and expect that the clinician will take away this wrenching pain. When the clinician fails to recognize the need for or fails to provide sufficient soothing, the patient is likely to react angrily or leave treatment. Not surprisingly, rapport and engagement into the treatment process occur only after a considerable period of mirroring and soothing. One of the reasons the establishment of rapport and engagement is difficult is clinician countertransference. The clinician can easily become bored, exasperated, and even angry during the initial interviews while listening to the patient's monologue of self-promotion. If the clinician can remain patient through this period and sufficiently mirror the patient, engagement can be achieved and the formal work of confronting and interpreting the grandiosity can begin.

Facilitating Collaboration

Developing a collaborative relationship with narcissistic patients can be extraordinarily challenging. The notion of collaboration is distasteful to them because collaboration implies some measure of equality, and they have a vested interest in maintaining their sense of superiority over everyone, including clinicians. Rather than view the treatment as a collaborative endeavor, narcissistic individuals are more likely to perceive it as a competitive endeavor in which they fight to establish and maintain their position of superiority. Not surprisingly, they will avoid, derail, or deride the clinician's efforts to directly influence them to collaborate. Furthermore, these individuals have usually had limited experience in cooperative interactions and very likely have skill deficits in cooperation and collaboration. Accordingly, the clinician will do well to mirror these individuals, "join" with their grandiosity, and not act out on their countertransference during the early period of treatment. Once the clinician passes this test, the patient is less likely to view the clinician as a competitor (Sperry, 2003). Then, the clinician will be more likely to convey to the patient that both might be able to work together in the best interests of the patient.

Transference and Countertransference

Common transferences involve idealization, devaluation, and projective identification. Narcissistic patients typically idealize clinicians when they provide patients mirroring and other emotional supplies, but they can quickly shift to devaluing clinicians when they are confronted or emotional supplies are withheld. Similarly, in projective identification, these patients exclude the clinician just as they were once excluded by their own parents. An aspect of the patient is projected onto the clinician, who identifies with that self before helping the patient to reintroject it (Gabbard, 2005).

Four countertransferences that can be activated in working with narcissistic patients are described by Gabbard (2005). First, failure of clinicians to recognize their own narcissistic needs may be operative as early as the initial session. Narcissistic patients may idealize their current clinicians while devaluing previous clinicians. Rather than viewing this as a defensive maneuver, clinicians who long for idealization may uncritically believe that they have unique talents that were lacking in the patients' previous providers. Another countertransference is boredom that can arise when the patient appears to be oblivious to the clinician's presence. When clinicians must endure serving as a sounding board for narcissistic patients during long sessions, they may easily experience boredom and subsequently respond critically or by not mirroring. In addition, clinicians may also struggle with feelings of being controlled by narcissistic patients. This occurs when patients interpret the clinician's body language and paralanguage as indicators of the clinician's rejection or boredom, resulting in the clinician feeling coerced into focusing entirely on the patient's every movement. Gabbard (1994) suggested that the clinician say something like: "It seems to hurt your feelings when I clear my throat or fidget in my seat because you feel I am not giving you my full attention" (p. 520). Finally, clinicians may have to contend with countertransference feelings, such as anger, hurt, or feeling impotent, in response to patients' devaluing comments.

☐ Pattern Analysis Strategies

Pattern analysis of individuals with NPD involves an accurate diagnostic and clinical evaluation of schemas, styles, and triggering stressors as well as level of functioning and readiness for therapeutic change. Knowledge of the optimal DSM-IV criterion along with the maladaptive pattern of these individuals is not only useful in specifying diagnosis but also in planning treatment that is tailored to their unique styles, needs, and circumstances. The optimal criterion specified for narcissistic personality disorder is that the patient has a grandiose sense of self-importance (Allnutt & Links, 1996). Both planned treatment goals and interventions should reflect this theme of grandiosity and specialness.

Pattern refers to the predictable and consistent style and manner in which a patient thinks, feels, acts, copes and defend the self. Pattern analysis involves both the triggers and the response—the "what"—as well as an explanatory statement—the "why"—about the pattern of a given narcissistic patient. Obviously, such a clinical formulation would be based on the *particular* schemas and temperamental styles unique to a given individual rather than on the more *general* ones that will be noted here.

Triggers

Generally speaking, the "triggers" or "triggering situations" for narcissistic individuals involve evaluations of self. This means that when these individuals are engaging in behaviors, discussing, or even thinking about being alone or relying on their own resources and become distressed, their disordered pattern is likely to be triggered, and their characteristic symptomatic affects, behaviors, and cognitions are likely to be experienced or exhibited (Sperry, 2003). For instance, an actual or perceived threat to the "I'm the only one that counts" can trigger rageful thoughts and affects, along with lowered self-esteem and compensatory self-centered and even retaliatory behavior.

Schemas

The underlying schemas generally involve a self view of grandiosity, specialness, and entitlement and a view of the world that demands special treatment and dispensation from the rules and regulations that govern others (Sperry & Mosak, 1996). Among the most frequently encountered schemas in narcissistic patients is the entitlement/self-centeredness schema. Occasionally, the insufficient self-control/self-discipline schema or abuse/mistrust also is observed, The entitlement/self-centeredness schema refers to the core set of beliefs that one is entitled to take or receive whatever is wanted, irrespective of the cost to others or to society. The insufficient self-control/self-discipline schema refers to the core set of beliefs that one has such limited control and ability to tolerate frustration that achieving goals or controlling impulses and emotional outbursts is unlikely. The abuse/mistrust schema is noted in the hypervigilant and suspicious narcissist. This schema refers to the core set of beliefs that others will hurt, humiliate, or take advantage of one (Bricker, Young, & Flanagan, 1993; Young, Klosko, & Weishaar, 2003).

Style/Temperament

There are three style or temperament dimensions that may need to be addressed in formulating treatment for narcissistic personality disorder: affective, behavioral–relational, and cognitive. Needless to say, these styles exacerbate and are exacerbated by their schemas. Narcissistic individuals are prone to overmodulated anger to the point of ragefulness. Behaviorally, they tend to be manipulative, and relationally, they are likely to have difficulty relating to others except in a superficial manner. In addition, they tend to have significant empathic deficits. Finally, their cognitive style is marked by the capacity for cognitive distortion and projective identification. When impulsivity is also present, it further exacerbates the other style dysregulations. The most notable skill deficit in this disorder is that of empathic responding. Other skill deficits that may be present include those of negotiation and conflict resolution (Sperry, 2003).

☐ Pattern Change Strategies

In general, the long-range goal of treatment for individuals with NPD is to increase their capacity and willingness to share and identify with others. Treatment strategies typically include challenging the individual's dysfunctional beliefs about specialness and grandiosity and helping them learn to become more empathic.

After the maladaptive pattern has been identified and analyzed in terms of schemas and style and skill deficits, the therapeutic process involves relinquishing that pattern and replacing it with a more adaptive pattern. Thus, the pattern change process involves modifying schemas and style and skill dimensions. The process of modifying the maladaptive schemas of patients with NPD usually follows efforts to modify style and skill-deficit dimensions because efforts at schema change early in the course of treatment are usually resisted by the patient.

Schema Change

The entitlement/self-centeredness schema is supported by such injunctive beliefs as "It's essential that I get others' admiration, praise, and recognition"; "Others should satisfy my needs"; "I'm not bound by the rules that apply to others"; "Others have no right to criticize me"; and, particularly, "Because I'm so superior, I'm entitled to special privileges and treatment" (Beck, Freeman, Davis, & Associates, 2004). In the schema change process, the clinician and patient work collaboratively to understand the developmental roots of the maladaptive schemas. Then, these schemas are tested through predictive experiments, guided observation, and reenactment of early schema-related incidents. Finally, narcissistic patients are directed to begin to notice and remember counterschema data about themselves and their social experiences.

Modification of the entitlement schema does not mean that these individuals become selfless and no longer believe themselves to have special talents or capacity to influence and control others. It means that while they continue to view themselves with some degree of specialness, they are able to use their talents and capacities to influence others more for the common good rather than for their own personal gratification.

Style/Temperament Change

Because narcissistic individuals tend to cognitively distort and overuse the defenses of splitting and projective identification, cognitive awareness training can be quite useful. With regard to the emotional style in which narcissistic rage is prominent, anger management training can be an effective intervention strategy. Because empathic deficits greatly affect relational style, empathy training and increasing intimacy-promoting behavior are indicated. And because impatience and impulsivity often exacerbate other style dysregulations, impulse control training may be necessary. As noted below, medication may also be a useful adjunct in modulating these style dimensions.

Medication Strategies

Stylistic or temperament treatment targets for this disorder usually are affective instability, interpersonal sensitivity, impulsivity, and aggression. The less their impulsivity, the more likely that these patients will be able to control their ragefulness and resulting projective identifications. Lithium and carbamezapine have been effective in treating affective instability, and serotonergic agents have been effective in treating impulsivity and aggressivity. Serotonergic agents, such as fluoxetine and sertraline, are effective for reducing the interpersonal sensitivity and reactivity. For those patients with rejection sensitivity, and who have shown good treatment compliance, a trial of a monoamine oxidase inhibitor (MAOI) can be considered if all other approaches have failed. Finally, serotonergic agents have some efficacy in lower-functioning narcissistic patients who exhibit impulsivity and affective instability (Reich, 2002).

Group Treatment Strategies

Group therapy has a role in the treatment of individuals with NPD. Alonso (1992) contended that group therapy is as effective as individual modes in the treatment of narcissistic personality disorder. Nevertheless, recent developments in conjoint marital therapy suggest that group treatment may have fewer indications than do individual and couples therapy (Sperry, 2003).

Several factors contribute to the effectiveness of group treatment for patients with NPD. First, peer feedback, rather than clinician feedback, tends to be more acceptable to the individual. Second, transferences—particularly negative transferences—tend to be less intense in group therapy compared with individual therapy. Working through intense effects is facilitated in groups because of the increased potential for positive attachments within the group and because of peer-group scrutiny of the individual's disavowed affects. Third, a group provides narcissistic individuals with sources of mirroring, objects for idealization, and opportunities for peer relationships. Finally, the group provides ready-made opportunities for narcissistic individuals to increase their ability to empathize with others and to enhance both self-esteem and self-cohesion.

Not surprisingly, narcissistic patients can make unreasonable demands for attention in group treatment. These demands can be very taxing for other group members, particularly in heterogeneous groups. Accordingly, it is advisable to begin narcissistic patients in individual therapy as a preparation for entry into group treatment. Even though the narcissistic pathology can strain efforts to achieve group cohesion, a properly run group can function as a container for splitting and projective processes. Nevertheless, the dropout rate among individuals with NPD is higher in long-term ongoing groups than in time-limited groups. Accordingly, concurrent individual psychotherapy that focuses on helping individuals remain in group therapy is often useful.

Horowitz (1987) outlined the following four indications and contraindications for group treatment of narcissistic individuals: (a) the presence of demandingness, (b) egocentrism, (c) social isolation and withdrawal, and (d) socially deviant behavior. While these traits may be taxing to both clinician and group members, Horowitz contended that patients with such traits tend to be quite responsive to group treatment. Finally, attending to the unique needs of the narcissistic individual usually means that the clinician will place less emphasis on interpreting overall group dynamics than on individual dynamics as they affect the group process (Sperry, 2003).

Marital and Family Therapy Strategies

Early reports on the use of family therapy for patients with NPD emphasized the treatment of adolescents in families with severe narcissistic pathology, wherein the adolescent was the identified patient on whom family members projected their own devalued views of themselves. More recent applications of family therapy to treatment of narcissistic personality disorder emphasize treating the entire family system from a systemic perspective (Jones, 1987).

Much has been published about marital therapy for the narcissistic spouse or couple. Solomon (1989; 1998) described a conjoint treatment strategy for narcissistic partners from a self-psychology perspective. Conjoint sessions are structured to functions as a "holding environment" for the distorted projections and other conflictual manifestations in the relationship. The therapist's empathic self is the basic tool in this kind of psychodynamic treatment.

Kalojera and his colleagues (Kalojera, Jacobson, Hoffman, et al., 1998) described an integrative blending of self-psychology and the systemic approach to the narcissistic couple that is noteworthy. Lachkar (1998) offered a number of clinically useful considerations for the treatment of couples where one partner meets the criteria for narcissistic personality disorder, while the other meets the criteria for borderline personality disorder. This type of couples are increasingly common today. Nurse (1998) described the dynamics and treatment strategies for another common variant of the narcissistic couple: One partner meets the criteria for narcissistic personality disorder, while the other meets the criteria for dependent personality disorder.

Relationship enhancement therapy has also been adapted to couples therapy for narcissistic spouses (Snyder, 1994). This approach emphasizes the learning and application of four basic interpersonal skills: (a) effective expression, (b) empathy, (c) discussion—mode switching between empathic and expresser roles, and (d) problem-solving/conflict resolution. The clinician's role is to explain, demonstrate, and teach each skill in the conjoint session, whereas the partner's role is to practice these skills during and between sessions with progressively difficult issues. It should not be surprising that empathic skills and the subjective aspect of the expresser skill are notably deficient in narcissistically prone couples. The clinician provides a "holding environment" in which narcissistic proneness is demonstrated and addressed productively rather than acted out. This results in both partners learning to express feelings with less risk of shame while increasing their capacity to empathize with their partner (Snyder, 1994).

Combined and Integrative Treatment Strategies

There is seldom a single treatment strategy, such as mirroring or empathy training, that can ensure positive treatment outcomes for narcissistic individuals. Rather, depending on the individual's overall level of functioning, temperamental patterns, defensive style, and skill deficits, a focused, specific, and sequentially coordinated tailored treatment protocol is usually necessary to accomplish treatment goals and objectives in a timely manner. As noted earlier, higher-functioning individuals who meet either the DSM-IV criteria or the dynamic criteria for a personality disorder have fewer troubling temperamental patterns, skill deficits, and defensive styles than do the lower-functioning individuals. Consequently, the higher the functioning and the fewer the skill deficits, the less likely it is that a combined approach is necessary; however, the lower the functioning and the more the skill deficits/ temperament dysregulations, the more likely it is that an integrative, tailored and combined approach is necessary. This section describes such integrative and combined strategies.

Generally, the psychodynamic approaches have largely emphasized the interpretation of narcissistic proneness to grandiosity and entitlement and the importance of soothing and mirroring frustrations to reduce narcissistic rage. The cognitive approaches have focused on modifying narcissistic proneness, emphasizing modification of schemas, moderating narcissistic expectations, and reducing cognitive distortions, particularly projective identification. The behavioral and psychoeducational approaches have emphasized skill training, particularly empathy training. Combining all three of these modalities is relatively easy to implement and quite acceptable to patients (Sperry, 1995). The usual time sequence for using these modalities is as follows: Begin with soothing and mirroring interpretations to engage the patient in treatment. Next, focus on reversing skill deficits and temperament dysregulation that would otherwise hinder the treatment process. This may include medication but almost always involves skills training, particularly empathy training (Snyder, 1994). This training can be accomplished in individual, group, or couples sessions. Then, continue with the schema change strategy and other interpretation strategies. The case example below illustrates this sequencing of modalities.

☐ Pattern Maintenance and Termination Strategies

Termination Issues

Planned termination is usually not particularly difficult for narcissistic patients. Rather, for the reasons described in the "Engagement" section, narcissistic patients tend to be premature terminators. There are some who, because of the clinician's early confrontative stance or failure to mirror sufficiently, experience treatment as another narcissistic injury and leave at the outset. But for all narcissistic patients, the therapeutic challenge is to be engaged in the treatment process long enough to achieve basic treatment objectives. To that end, it may be necessary to conceptualize the treatment process as a series of discrete phases and establish treatment contracts for these phases. The initial phase usually involves resolution of distress. Many narcissistic individuals present for treatment with sufficient distress that they will remain until it has lessened. For instance, they come for treatment because of depression, a serious narcissistic injury, or because of the distress they have created in the lives of others, such as a spouse who threatens divorce if treatment is not sought. These individuals will likely remain in treatment until they have achieved sufficient soothing or alleviation of their anxiety or depressive symptoms. Many of them terminate treatment after experiencing relief of their distress. Accordingly, it is advisable to establish a treatment agreement for a given number of sessions focused on distress resolution and then reevaluate and renegotiate another series of sessions to focus on more general concerns. The clinician's challenge is to sufficiently "join" with the patient's entitlement so that the patient comes to believe that therapeutic change is in his or her best interests (for an illustration of these points, see "Case Example" below).

Relapse Prevention Strategies

Relapse prevention is essential in the effective treatment of narcissistic individuals. Even though effective treatment greatly reduces their interpersonal sensitivity and narcissistic tendency, these individuals are still prone to narcissistic injury. The final phase of treatment should therefore emphasize relapse prevention. An important goal of relapse prevention is predicting likely difficulties in the time period immediately following termination. The patient needs to be able to analyze specific factors, such as persons, places, and circumstances, as well as specific narcissistic beliefs, that can trigger their maladaptive pattern. Once these have been predicted, the patients can develop a contingency plan to deal with these stressors.

☐ Case Example

James K. was 49 years old, married, and chairman of the department of plastic and reconstructive surgery at a university school of medicine. He grudgingly came for psychotherapy because of his depressive symptoms and because of ultimatums from his wife and boss. His wife had demanded that he get help or she would divorce him. He had been married for 7 years to his current wife and prior to that had been married to another woman for approximately 5 years, during the last 2 years of medical school and the first 3 years of his surgical residency. Recently, his wife had complained that she would no longer tolerate his constant need for attention or his increasing rage and verbal abuse, which consisted of blaming, insults, and name-calling. Lately, their time together had been marked by either destructive conflict or cold distancing for days to weeks. In addition, the dean of the medical school had also warned him that if he did not adopt a "more consultive management style," he would be removed from his position as chair of his department. Apparently, Dr. K. had increasingly alienated a number of his faculty over the past few years with his arrogant, demanding style and because he had recently fired two junior faculty members for insubordination. The university grievance committee that reviewed the dismissals had found that due process had not been followed and had recommended that the two members be reinstated. Dr. K. had been furious with the committee's recommendation and had demanded that the dean ignore it. It was then that the dean had given him the ultimatum. Dr. K.'s rage turned to depression manifested by dysphoria, insomnia, some anhedonia, and loss of energy. Although he had refused his wife's demand for couples therapy, he reluctantly agreed to individual psychotherapy.

Engagement Process

Like many narcissistic individuals who enter treatment, Dr. K. was narcissistically wounded deeply and depressed mildly to moderately. Nevertheless, such patients usually seek treatment with great reluctance and demand that it be on their terms. Dr. K. announced during the first session that he was there against his better judgment and that he had no problems except for a wife who was a "bedeviling shrew" and a boss who was a "wimpish idiot." Reluctantly, he admitted that he was embarrassed and hurt by recent events, particularly at the medical school, but said these would pass. Mainly, he was concerned about his depressive symptoms, which were worsening over the past 3 weeks. He wanted an antidepressant. By the second session, he reported that his sleep was normalizing and that he was more energetic but still felt quite wounded. He responded to the clinician's mirroring and attentiveness and agreed to return for a third session. The clinician, a member of the school's psychiatry faculty, had to respond to an emergency and therefore was about 6 minutes late for Dr. K.'s third appointment. Dr. K. immediately launched into an attack on the clinician's character and competence and stated that he should never have trusted himself to the care of a junior faculty member when he should have been seen by the chair of the department or at least a faculty psychiatrist who was listed in *Best Doctors in America.* The clinician successfully soothed Dr. K. and apologized for the delay. Later during that session, Dr. K. announced that his depression had lifted and he no longer needed treatment. The clinician offered a mirroring interpretation and suggested that it might still be in Dr. K.'s best interests to consider some alternative ways of dealing with his wife, his colleagues, and the dean that would ease the current situation and prevent its recurrence. Dr. K. agreed that it was in his best interests to "do some damage control" and committed to eight additional sessions after which the treatment contract would be reviewed.

Pattern Analysis

Although Dr. K. did not meet the criteria for major depressive disorder, he did meet the criteria for minor depressive disorder as well as narcissistic personality disorder. A review of his early childhood and later developmental history as well as his early recollections indicated a self view of specialness and a world view in which others were expected to cater to all of his needs. His maladaptive pattern involved increasing self-aggrandizement, manipulation, and demands made on others whenever he felt the slightest discomfort or lack of others' recognition. When criticized or otherwise narcissistically wounded, he would engage in projective identification and ragefulness. This pattern reflected the maladaptive schema of entitlement/self-centeredness and, to some extent, the schema of insufficient self-control/self-discipline. This pattern also reflected style/skill deficits in accurate attributions, impulse control, and empathic communication. Figure 7.1 summarizes these style features.

Pattern Change

The eight sessions were arranged to include four individual weekly sessions and four weekly conjoint sessions. The individual sessions focused on cognitive awareness training and impulse control training skills. Even though Dr. K. had previously refused couples therapy, he was receptive to conjoint sessions because the focus would be limited to interpersonal skills. Dr. K. agreed that the purpose of these sessions was to give him "another set of people skills" that he could "use when it was expedient." After all, he was proud of his persona of toughness and arrogance and did not want

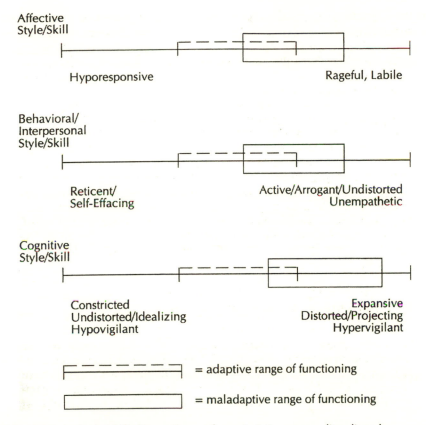

FIGURE 7.1. Style/skill dimensions of narcissistic personality disorder.

to give it up. Empathy training exercises were the focus of four such conjoint sessions. In these sessions, both spouses were helped to understand the patient's narcissistic tendency, expectations, and needs underlying the narcissistic defense. The clinician modeled empathic listening as well as empathic responding for them and coached them in both listening and responding from the others' frame of reference. In part, this was accomplished by role-playing and role reversal in which Dr. and Mrs. K. played themselves expressing their feelings and concerns and then reversed roles. They agreed to practice these skills at least 30 minutes per day.

During the last of the four individual sessions, the eight-session treatment agreement was reviewed. The focal intensity of the individual and conjoint sessions as well as the couple's daily skill practice had resulted in a significant shift in the couple's relationship. It had become much more respecting and caring, and they had been able to handle the few conflicts that had arisen in a more adaptive fashion. Dr. K. was pleased that his work relationships were also less charged, and he congratulated himself for "reinventing myself," by which he meant he now had a "good guy persona," too. Through mirroring interpretations, the clinician set the stage for discussing a continuation of the treatment contract. The modality would be individual psychotherapy, with a focus on further enhancement of the skills and understanding of self that had already been started. Not surprisingly, Dr. K. declined the invitation saying he had gotten what he had come for and was fine. The clinician offered to resume treatment if and when Dr. K. might find it beneficial.

Approximately 5 months later, Dr. K. was back in treatment. Two weeks earlier, following a stormy confrontation with him, Mrs. K. had filed for divorce. Dr. K. was crushed. He was dysphoric and panicky at the prospect of losing "the jewel of my life." Furthermore, he had begun experiencing palpitations that were diagnosed as cardiac arrhythmia, and he had been prescribed medication for it. He was agreeable to anything now, even couples therapy. Individual psychotherapy was begun with a focus on maladaptive schemas. The antidepressant was reintroduced for a short time until depressive and anxiety symptoms were alleviated. Twice weekly sessions were scheduled. These sessions continued for the next 11 months, after which they were reduced to weekly sessions for an additional 3 months.

Pattern Maintenance and Termination

During the course of this treatment period, Mrs. K. dropped the divorce action. A planned termination ensued. Dr. K. had developed considerable insight into his need for specialness and control along with concomitant changes in his behavior. Dr. K. did not believe a scheduled follow-up appointment was necessary but agreed to call the clinician in 6 months. At that time, he reported that things were going reasonably well at work and even better at home. His son, who got married just after Dr. K. had started the long-term therapy, had just visited with his wife and infant daughter. He and Mrs. K. were quite excited to be grandparents.

☐ Summary

Effective treatment of narcissistic personality disorder requires the establishment of a trusting patient–clinician relationship fostered by focal treatment interventions to modify the maladaptive pattern and to maintain the new pattern. Because these patients may have considerable difficulty engaging in and profiting from traditional psychotherapy, an integrative

TABLE 7.2. Treatment Interventions for Narcissistic Personality Disorder

Phase	Issue	Strategy/Tactic
Engagement	Demanding mirroring; easily narcissistically wounded	Mirroring; minimizing
Transference	Idealizing to devaluating; projective identification	Mirroring interpretation
Countertransference	Not recognizing one's own narcissistic needs; boredom; feeling controlled by the patient; angry, hurt, impotent	Monitoring and interpreting
Pattern Analysis	Trigger: evaluation of self	
Pattern Change	Treatment Goal: increased awareness and responsiveness to others' needs	
Schema/Character	Entitlement/self-centeredness; insufficient self-control/ self-discipline; abuse/mistrust	Interpretation or schema change strategy
Style/Temperament		
a. Affective Style	Narcissistic rage	Anger management
b. Behavioral/ Relational Style	Empathic deficits	Empathy training
c. Cognitive Style	Cognitive distortion; projective identification; hypervigilance	Cognitive awareness training; sensitivity reduction training
Maintenance/ Termination	Premature termination	"Join" patient's entitlement

and combined approach that focuses on characterological, temperament, and skill dimensions may be essential for effective treatment outcomes. The case example illustrated the common challenges that these patients present and the kind of flexibility, resourcefulness, and level of competence required from the clinician. Table 7.2 summarizes the treatment intervention strategies most likely to be effective in treating this disorder.

Histrionic Personality Disorder

Histrionic personality disorder (HPD), as delineated by DSM-IV, is not synonymous with hysterical personality disorder that is described in the psychoanalytic literature. Rather, the description and criteria of HPD reflect a more primitive entity than the higher-functioning hysterical personality. Needless to say, the treatment of HPD is more challenging than the treatment of hysterical personality disorder. Nevertheless, individuals with HPD can be effectively treated. This chapter describes specific engagement, pattern analysis, pattern change, and pattern maintenance and termination strategies for effectively managing and treating this disorder. In addition to individual psychotherapeutic strategies and tactics, group, marital, family, medication, and integrative and combined treatment strategies are detailed. An extensive case example illustrates the treatment process. Before turning to treatment strategies, the DSM-IV description and criteria are briefly presented.

Clinical Conceptualization of Histrionic Personality Disorder

Behavioral Style:	Charming/excitement-seeking; labile, capricious, superficial
Interpersonal Style:	Attention-getting/manipulative; exhibitionistic/flirtatious
Cognitive Style:	Impulsive, thematic, field-dependent; avoid awareness of their hidden dependencies
Feeling Style:	Exaggerated emotional display

Temperament:	Hyperresponsive infantile pattern externally oriented for gratification
Attachment Style:	Preoccupied
Parental Injunction:	"I'll give you attention when you do what I want."
Self View:	"I need to be noticed"; externally-oriented for gratification
World View:	"Life makes me so nervous, so I'm entitled to special care and consideration."
Maladaptive Schemas	Approval-seeking; emotional deprivation; defectiveness
Optimal DSM-IV-TR	
Criteria:	Is uncomfortable in situations in which he or she is not the center of attention.

☐ DSM-IV Description and Criteria

DSM-IV offers this description and criteria for histrionic personality disorder (Table 8.1):

TABLE 8.1.   DSM-IV Description and Criteria for Histrionic Personality Disorder

301.50 Histrionic Personality Disorder

A pervasive pattern of excessive emotionality and attention-seeking, beginning by early adulthood and present in a variety of contexts, as indicated by five (or more) of the following:

(1) Is uncomfortable in situations in which he or she is not the center of attention

(2) interaction with others is often characterized by inappropriate sexually seductive or provocative behavior

(3) displays rapidly shifting and shallow expression of emotions

(4) consistently uses physical appearance to draw attention to self

(5) has a style of speech that is excessively impressionistic and lacking in detail

(6) shows self-dramatization, theatricality, and exaggerated expression of emotion

(7) is suggestible, that is, easily influenced by others or circumstances

(8) considers relationships to be more intimate than they actually are

☐ Engagement Strategies

Early Session Behavior

Interviewing histrionic individuals is usually enjoyable, but it is always quite challenging. The challenge is that these individuals are more interested in admiration and approval than in establishing a therapeutic relationship. The clinician can expect exaggerated emotionality, vagueness, and superficiality in the first session. Histrionic females are likely to be flirtatious, obsequious, or playful with a male clinician, whereas they are more likely to engage in a power struggle with a female clinician (Sperry, 1995). Eliciting sufficient history and information to complete the diagnostic evaluation usually requires the clinician to neutralize the histrionic individual's vagueness, dramatics, or control. The clinician's use of open-ended and unstructured questions should be limited or avoided because these patients easily become sidetracked. Rather, it is more productive to pursue a basic theme, such as interpersonal conflict or a work issue and then elicit specific examples while curbing the patients' ramblings and contradictions. Confronting their contradictions may result in hostility and even loss of rapport, and thus, it is preferable to express empathy and understanding. It should be anticipated that when the patients experience a diminishing of empathy and understanding, they will return to vagueness or dramatization (Othmer & Othmer, 2002).

Because histrionic patients tend to regard the self as a recipient of the actions of others rather than as an agent of action, they report symptoms as caused or represented outside of the self. Accordingly, through repetitions and structured questioning, the clinician can begin assisting these patients to clarify their experiences, to provide everyday labels for them, and to recognize that thoughts and feelings come from within the self (Horowitz, 1995).

Facilitating Collaboration

Establishing a collaborative relationship with histrionic patients is somewhat similar to establishing such a relationship with patients with dependent personality disorder. At the outset of treatment, both types of patients are likely to view clinicians as all-powerful rescuers who will make everything better for them. And because of their global, impressionistic cognitive style and sense of specialness, histrionic patients tend to believe and expect that clinicians will somehow intuitively be able to appreciate and understand their needs and concerns without any or much intrapsychic exploration of these needs and concerns. For this reason, it is essential that the clinician assume an active role at the outset of treatment (Othmer & Othmer, 2002). The more this active role is evidenced, the quicker the fantasy of the all-powerful rescuer will fade.

Histrionic patients must undergo a socialization process in which they experience the phenomenon of collaboration, which is quite foreign to them. Whenever histrionic patients beg and demand that they be helped or rescued, clinicians use questioning to assist them in arriving at their own solutions. Furthermore, clinicians must reinforce every instance of assertive and competent behaviors manifest in the early phase of treatment rather than reinforcing the helping–demanding behaviors. The cognitive therapy strategy of guided discovery in which clinicians work with patients to understand the connection between patients' thoughts, images, feelings, and behaviors is particularly effective in facilitating collaboration with histrionic patients (Beck, Freeman, Davis, & Associates, 2004).

Transference and Countertransference

Two common transferences noted in histrionic patients are rescue fantasy and the erotic or eroticized transferences. When histrionic patients bring a series of problems to clinicians expecting quick solutions, or otherwise feign helplessness, it is easy for clinicians to respond to their rescue fantasies by assuming an all-powerful/messianic or rescuer role. In the role of rescuer, clinicians may provide advice, give in to specific demands, make decisions, and even assume blame for their patients' failure to work toward change. As a result, clinicians may feel angry, manipulated, and deceived. Not surprisingly, by assuming the rescuer role, clinicians not only inadvertently reinforce feelings of helplessness among these patients but also become embroiled in a reenactment of their earliest relationship pattern (Beck, Freeman, & Associates, 1990). Redirecting and refocusing the patients toward finding their own solutions is recommended.

In hysterical patients, the erotic transference—or transference love, which is a mixture of tender, erotic, and sexual feelings toward the clinician— tends to develop over a gradual period of time along with feelings of shame and embarrassment. On the other hand, individuals with HPD can develop an eroticized transference, which, unlike transference love, is characterized by the expectation of sexual gratification. Typical countertransferences with erotic and eroticized transferences are aloofness, anxiety, and exploitation. Essentially, these transferences need to be analyzed and understood, and the countertransferences monitored rather than acted out. A detailed discussion of the resolution of these erotic/eroticized transference–countertransferences can be found in Gabbard (2005).

☐ Pattern Analysis Strategies

Pattern analysis of individuals with HPD involves an accurate diagnostic and clinical evaluation of schemas, styles, and triggering stressors, as well as level of functioning and readiness for therapeutic change. Knowledge of the optimal DSM-IV criterion along with the maladaptive pattern of the individual with HPD is not only useful in specifying diagnosis but also in planning treatment that is tailored to the histrionic patient's unique style, needs, and circumstances. The optimal criterion specified for histrionic personality disorder is discomfort in situations in which the patient is not the center of attention (Allnutt & Links, 1996). Both planned treatment goals and interventions should reflect this theme of attention-getting and specialness.

Pattern refers to the predictable and consistent style and manner in which a patient thinks, feels, acts, copes, and defends the self. Pattern analysis involves both the triggers and the response—the "what"—as well as an explanatory statement—the "why"—about the pattern of a given histrionic patient. Obviously, such a clinical formulation specifies the *particular* schemas and temperamental styles unique to a given individual rather than the more *general* ones that will be noted here.

Triggers

Generally speaking, the "triggers" or "triggering situations" for histrionic patients are stressors related to heterosexual relationships (Othmer & Othmer, 2002). This means that when histrionic individuals are engaging in behaviors, discussing, or even thinking about certain opposite-sex relationships and they become distressed, their disordered or maladaptive pattern is likely to be triggered, and their characteristic symptomatic affects, behaviors, and cognitions will be experienced or exhibited. While histrionic patients generally tend to engage in help-seeking, seductive, or attention-getting behaviors with opposite-sex individuals, they are more likely to engage in power struggles with same-sex individuals.

Schemas

The underlying schemas in HPD involve a self view of needing to be noticed by others and a view of the world as the provider of special care and consideration because life makes these patients nervous (Sperry & Mosak, 1996). Among the most frequently encountered schema in histrionic patients is the entitlement/self-centeredness schema. Often, features of the emotional deprivation schema are also noted. The entitlement/self-centeredness schema refers to the core set of beliefs that one is entitled to take or receive whatever is wanted irrespective of the cost to others or society. The emotional deprivation schema refers to the core set of beliefs that one's need for nurturance and emotional support will never be met by others (Bricker, Young, and Flanagan, 1993; Young, Klosko, and Weishaar, 2003).

Style/Temperament

There are three style or temperament dimensions that may need to be addressed in formulating treatment for the histrionic patient: affective, behavioral–relational, and cognitive. These styles exacerbate and are exacerbated by their schemas. Histrionic individuals are prone to superficial, overmodulated affects. Behaviorally, they tend to be unfocused and inconsistent, and relationally they are likely to have difficulty relating to others except in a superficial, manipulative manner. In addition, they tend to have empathic deficits. Finally, their cognitive style is marked by the capacity for global, impressionistic thinking and vividness of imagination (Sperry, 2003). They also experience considerable difficulty focusing on specifics and details. When impulsivity is also present, it further exacerbates the other style dysregulations. The most notable skill deficits in this disorder are problem-solving skills and self-management skills. Other skill deficits that may be present include deficits in empathy and time and money management.

☐ Pattern Change Strategies

In general, the overall goal of treatment for individuals with HPD is to increase their capacity for reflection, interdependence, and self-management. In other words, the first goal is to "feel less and think more," which is the converse of the goal for treatment of obsessive-compulsive personality disorder. The goal of interdependence is met when the histrionic individual is able to establish and maintain more functional intimate relationships. That means that instead of relating to others in the demanding but distancing role of princess or sex object, the female histrionic can relate more as an intimate, equal partner taking the risks that mutually giving relationships require. Accomplishing these goals involves modifying maladaptive beliefs about specialness and attention-getting, and learning ways in which to increase self-management.

After the maladaptive pattern has been identified and analyzed in terms of schemas, style and skill deficits, the therapeutic process involves relinquishing that pattern and replacing it with a more adaptive one. Thus, the pattern change process involves modifying schemas, modulating style dysregulations, and reversing skill deficits. The process of modifying the maladaptive schemas of patients with HPD usually follows efforts to modify style and skill-deficit dimensions because schema change early in the course of treatment is often resisted by the patient.

Schema Change

The entitlement/self-centered schema is supported by such injunctive beliefs as "I'm interesting and exciting"; "Intuition and feeling are more important than rational planning"; "If I'm entertaining, others won't notice my weaknesses"; and, particularly, "To be happy, I need other people to pay attention to me" (Beck, Freeman, Davis, & Associates, 2004). The emotional deprivation schema fosters such histrionic beliefs as "I'll never get enough love and attention" and "I'm only capable of having superficial relationships" (Young, Klosko, & Weishaar, 2003). In the schema change process, the clinician and patient work collaboratively to understand the developmental roots of the maladaptive schemas. Then, these schemas are tested through predictive experiments, guided observation, and reenactment of early schema-related incidents. Finally, histrionic patients are directed to begin to notice and remember counterschema data about themselves and their social experiences.

Style/Temperament Change

Because histrionic individuals tend to exhibit superficial but intense and overly modulated affects, emotional awareness training along with "dramatic behavioral experiments" can be effective interventions. Because of their flair for the dramatic and their dread of protocol and detail, histrionic patients will likely respond to homework assignments if they are given permission to use their vivid imaginations, particularly with behavioral experiments and behavioral rehearsals. Beck, Freeman, Davis, and Associates (2004) illustrated the use of dramatic behavioral experiments with histrionic patients.

Problem-solving training can be effective in assisting histrionic patients to become more organized and exert more consistent effort in daily life. Adding a measure of structure in their lives can reasonably modulate their free-spirited, inconsistent, and manipulative style (Marra, 2005). Because impulsivity is usually part of this style and can also exacerbate other style dysregulation, impulse control training may be necessary. Furthermore, these patients tend to have some deficits in assertiveness, empathy, and intimacy, and therefore, assertive communication training, empathy training, and intimacy promoting activities may be indicated.

Setting specific treatment goals and learning the skill of listing advantages and disadvantages, or pros and cons, are common cognitive therapy interventions for modifying the histrionic personality's cognitive style (Beck, Freeman, Davis, & Associates, 2004). As noted below, medication may also be a useful adjunct in modulating these style dimensions.

Medication Strategies

Individuals with HPD may exhibit Axis I symptoms, including anxiety, depression, and somatoform symptoms. When moderate to severe anxiety or depression is the presenting Axis I symptom, antidepressants may be indicated. When the presentation involves attention-craving, exquisite rejection sensitivity, demanding behavior, and hypersomnia, the clinician should rule out the possibility that "hysteroid dysphoria" may be present; therefore, a monoamine oxidase inhibitor (MAOI) might be considered. When no obvious Axis I symptom is present but affective instability and impulsivity are noted—often in lower-functioning histrionic patients— sertraline, fluoxetine, or other selective serotonin reuptake inhibitors (SSRIs) have shown some benefit with such histrionic patients (Kavoussi, Liu, & Chaucer, 1994). However, often, temperament or style dysregulations can be effectively modulated only with skills training.

Group Treatment Strategies

Group treatments have a number of advantages over individual treatment for HPD. First, group treatment frustrates the histrionic patient's wish and demand for the exclusive attention of the therapist. Group dynamics inevitably challenge the approval-seeking posture of these patients. Accordingly, the likelihood of an eroticized transference developing is relatively less compared with individual therapy. Second, the histrionic patient's global cognitive style and related defenses of denial and repression can be more effectively modified in a group treatment context rather than in an individual treatment context. These features are frustrating for other group members who will subsequently confront the histrionic patient's distorted self-perceptions, omission of details, and thematic thinking. Third, because histrionic patients crave positive maternal transference, they expect, and even demand, that the group provide them with the maternal nurturance they missed in their childhood. While the nurturing maternal transference can be particularly challenging in individual therapy, the group treatment context effectively diminishes this transference (Gabbard, 2005). These advantages are particularly relevant with lower- to moderate-functioning histrionic patients.

The following are some indications and contraindications for group treatment of histrionic personality disorder. Indications for group treatment include higher-functioning histrionic individuals who can express affects directly and spontaneously and those who can draw others out and manifest concern for other group members. Such individuals tend to be highly valued by other group members. Contraindications include histrionic patients who cannot participate in a group process without monopolizing or disrupting it. Nevertheless, clinical experience suggests that concurrent individual psychotherapy and group therapy can be useful for histrionic patients who are likely to monopolize or be disruptive in group settings. It should also be noted that skill-oriented groups are well suited for lower-functioning histrionic patients, particularly in partial hospitalization and day-treatment programs.

Marital and Family Therapy Strategies

Little has been written about family therapy, per se, for histrionic patients. However, there is considerable literature on couples therapy for histrionic patients. Typically, the marriage consists of a histrionic wife and an obsessive-compulsive husband, wherein the obsessive-compulsive partner has assumed increasing responsibility for the relationship, while the histrionic partner has assumed an increasingly helpless or irresponsible role (Sperry & Maniacci, 1998). Treatment is often sought after a primitive outburst, which usually involves some actual or threatened self-destructive behavior, often in the context of a separation or divorce. The perceived or actual loss of a stable, dependent person in their lives is a major stressor for histrionic patients. Thus, they will engage in various forms of attention-seeking behavior—including suicide gestures and promiscuity—in an effort to get the other partner's attention (Harbir, 1981). Generally, the goal of treatment is to change this pattern and redirect the energies of both partners. Usually, this goal can be better accomplished in conjoint treatment rather than individual treatment. Sperry and Maniacci (1998) described an integrative dynamic, cognitive–behavioral, and systems treatment approach for this type of couples.

Combined and Integrated Treatment Strategies

Integrated and combined treatment strategies are not only useful for higher-functioning histrionic patients, they can also considerably shorten the course of treatment. However, with lower- to moderate-functioning histrionic patients, integrated and combined treatment strategies are essential for effective treatment outcomes. The most common combination of treatment modalities for moderate- to higher-functioning histrionic patients are (a) individual therapy with couples or marital therapy, and (b) individual therapy with heterogeneous group therapy. For lower-functioning histrionic patients, skill-focused group treatment is particularly useful. Typically, this modality is combined with individual treatment. As mentioned earlier, concurrent individual psychotherapy is a necessary adjunct to group therapy for histrionic patients who monopolize the group process or are otherwise disruptive in group settings. Finally, medications may be a useful adjunct to psychotherapy, either sequentially or in tandem, if specific Axis I or Axis II target symptoms are prominent.

☐ Pattern Maintenance and Termination Strategies

Termination Issues

Treatment termination can be difficult and challenging for the clinicians and for the histrionic patients, largely because the therapeutic relationship provided patients with undivided attention and concern. As the termination phase begins, a repetition of the maladaptive histrionic pattern is inevitable as the patients begin to realize that they must soon relinquish the attention and nurturance that treatment had come to represent. Fantasies of rescue and nurture that previously had remained veiled will now be disclosed. Particularly prominent are fantasies of a continued relationship with the clinician following termination. But since the patients have already relinquished much of their maladaptive pattern, these fantasies and yearnings are no longer as compelling as before. Presumably, these individuals have also developed more adaptive relationships with significant others since treatment began. Accordingly, they can better tolerate the perceived loss of the therapeutic relationship. Subsequently, residual symptoms will finally be relinquished during this last phase of treatment, particularly those symptoms that were maintained because of secondary gain.

Allen (1977) noted that "the patient may have a covert wish for indefinite continuation of treatment, and only in the termination phase is it possible to examine and resolve the desperate need for an enduring, sustaining relationship" (p. 320). Furthermore, all of the patients' dilemmas about relating to others, getting attention, and authentic sexuality can now be reviewed in the context of terminating the therapeutic relationship. Not surprisingly, as termination nears and their anxiety mounts, some patients attempt to continue a transference as a defense against the risk of establishing and maintaining real relationships outside the treatment context.

Two therapeutic strategies can facilitate the termination process. First, the clinician can offer the predictive interpretation that attention-getting and dependency needs may complicate the termination process. Conveying this prediction to the patient in a matter-of-fact, nonjudgmental fashion can preempt the patient's conscious or unconscious wish to subvert termination and continue therapy indefinitely, and also provide the patients with useful feedback regarding the ways in which their strivings can adversely affect other important interpersonal relationships. Second, spacing out sessions allows patients to become less reliant on their relationship with the clinician and more on relationships outside the treatment context. As they become increasingly able to tolerate this separation, their maladaptive pattern shifts to a more adaptive and healthier pattern of interdependence.

Relapse Prevention Strategies

Another essential aspect of the treatment plan and process is relapse prevention. Because histrionic patients can easily revert to their maladaptive pattern, it is necessary to predict and plan for relapse. The final phase of treatment should largely focus on relapse prevention. An important goal of relapse prevention is predicting likely difficulties in the time period immediately following termination. Histrionic patients need to be able to analyze specific external situations, such as persons, times, and places, and internal states, such as specific histrionic beliefs, fears, and other vulnerabilities that increase the likelihood of their responding with histrionic behavior in the face of predictable triggers. Once predicted, a contingency plan to deal with these stressors can be developed. Clinicians may find it useful to have patients think and talk through the following questions: What can I do if I find myself wanting to impress others or show off? What should I do if I start placing unreasonable demands on important relationships? What should I do if I start believing in my old histrionic beliefs more than in my new beliefs? What should I do if I relapse? Finally, because interpersonal relationships are triggers for the histrionic pattern, the relapse plan should also include provisions for increasing and maintaining intimacy and commitment.

☐ Case Example

Kristy G. is a 44-year-old, married female, who worked as a beauty consultant for a major cosmetics distributor. She had been married to Warren G. for 19 years, and they had an 18-year-old son. For the past 5 years, Kristy had been in psychiatric treatment for chronic, recurrent depression. Irrespective of the medications used, she experienced only partial remission of her symptoms and reported episodic periods of dysphoria, vague suicidal ideation, and chronic dissatisfaction with her life. She had also received adjunctive supportive psychotherapy from a social worker, who claimed that "adjustment to her condition" was all she could expect from treatment. During her third year of treatment, Kristy realized that she was not improving and her marriage was deteriorating. Her husband, who had always been a pillar of strength for her, was becoming quite symptomatic himself, and their relationship had become even more distant. So, Kristy decided to stop her current treatment and try couples therapy. Subsequently, she and her husband met with a couples therapist, who, after evaluating them as a couple in a conjoint session and then also individually, recommended a course of conjoint couples therapy and also dynamically oriented individual psychotherapy for both spouses. The course of therapy for this couple is described in some detail in conjunction with the individual therapy of Warren G. in Chapter 9 of this book, and the course of individual treatment for Kristy is described here.

Engagement Process

Kristy was an attractive woman who was quite fashionably dressed, and yet she appeared somewhat older than her stated age. She seemed considerably pleased with the prospect of working with a male clinician. Despite her somewhat depressed mood, she forced her smiles, gesticulated with her hands and made facial expressions in an exaggerated manner, and gave the impression that she was performing for an admiring but unseen audience. Initially skeptical of combining dynamically oriented individual therapy with couples sessions, Kristy eventually agreed to the treatment plan.

Pattern Analysis

Kristy was the youngest of four siblings and a prized daughter, particularly of her father. She was especially cute and received considerable attention for her brightness and vivaciousness. Shortly after her third birthday, her mother was admitted for the first of several hospitalizations for depression. This illness took its toll on the rest of the family. The father was forced to take on an additional job and withdrew much of his attention from Kristy. While she was still the favorite grandchild of her grandparents, she secretly envied her mother's new, privileged position. Mother gained considerable sympathy and seemed to be excused from much of the burden of being a housewife and mother. Her needs always seemed to prevail, and, not surprisingly, the family byword was "Don't upset your mother!" Kristy's first episode of depression occurred when she 15 years old following the breakup of an intense relationship with her 18-year-old boyfriend who had left town to attend university. She had felt devastated and claimed to have never fully gotten over this loss. She eventually completed training as a cosmetologist, after which she had been successfully employed as a beauty consultant.

Kristy's earliest memory involved her fourth birthday party: She was wearing a beautiful dress and everyone was looking admiringly at her. She felt special and loved and was amazed at all the gifts and the cake placed before her. Her next memory involved her first day of school: She recalled walking into class, feeling pretty in a new dress. The female teacher told her that she needed to take a seat near the back of the room, since her name was near the end of the alphabet. Her first reaction was to look at the teacher, but then at herself, thinking she was not dressed "nice enough" to sit in the front of the class. She felt angry and sad. These early recollections, along with other data on her developmental history, suggested that Kristy had internalized the schemas of entitlement/self-centeredness and emotional deprivation indicative of the histrionic personality. Her overmodulated affects, impressionistic thinking, and deficits in intimacy, empathy, and other interpersonal skills were also indicative of the histrionic personality. She met the criteria for dysthymic disorder as well as those for histrionic personality disorder with narcissistic features. Her current level of functioning was fair (Global Assessment Functioning [GAF] score of 55), although she had functioned better earlier in the year (GAF score of 67). The current level of distress she was experiencing in herself and in her family, along with her husband's willingness to seek couples therapy with her, suggested that her motivation and readiness were reasonably high and predictive of a positive treatment outcome.

The following pattern formulation served as the basis for planning individual treatment. Kristy had grown up feeling special but cheated. Although she was aware that she could get attention for her special-ness, she was also aware how fleeting it could be. Getting attention was wonderful, but being able to hold on to it was another matter. She mea-sured life and others by how much they could care for her and notice her. Not surprisingly, she mastered the art of attracting others' attention. As she grew older, she thought her specialness—particularly, her beauty, youth, and energy—was beginning to fade. She felt abandoned by her husband who worked long hours and anticipated that she would also be abandoned by her son who would soon be leaving for college, as her first love had. She was using depression as a coping device to deal with life, to draw others to her as she had seen modeled by her mother. She was probably genetically loaded for depression and had become skilled, like her mother, in using it to rally support for herself. Figure 8.1 summarizes these style features.

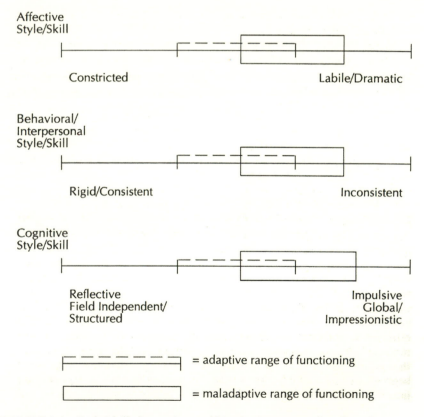

FIGURE 8.1. Style/skill dimensions of histrionic personality disorder.

Pattern Change

Since Kristy had experienced only partial symptomatic relief from several antidepressant trials over the last 5 years, her depressive symptoms were framed as persistent symptoms that were more likely to respond to psychosocial interventions, such as symptom management training and cognitive therapy. Accordingly, individual treatment sessions initially focused on learning the symptom management skill of distraction, which Kristy agreed to practice between sessions. Concurrently, treatment also focused on her dysthymic features, using the short-term cognitive therapy treatment protocol for dysthymia described by Freeman (1992). Kristy was helped to identify her negative thoughts and cognitive distortion and challenge them. The 26 individual sessions, supported by couples therapy, allowed Kristy to gain considerable control over her chronic depression and dissatisfaction. Her scattered, inconsistent behavior style, which had been reinforced by her impressionistic cognitive style, was modulated to some degree through problem-solving training and assertive communication training. In the course of in-session and between-session activities, Kristy learned to take more control of her life by being better organized and more decisive. Empathy training and work on intimacy skills were accomplished in conjoint sessions with her husband (refer to the case example in Chapter 9). Finally, schema change strategies were used to modify her entitlement/self-centeredness and emotional deprivation schemas.

Pattern Maintenance and Termination

During the termination phase, Kristy's dysthymia was brought more under control, and she experienced more satisfaction in life, especially in her marriage. Her relationship with her husband greatly improved, in part because of the couples therapy and in part because her husband was now working out of a home office, which meant that he and Kristy were able to spend more time together. She also reported being less fearful about her future, her marriage, and her son. She began to feel more consistency and balance in her life. While she still enjoyed dressing fashionably and remained free-spirited, she experienced herself as being more connected and valued as a person. A planned termination from individual treatment occurred after 26 sessions. These sessions had been spaced over a period of 18 months. Four months prior to termination, the couples therapy had been terminated. Kristy and her clinician agreed that quarterly follow-up sessions would be scheduled for the following year.

☐ Summary

Effective treatment of histrionic personality disorder requires that patients with this disorder become sufficiently committed to a treatment process that is tailored and focused on modifying their maladaptive histrionic pattern. Because these patients tend to have considerable difficulty engaging in and profiting from traditional psychotherapy, an integrative-combined approach that focuses on characterological, temperament, and skill dimensions is usually essential for effective treatment outcomes. The case example illustrates the common challenges that these patients present and the kind of clinician flexibility and competence as well as treatment resources required. Table 8.2 summarizes the treatment intervention strategies most likely to be effective in treating this disorder.

TABLE 8.2.   Treatment Interventions for Histrionic Personality Disorder

Phase	Issue	Strategy/Tactic
Engagement	Quickly develop therapeutic alliance; believe clinician should be able to understand them intuitively, nonverbally, without intrapsychic exploration	Role induction and socialization; reflection vs. impressionistic reporting
Transference	Rescue fantasy; erotic or eroticized transference	Redirect and refocus; analyze and explain
Countertransference	Messiah/rescue role; aloofness, anxiety; exploitation	Monitor and refrain from acting out
Pattern Search	Triggers: opposite-sex relationships	
Pattern Change	Treatment Goals: feel less, think more; increased interdependence and self-management	
Schema/Character	Entitlement/self- centeredness schema; emotional deprivation schema	Schema change strategy; interpretation strategy
Style/Temperament		
a. Affective Style	Superficial, over-modulated affects	Emotional awareness training; dramatic behavioral experiments; externalization of voices
b. Behavioral/ Relational Style	Inconsistency; over/underassertive; empathy and intimacy deficits	Problem-solving training; intimacy skills; empathy training
c. Cognitive Style	Global/impressionistic impulsivity	Set specific treatment goals; pros and cons analysis; impulse control training
Maintenance/Termination	Fantasies of a continuing relationship; fear of termination	Predictive interpretation; weaning, spaced sessions; encourage other healthy relationships

9

Obsessive-Compulsive Personality Disorder

Obsessive-compulsive personality disorder is characterized by rigidity, stubbornness, and judgmentalness—all factors that can impede personal change. Nevertheless, these individuals can be effectively treated, although the treatment of obsessive-compulsive personalities involves some unique therapeutic challenges. This chapter describes specific engagement, pattern analysis, pattern change, and pattern maintenance and termination strategies for effectively managing and treating this disorder. In addition to individual psychotherapeutic strategies and tactics, group, marital, family, medication, and integrative and combined treatment strategies are detailed. An extensive case example illustrates the treatment process. Before turning to treatment strategies, the DSM-IV description and criteria are briefly presented.

Clinical Conceptualization of Obsessive-Compulsive Personality Disorder

Triggering Event(s):	Authority; unstructured situations, and/or demands of intimate and close relations
Behavioral Appearance:	Workaholic, dependable, stubborn, possessive; procrastinating, indecisive, perfectionistic
Interpersonal Behavior:	Autocratic to peers and subordinates but deferential to superiors; polite and loyal

Cognitive Style:	Constricted—rule-based, unimaginative; assertive (defiance) vs. pleasing (obedience)
Feeling Style:	Grim and cheerless, feeling avoidance
Temperament:	Irritable, difficult, or anxious
Attachment Style:	Preoccupied
Parental Injunction:	"You must do/be better to be worthwhile."
Self View:	"I'm responsible if something goes wrong."; sees self as reliable, competent, righteous
World View:	"Life is unpredictable and expects too much. Therefore, be in control, be right and proper, and don't make mistakes."
Maladaptive Schemas:	Unrelenting standards; punitiveness; emotional inhibition
Optimal DSM-IV-TR Criteria:	Shows perfectionism that interferes with task completion

☐ DSM-IV Description and Criteria

DSM-IV offers the following description and criteria for obsessive-compulsive personality disorder (Table 9.1):

TABLE 9.1. DSM-IV Description and Criteria for Obsessive-Compulsive Personality Disorder

301.4 Obsessive-Compulsive Personality Disorder

A pervasive pattern of preoccupation with orderliness, perfectionism, and mental and interpersonal control, at the expense of flexibility, openness, and efficiency, beginning by early adulthood and present in a variety of contexts, as indicated by four (or more) of the following:

(1) Is preoccupied with details, rules, lists, order, organization, or schedules to the extent that the major point of the activity is lost

(2) shows perfectionism that interferes with task completion (e.g., is unable to complete a project because his or her own overly strict standards are not met)

(3) is excessively devoted to work and productivity to the exclusion of leisure activities and friendships (not accounted for by obvious economic necessity)

(4) is overconscientious, scrupulous, and inflexible about matters or morality, ethics, or values (not accounted for by cultural or religious identification)

(5) is unable to discard worn-out or worthless objects even when they have no sentimental value

(6) is reluctant to delegate tasks or to work with others unless they submit to exactly his or her way of doing things

(7) adopts a miserly spending style toward both self and others; money is viewed as something to be hoarded for future catastrophes

(8) shows rigidity and stubbornness

☐ Engagement Strategies

Early Session Behavior

The characteristic features of circumstantiability, perfectionism, and ambivalence make interviewing obsessive-compulsive individuals difficult and challenging. Their preoccupation with details and their need for control often results in a seemingly endless struggle with regard to facts, issues, and power conflicts. Clinicians who persist in asking open-ended questions will note that while they become frustrated, obsessive-compulsive individuals will become confused. These patients are better able to handle more focused questions, although they have a tendency to interpret them too narrowly. They may bring copies of past treatment records or notebooks that detail their medical histories, diets, exercise patterns, and possibly their dreams. Usually, they expect the clinician to review these documents or topics in detail. Because these details are important to the obsessive-compulsive patient's self-definition, it is important that the clinician acknowledges this offer rather than preemptively dismissing it. Expressing affects are difficult because these individuals believe emotional expression is dangerous or at least suspect. Although they may admit that affects are associated with details, they will discount the value of expressing those affects, much less talking about them. Furthermore, it is difficult for them to overcome their ambivalence because they will not easily accept the clinician's assurance that their problems are solvable or that relinquishing control of their life is tolerable.

Because they insist they are objective and have no feelings, these patients are perturbed at the clinician's expression of empathy and reject it as irrelevant. The clinician's only effective therapeutic leverage with these patients is to get and keep them in touch with their anger and other affects. Initially, they will defend against or deny these affects and use additional obsessionality to neutralize such therapeutic leverage. In sum, forming a therapeutic alliance with these obsessive-compulsive individuals is difficult, and early sessions may consists of aborted attempts, frustrations, and struggles (Othmer & Othmer, 2002).

Facilitating Collaboration

True collaboration is extremely difficult to achieve early in the course of treatment of obsessive-compulsive personality disorder. Rather, pseudo-collaboration tends to occur quickly. *Pseudocollaboration* refers to behaviors that, at first, may appear to be collaborative and cooperative but, in fact, are not. These patients may appear to be eager to be "model" patients and attempt to please the clinician by being "prepared" for sessions. For example, they may come to sessions with lists of items that they are pre-pared to discuss, diaries that detail dreams, and so on, or they may have overachieved on a between-session or homework assignment. However, the veneer of their "collaboration" quickly disappears when the clinician endeavors to find out about their feelings and fears or attempts to focus on the present rather than the past. Typically, the patients will resist requests to share affects and are uncomfortable commenting on the "here and now" of the clinician–patient relationship. Such responses are reflective of their ambivalence, their need to please vs. their need to control, as well as their belief that because life is unpredictable, they must take control or, at least, resist efforts to be controlled. For the obsessive-compulsive individual, rational expression is much more predictable and comfortable than expres-sion of affects, which are much less predictable and comfortable. Whereas facts can bolster their perceived sense of self-worth, feelings threaten to embarrass or even injure them. Similarly, these patients will "structure" sessions with their planned agenda to reduce the unpredictable.

True collaboration will occur only when the obsessive-compulsive patient experiences minimal threat in treatment. Accordingly, the clini-cian should establish a "collaborative contract," based on the patient's goal for treatment. The goal, a method for achieving that goal, and specific role expectations for both clinician and patient should all be determined (Sperry, 2003). For example, the patient's goal might be "to increase my efficiency," and problem-solving could be indicated as the primary treat-ment strategy or method to achieve that goal. A problem-solving treatment strategy is an excellent way of operationalizing the collaborative contract. It consists of stating a goal or analyzing a problem, identifying options, weighing the options, deciding on a course of action, and then imple-menting it. Besides being effective, this treatment strategy is usually quite acceptable to the obsessive patient, since it is rational and is relatively non-threatening. In addition, the clinician needs to structure sessions in such a way that threat is minimized and treatment goals can be achieved. This means focusing on one topic at a time and confronting resistances as they arise. Not surprisingly, the cognitive-behavioral approach is well suited for working with obsessive-compulsive patients.

Transference and Countertransference

Predictable transference and countertransference problems are noted in treating individuals with obsessive-compulsive personality disorder. Perhaps the most common transference involves their tendency to engage in rambling speech, often in a monotone. The defenses of intellectualization and isolation of affect are commonly noted. In the process, they wander from their original point and create an "anesthetizing cloud," which serves both as a smokescreen to mask their feelings and to sidetrack the clinician's attention (Gabbard, 2005). Not surprisingly, the countertransference to this rambling is boredom, daydreaming, and disengagement. Sometimes, these monologues may have high interest for the clinician, and the clinician may be tempted to reinforce or collude with the patient's intellectualization and isolation of affect. The clinician does well to interrupt, interpret, or redirect these rambling accounts by saying, "Let's just stop for a moment. What are you feeling right now?" This can refocus and set the stage for interpreting resistance.

For some obsessive-compulsive patients, clinical and transference interpretations can be quite threatening and are consequently vigorously resisted. A related transference involves patients discounting the clinician's interpretations (Gabbard, 2005). Patients may quickly respond to interpretations saying that these interpretations are completely wrong or that they have thought about or heard about them before and did not agree with them then or now. The clinician's countertransference may range from self-doubt and cautiousness to anger and hostility at the patient's impertinence and unappreciativeness.

☐ Pattern Analysis Strategies

Pattern analysis with obsessive-compulsive individuals involves accurate diagnostic and clinical evaluations of schemas, styles, and triggering stressors, as well as level of functioning and readiness for therapeutic change. Knowledge of the optimal DSM-IV criterion along with the maladaptive pattern of the individual is not only useful in specifying diagnosis but also in planning treatment that is tailored to the obsessive-compulsive patients' unique styles, needs, and circumstances. The optimal criterion specified for obsessive-compulsive personality disorder is showing perfectionism that interferes with task completion (Allnutt & Links, 1996). Both planned treatment goals and interventions should reflect this theme of perfectionism.

Pattern refers to the predictable and consistent style and manner in which a patient thinks, feels, acts, copes, and defends the self. Pattern analysis involves both the triggers and the response—the "what"—as well as an explanatory statement—the "why"—about the pattern of a given obsessive-compulsive patient. Obviously, such a clinical formulation specifies the *particular* schemas and temperamental styles unique to a given individual rather than the more *general* ones that will be noted here.

Triggers

Generally speaking, the "triggers" or "triggering situations" for obsessive-compulsive patients are stressors related to authority, unstructured situations, or close relationships (Othmer & Othmer, 2002). This means that when these individuals are engaging in behaviors, are discussing or even thinking about the demands of authority figures or close relationships, or are in situations where expectations for them are unclear and they become distressed, their disordered or maladaptive pattern is likely to be triggered and characteristic symptomatic affects, behaviors, and cognitions are likely to be experienced or exhibited.   ·

Schemas

The underlying schemas involve a self view of being responsible for not making errors and a view of the world as overly demanding and unpredictable (Sperry & Mosak, 1996). Among the most frequently encountered schemas in obsessive-compulsive patients is the unrelenting/unbalanced schema. Occasionally, the emotional inhibition schema is also observed. The unrelenting/unbalanced schema refers to the core set of beliefs about the relentless striving to meet high-flown expectations of oneself at the expense of happiness, health, and satisfying relationships. The emotional inhibition schema refers to the core set of beliefs that emotions and impulses must be inhibited in order to not lose self-esteem or not harm others (Bricker, Young, & Flanagan, 1993; Young, Klosko, & Weishaar, 2003).

Style/Temperament

There are three styles/temperaments that may need to be addressed in formulating treatment for patients with obsessive-compulsive personality disorder: affective, behavioral–interpersonal, and cognitive. Needless to say, these styles exacerbate and are exacerbated by their schemas. The affective style of obsessive-compulsive individuals is characterized by constriction and isolation of affect. Their cognitive style is ruminative and overly reflective, which predisposes them to preoccupation with details and minutia and to worrying. Behaviorally, their style is rigid and calculating, which, together with their ruminative style, predisposes them to procrastination and indecisiveness. Relationally, they are inhibited and ill at ease. Often, they are also deficient in empathy and other interpersonal skills (Sperry, 2003).

☐ Pattern Change Strategies

At the outset of treatment, it would not be unusual for obsessive-compulsive individuals to have their own personal goal of treatment—to become asymptomatic and more productive while retaining their maladaptive pattern. This contrasts with the therapeutic treatment goal, which is to change the maladaptive pattern. More specifically, the general treatment goal for obsessive-compulsive individuals is to achieve a balance between being perfectionistic and driven and being easygoing and carefree, to become introspective without being preoccupied and ruminative, and to better tolerate the humanness they observe in themselves and others. In other words, the goal is to "think less and feel more," which is the converse of the goal for patients with histrionic personality disorder.

Treatment begins after the maladaptive pattern has been identified and analyzed in terms of schemas, style, and skill deficits. The therapeutic process involves relinquishing that pattern and replacing it with a more adaptive pattern. This pattern change process involves modifying schemas, modulating style dysregulations, and reversing skill deficits. The process of modifying the maladaptive schemas usually follows efforts to modify style and skill-deficit dimensions because schema change early in the course of treatment is often resisted by the patient. Because of this, as noted in the section on facilitating collaboration, treatment should begin by using a problem-solving treatment strategy. This strategy is not only effective in establishing a collaborative relationship but also for making initial changes in pattern. This strategy is greatly appreciated by obsessive patients because it is rational and systematic and is much less threatening and anxiety-producing than dynamic or experiential intervention strategies.

Schema Change

The unrelenting/unbalanced standards and emotional inhibition schemas are supported by such injunctive beliefs as "Nothing I do is really good enough, I must always do better"; "I need to be in total control of my feelings"; "Details are extremely important"; "If I don't perform at the highest possible level, I'm a failure"; and "Mistakes, errors, and defects are absolutely intolerable" (Beck, Freeman, Davis, & Associates, 2004; Young, Klosko, & Weishaar, 2003).

In the schema change process, the clinician and patient work collaboratively to understand the developmental roots of the maladaptive schemas. Then, these schemas are tested through predictive experiments, guided observation, and reenactment of early schema-related incidents. Finally, obsessive-compulsive patients are directed to begin to notice and remember counterschema data about themselves and their social experiences.

Style/Temperament Change

Because obsessive-compulsive individuals are characterized by an affective style of constriction and isolation of affect, emotional awareness training can be an effective intervention. Thought-stopping can be useful in reducing ruminative thinking. Furthermore, because these patients tend to have behavioral and relational styles that are somewhat inhibited and stiff and often have deficits in empathy, interpersonal skills training and empathy training may be indicated. Furthermore, activity-scheduling (Freeman, Pretzer, Fleming, & Simon, 1990; KIolsko & Young, 2004) can be effectively used in reducing procrastination and improving time management.

Medication Strategies

Style or temperament treatment targets for this disorder usually are anxiety or fearfulness, interpersonal sensitivity, and ruminations. There is currently no indication for the use of medication to treat this disorder, unless there is a concurrent Axis I diagnosis. While clinical lore suggests that this personality disorder commonly coexists with obsessive-compulsive disorder, research does not support this belief. Actually, obsessive-compulsive disorder is more likely to occur with dependent and avoidant personality disorders than with obsessive-compulsive personality disorder (Baer & Jenike, 1992). For individuals with ruminations but without impulsive behavior, it is reasonable to begin an SSRI (selective serotonin reuptake inhibitor) trial, particularly, Effexor. If there is partial response, a long-acting benzodiazepine or clonazepam can be added or even used as the sole medication following a multiple SSRI trial. If these fail, the use of beta blockers or atypical antipsychotics can be considered (Reich, 2005).

Group Treatment Strategies

A major deficit of obsessive-compulsive personality disorder is the inability to share tenderly and spontaneously with others. Thus, group treatment can be particularly useful with obsessive-compulsive patients. Nevertheless, because these patients tend to be competitive and controlling, certain complications can arise, which the clinicians would do well to keep in mind. For instance, these patients will dominate a group with their rambling and excessive speech patterns, if not redirected. Because they may initially experience the affective atmosphere in a group to be overwhelming, they may become more socially isolated or intellectually detached. Thus, the clinician does well to intervene to avoid unnecessary power struggles. When this is accomplished, these patients are usually able to vicariously model the emotional expressiveness of others in the group.

Group therapy offers a number of advantages over individual therapy for the obsessive-compulsive patients. First, this personality pattern tends to make the individual therapy process tedious, difficult, and unrewarding, particularly early in treatment when clinicians commonly err with premature interpretations or behavioral prescriptions. Second, the group process tends to diffuse the intensity of the obsessive-compulsive patient's impact, particularly in a heterogeneous group. Third, group treatment also tends to neutralize transferences and countertransferences because patients more easily accept feedback from peers than from a clinician. Finally, group therapy activates these patients into "experiencing" their problems rather than just talking about them.

There are, however, some contraindications for outpatient group therapy for obsessive-compulsive patients: severe depression or high suicidality; impulse dyscontrol; strong paranoid propensities; acute crisis; difficulty in establishing trust; fear of relinquishing obsessive-compulsive defenses; the need to establish superiority; and the use of "pseudo-insight" to avoid dealing with both hostile and tender feelings (Wells, Glickhauf-Hughes, & Buzzel, 1990). Nevertheless, such patients or other lower-functioning obsessive-compulsive patients may still be candidates for skill-oriented group treatment in partial hospital or day programs.

Wells et al. (1990) described a group treatment approach well suited for obsessive-compulsive patients. This approach combines both interpersonal and psychodynamic interventions. The treatment process involves the following goals: modifying cognitive style, resolving control issues, expanding decision-making and action-taking capacities, modifying harsh superego, increasing comfort with emotional expression, and modifying interpersonal style.

Marital and Family Therapy Strategies

Harbir (1981) reported that obsessive-compulsive individuals usually agree to family treatment because close family members have become angry with their rigidity, procrastination, constricted affect, perfectionism, and pessimistic outlook. Likewise, the obsessive-compulsive individual may agree to couples therapy only after being threatened with divorce by their partner. Often, a threat of separation or divorce may be the only motivation to start treatment. The anxiety of the complaining partner may be the only leverage for treatment, and the clinician may need to work with that partner to deal more effectively with the other partner's obsessive-compulsive personality pattern. Clinical experience suggests that obsessive-compulsive individuals tend to marry histrionic individuals (Sperry & Maniacci, 1998).

Salzman (1989) noted that obsessive-compulsive patients who are highly anxious may be unable to participate in marital or family therapy until their anxiety has been sufficiently quelled in individual psychotherapy or combined psychotherapy and pharmacological treatment. Even when excessive anxiety is not particularly bothersome, these patients can be tyrants in family sessions and may immobilize other family members to such an extent that treatment is jeopardized. When this occurs, structural and strategic interventions directed at redistributing power may be particularly advantageous in such situations (Sperry, 2003).

Combined and Integrated Treatment Strategies

Salzman (1989) contended that a combined and integrated approach is essential in the treatment of obsessive-compulsive disorder, particularly in moderately severe cases. He insisted that the various treatment modalities and methods must be viewed as mutually inclusive rather than mutually exclusive.

Combined treatments tend to be more effective when based on a protocol. Because high levels of anxiety or depression will limit the patients' participation in psychotherapy, an appropriate trial of medication may be necessary at the onset of treatment. When rituals or obsessions are prominent, specific behavior interventions are probably indicated. The dynamics of perfectionism, indecisiveness, and isolation of affect are best addressed with specific psychotherapeutic interventions. Decisions about the use of the individual, group, marital, or module format, or a combination of modalities should be based on the severity of the disorder, particular treatment targets, and specific contraindications to treatments.

In short, a fuller understanding and appreciation of the obsessive-compulsive personality usually requires an integration of several modalities because "the resolution of the disabling disorder demands cognitive clarity plus behavioral and physiologic alterations. Each modality alone deals with only a piece of the puzzle. A therapist who can combine all these approaches will be the most effective" (Salzman, 1989, p. 2782).

☐ Pattern Maintenance and Termination Strategies

Termination Issues

Just as establishing a collaborative relationship with obsessive-compulsive patients can be extremely difficult, so also is terminating treatment. Assuming they have achieved some level of balance between being perfectionistic and driven and being easygoing and carefree, terminating treatment can be considered. Unfortunately, ambivalence, which is a core feature of the obsessive-compulsive pattern, is commonly observed during the termination process. Initially, these patients may press to leave treatment and function on their own. Soon thereafter, they begin expressing great reluctance to relinquish the security of therapy for the exigencies of the real world until there is absolute certainty that insurmountable problems will not occur. Consequently, they will insist on remaining in treatment. Salzman (1980) contended that these patients cannot be relied on to initiate discussion on or press for termination. The clinician task is to raise the issue of readiness for termination and then coax and prod these patients into the real world. Nevertheless, termination must be a gradual and empirical process. Unlike the fixed planned termination date that might be established in the case of patients with dependent personality disorder, some measure of flexibility is more therapeutic with the obsessive-compulsive patients. Insistence on setting strict deadlines and appointment scheduling would be an enactment of the rigidity and perfectionism that the clinicians are trying to modify in these patients.

Reducing the length of a session or spacing out sessions over a reasonable period of time allow these patients to more safely reenter the real world. This reduction can begin when patients become comfortable enough for the patients to accept some uncertainty and reverses in their lives without experiencing intolerable symptoms. For many obsessive-compulsive patients, the termination process can be expected to engender anxiety and somatic symptoms. They must come to understand and accept that such symptoms will occasionally occur throughout life and that treatment does not guarantee symptom-free living.

Relapse Prevention Strategies

After treatment is formally terminated, the option for occasional appointments or even brief contacts during times of crisis should be discussed. Some obsessive-compulsive patients will appreciate the offer of one or more planned follow-up visits in the subsequent 12 months. The hope, however, is that these patients will be able to function as their own clinicians. To this end, it is helpful for clinicians and patients to collaboratively develop a plan of self-therapy and relapse prevention following termination. It is recommended that these patients set aside an hour a week to engage in activities that continue the progress made during formal treatment. They might work on selected exercises. They might look ahead at the coming week and predict which situations could be troublesome. The goal of such efforts is to maintain treatment gains, particularly the patients' newly acquired pattern. They should expect to cope much more effectively than prior to treatment because they have developed sufficient personal and relational skills to be introspective, without being preoccupied and ruminative, and to be more tolerant of the humanness they observe in themselves and others. And when they find themselves slipping or regressing, they will know how to refocus on their goals and redirect themselves.

The relapse plan will help them analyze specific external situations (such as persons, times, and places) and internal states (such as specific obsessive-compulsive beliefs and fears) and other vulnerabilities that increase the likelihood of their responding with obsessive-compulsive behavior in the face of predictable triggers. Once predicted, a contingency plan to deal with these stressors can be developed. Clinicians may find it useful to have patients answer these questions: What can I do if I find myself ruminating? What should I do if I start placing unreasonable demands or expectations on others to be more perfect? What should I do if I start believing in my old obsessive-compulsive beliefs more than in my new beliefs? What should I do if I relapse? Finally, because relational demands, unstructured situations, and authority issues can trigger the obsessive-compulsive pattern, the relapse plan should also include provisions for increasing and maintaining playfulness and spontaneity.

☐ Case Example

Warren G., a 41-year-old accountant, presented with his wife, Kristy G., for couples therapy. They had been married for 19 years and had an 18-year-old son who would soon be finishing high school and move away to attend college. Warren complained of worsening insomnia and decreased energy. In addition, his acrophobia had also worsened. He now had become so anxious crossing bridges and taking escalators, especially glass elevators, that he had to take a longer route to get to his office building and would walk up seven flights of stairs to reach his office. He had been prescribed Ativan by his family physician but rarely used the medication fearing he would become addicted.

Warren reported significant strains in the marriage. He was concerned about his wife's safety, having observed that she seemed more depressed and hopeless. He described Kristy as increasingly moody, unpredictable, and given to outbursts, which frustrated and frightened him. She would pursue him relentlessly with demands, and all he could do was clam up and retreat. He hesitatingly admitted that it was a relief to stay late at his office so as to avoid facing her fury. Lately, he feared he might lose his mind if this continued. His only display of emotion during the entire interview occurred at that point in his narration: He was briefly silent as tears welled in his eyes, but then he quickly regained composure.

Engagement Process—Warren

As part of the evaluation phase of couples therapy, Warren was scheduled for an individual evaluation session. During this session, he seemed more at ease discussing concerns about his marriage than he had been in the conjoint session. Nevertheless, he was somewhat reluctant in disclosing personal information. He was a methodical historian of the various details of his life. He spoke in a slow, deliberate monotone with little change in affect or mood. The clinician recommended individual therapy in addition to couples therapy to help Warren understand the marriage relationship and the effect it was having on him. Initially, he balked at the suggestion of individual sessions, stating that he was more concerned about his wife's well-being and that she was his first priority. Recognizing that Warren was likely resisting individual treatment in the belief that he had to be dutiful and unselfish, the clinician made the following observations to Warren. He stated that it was commendable to put his wife's concerns first but Warren also had worsening symptoms that were greatly worrisome to his wife. He gently reminded Warren that during their conjoint session, Kristy had hoped that he would be receptive to individual sessions. Furthermore, the clinician emphasized that focusing on these matters from both individual and couples perspectives would be the most "efficient" approach. Warren liked that concept and agreed to the plan.

Engagement Process—Couple

It seemed clear that both partners wanted and needed help. However, because Kristy had been in long-term psychiatric treatment and so was perceived as a "patient," the clinician thought it necessary and useful to socialize Kristy and Warren to a systems perspective for the conjoint treatment. The clinician presented the concept that neither of them was "sick" and that each was simply expressing, in his or her characteristic style, what neither had "permission" or the "ability" to say openly. Both responded positively to this perspective. Warren was fascinated by the prospect that anything could occur beyond one's control. He knew it happened, he had seen it at work many times, but he never thought that any such process could be going on inside himself without his knowing. Kristy was amused by his comment and pointed out that if he "knew" he was doing such things, he would not be able to do them. She beamed at the clinician, as if waiting for a reward or praise. The clinician also presented to them that neither was "crazy" but, rather, both were attempting to communicate with the other. Not only did the receiving partner not understand the communication, but the other partner was also not completely aware of the message he or she was sending. Thus, the first goal of treatment was for them both to accept responsibility for sending any message, that is, acknowledge that a message was being sent, and to then clarify the message. Only then, could each decide how to respond positively to the message being sent.

Pattern Analysis—Warren

Warren described his childhood as "reasonably good" but went on to describe his father as a violent alcoholic with unpredictable mood swings and his mother as a long-suffering woman who leaned on Warren as her sole support. Warren had a younger sister who had cerebral palsy, and he recalled his father's frequent threats to institutionalize her. He took it on as his mission to keep her out of an institution and so became her surrogate parent, teacher, and friend. He worked outside the home from the age of 15.

His first job had been on a loading dock amid much squalor. These experiences had led him to vow to make a better life for himself and to never lose his temper or drink like his father. He eventually completed a GED, went on to college, studied for and passed his CPA exam, and found employment with a small accounting firm. Although he agreed that he worked too many hours, he liked his job. There was little room for upward mobility there, but he was proud that his boss entrusted him with complicated and sensitive projects that no one else could do as well as Warren could.

His earliest memory was about an incident when he was 5 years old; he was on the fire escape of the family apartment, and as he was admiring the view from there, he heard a scream. His mother rushed out and pulled him back into the apartment, yelling that it was too dangerous to be out on the fire escape. He felt confused but vowed to be more careful and never to upset her again.

Needless to say, Warren grew up believing that he had to be careful and conscientious or bad things would happen. Gradually, the line between conscientiousness and control began to blur; unless he was in total control of his life, as well as others', he felt an uneasy, impending doom. His solution was to work harder, to control more, and to be careful. The only dispensation he allowed himself from this rigid agenda was illness. For reasons of being afraid of heights and unable to sleep, he could ask for a break and take some time for himself without having to admit that he was shirking responsibility.

An evaluation of Warren's developmental history and clinical observation of interactions with Kristy indicated an obsessive-compulsive pattern. His pattern was notable for both the unrelenting/unbalanced schema and the emotional inhibition schema. His style dimensions, such as constricted affect, rigidity, empathic and interpersonal deficits, and analytic, ruminative cognitive style, also suggested an obsessive-compulsive pattern.

Warren met the criteria for minor depressive disorder as well as obsessive-compulsive personality disorder. His current level of functioning was *fair* to *good* (GAF score of 61) and his best functioning in the past year had been *good* to *very good* (GAF score of 73). Because of his willingness and efforts to make personal and relational changes, his motivation and readiness for treatment were rated as high. Figure 9.1 summarizes these style features.

Pattern Analysis—Couple

The interlocking dynamics gradually became clear to both Warren and Kristy. The clinician reframed Kristy's depression as her way of asking to be cared for and her "moodiness" as her attempt to keep the relationship together. She valued love, marriage, and family, and she wanted them both

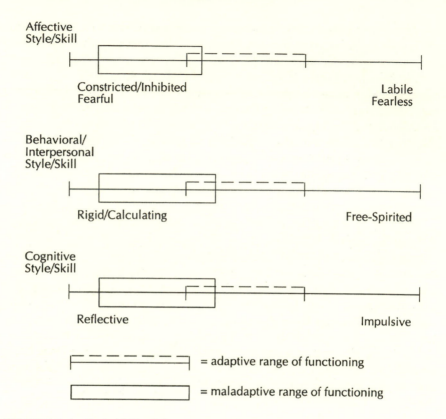

FIGURE 9.1. Style/skill of dimensions of obsessive compulsive personality disorder.

to be happy. She was trying to keep them together and to look out for her husband and his health. Warren was trying to keep his family together, too. The clinician reframed his long work hours as his way of showing care and concern. The clinician told them that their symptoms were, in effect, serving the same purpose, just in different ways. The challenge for both of them was to communicate their desires in more direct, constructive ways.

Pattern Change—Couple

Pattern change involved rebalancing their relationship pattern. This proved exceedingly challenging because power was rather evenly distributed: Warren was aloof, didactic, and in charge, until Kristy became upset and "hysterical," at which point she would take over power in the relationship. Then, Warren would bring calm to the situation by arranging things the way she wanted. In the process, he would organize and structure the necessary changes and, thus, assume power again. She would allow this until she felt he cared more about his work than her, and then she would grow impatient, become upset, and the cyclic pattern would repeat itself.

The clinician pointed out this cyclic pattern to Warren and Kristy. Warren immediately grasped it and its ramifications, but Kristy found it harder to comprehend. The clinician's verbal explanation was well suited to Warren's analytic style but did not match Kristy's more global-impressionistic style. Furthermore, their maladaptive cyclic pattern was being enacted in the session. Warren shifted into his parental mode and began lecturing her, while Kristy shifted into her childish mode and tried to follow his explanation but could not. At that point, the clinician graphically illustrated their interaction pattern, and Kristy was then able to readily grasp it.

Boundaries and intimacy were not as easily addressed by the couple. A triangle existed, with their son vacillating between being a husband-surrogate for his mother when Warren was away from home and his acting like a friend to his father when Warren was home. His presence both fueled the maladaptive cyclic pattern and perpetuated the very problems that might be resolved without his presence. The next several weeks of conjoint treatment focused on these issues. While there might be value in switching to a family therapy mode, there were inherent dangers as well. Introducing the son into the conjoint sessions would further perpetuate the issue being considered: intrusion on the couple's relationship. Instead, efforts were undertaken to strengthen the couple's bond without including the son in the session. Warren and Kristy were started on interpersonal skills training. One component of the training was for the couple to go out on a date after each session. Relating intimately had been problematic for Warren because of deficits in empathic responding. Accordingly, three conjoint sessions focused on empathy training. In addition, the clinician suggested to Warren that his son needed to "have space to find himself," while Warren needed to expand his own social network. To Kristy, it was suggested that by encouraging her son to "separate," she would be strengthening her marriage as well as her son's future. Both Warren and Kristy agreed to a "weaning" process that was aided by the son's moving out of the city to attend college.

Warren's controlling behavior and Kristy's emotionality were mutually complementary. She was encouraged to "teach" him to be more passionate, and he was urged to be her consultant on matters of organization. They grasped this way of working, and though they still experienced some conflict, they were able to become more affectionate toward each other.

Pattern Change—Warren

A brief course of cognitive behavior therapy for Warren's phobic issues— with his wife as coach—worked very well. Within a short time, he found himself crossing bridges and riding escalators and elevators with relatively little or no anxiety. Similarly, a psychoeducational approach to insomnia was introduced. By modifying his evening schedule and attending to other aspects of sleep hygiene, his chronic insomnia gradually gave way to restful sleep within 3 weeks. Efforts to modulate his constricted affect and to reverse his interpersonal and empathic deficits were addressed in conjoint sessions. Thought-stopping training was used in individual sessions and in prescribed homework to modulate and better control his ruminations. Finally, schema change strategies were used to modify his unrelenting/unbalanced schema and the emotional inhibition schema.

Pattern Maintenance and Termination—Couple and Warren

As Kristy's dysthymia became more under control, she experienced more satisfaction in her relationship with Warren. He was encouraged to go into business for himself, and after some hesitancy, he did. He began to work out of his home, and within 6 months, his accounting practice was thriving. He gained greater control over his schedule, worked less hours and more efficiently, and found more pleasure at home. These dynamics were worked on in individual and couple therapies. After 30 conjoint sessions over a period of 14 months, the couple progressed to the point of conjoint quarterly follow-up sessions. Kristy also had individual quarterly follow-up sessions. Warren scheduled occasional individual follow-up sessions to reflect on the level of balance in his life. Each of them reported considerably more satisfaction with their marriage and minimal conflict. Warren learned to be less rigid and controlling, and Kristy, while still somewhat given to dramatics, felt more connected and valued.

☐ Summary

Effective treatment of obsessive-compulsive personality disorder requires that the patients become sufficiently committed to a treatment process that is tailored and focused on modifying their maladaptive obsessive-compulsive pattern. Because these patients tend to have considerable difficulty engaging in and profiting from traditional psychotherapy, an integrative-combined approach that focuses on characterological, temperament, and skill dimensions is usually essential for effective treatment outcomes. The case example illustrated the common challenges that these patients present and the kind of clinician flexibility and competence as well as treatment resources required. It also demonstrated the process

TABLE 9.2. Treatment Interventions for Obsessive-Compulsive Personality Disorder

Phase	Issue	Strategy/Tactics
Engagement	Appearing eager to complete assignments	Establish collaborative contract based on patient's goal, and confront resistances; Structure sessions with a problem-solving focus
Transference	Obsessive rambling; discounting clinician	Interrupt; Interpret; redirect
Countertransference	Disengagement; isolated affect; anger; collusion with patient's defenses	Self-monitor
Pattern Analysis	Triggers: Authority; unstructured situations; close relationships	
Pattern Change	Treatment Goal: "Think less, feel more"; less perfectionistic; more spontaneous and playful	
Schema/Character	Unrelenting/unbalanced standards schema; emotional inhibition schema	Schema change strategy; confrontation; interpretation
Style/Temperament		
a. Affective Style	Constricted/isolated affect	Emotional awareness training
b. Behavioral/ Relational Style	Procrastination; empathic deficits; rigidity; interpersonal deficits.	Activity scheduling; empathy training; interpersonal skills training
c. Cognitive Style	Ruminative; reflective	Thought-stopping training
Maintenance/ Termination	Ambivalence about termination	Wean, and space out sessions

of combining individual therapy with couples therapy for the treatment of a couple who presented with two different personality disorders. Table 9.2 summarizes the treatment intervention strategies most likely to be effective in treating this disorder.

REFERENCES

Adler, A. (1956). *The individual psychology of Alfred Adler.* H. Ansbacher & R. Ansbacher (Eds.). New York: Harper & Row.

Alden, L. (1989). Short-term structured treatment for avoidant personality disorder. *Journal of Consulting and Clinical Psychology, 57,* 756–764.

Alden, L. (1992). Cognitive–interpersonal treatment of avoidant personality disorder. In P. Keller & S. Heyman (Eds.), *Innovations in clinical practice: A sourcebook* (Vol. 2, pp. 5–2). Sarasota, FL: Professional Resources Exchange.

Alden, L. (2002). Avoidant personality disorder: Current status and future directions. *Journal of Personality Disorders, 16,* 1: 1–29.

Allen, D. (1977). Basic treatment issues. In M. Horowitz (Ed.), *Hysterical personality* (pp. 283–328). New York: Jason Aaronson.

Allnutt, S., & Links, P. S. (1996). Diagnosing specific personality disorders and the optimal criteria. In P. S. Links (Ed.), *Clinical assessment and management of the severe personality disorders* (pp. 21–47). Washington, DC: American Psychiatric Press.

Alonso, A. (1997). The shattered mirror: Treatment of a group of narcissistic patients. *Group, 16,* 210–219.

Altamura, A., Piolo, R., Vitto, M., & Mannu, P. (1999). Venlafaxine in social phobia: A study in selective serotonin reuptake inhibitor non-responders. *International Clinical Psychopharmacology, 14,* 239–245.

American Psychological Association. (1994). *Diagnostic and statistical manual of mental disorders* (4th ed.). Washington, DC: Author.

American Psychological Association. (2000). *Diagnostic and statistical manual of mental disorders, text revision (DSM-IV-TR)* (4th ed.). Washington, DC: Author.

Barber, J. Morse, J., Kakauer, I., et al. (2002). Change in obsessive-compulsive and avoidant personality disorder following time-limited supportive-expressive therapy. *Psychotherapy, 34,* 133–143.

Barlow, D., & Waddell, M. (1985). Agoraphobia. In D. Barlow (Ed.), *Clinical handbook of psychological disorders: A step-by-step treatment manual* (pp. 1–68). New York: Guilford.

Bateman, A., & Fonagy, P. (1999). Effectiveness of partial hospitalization in the treatment of borderline personality disorder: A randomized controlled trial. *American Journal of Psychiatry, 156,* 1563–1569.

Bateman, A., & Fonagy, P. (2001). Treatment of borderline personality disorder with psychoanalytically oriented partial hospitalization: An 18-month follow-up. *American Journal of Psychiatry, 158,* 36–42.

Beck, A. (1964). Thinking and depression: II: Theory and therapy. *Archives of General Psychiatry, 10,* 561–571.

Beck, A. (1976). *Cognitive therapy and the emotional disorders.* New York: International Universities Press.

Beck, A., Freeman, A., & Associates (1990). *Cognitive therapy of personality disorders.* New York: Guilford.

Beck, A., Freeman, A., Davis, D., & Associates. (2004). *Cognitive therapy of personality disorders* (2nd ed.). New York: Guilford.

Beck, J. (1997). Personality disorders: Cognitive approaches. In. L. Dickstein, M. Riba, & J. Oldham (Eds.). *American Psychiatric Press review of psychiatry* (Vol. 16). Washington, DC: American Psychiatric Press.

Beitman, B. (1991). Medication during psychotherapy: Case studies of the reciprocal relationship between psychotherapy process and medication use. In B. Beitman & G. Klerman (Eds.), *Integrating pharmacotherapy and psychotherapy* (pp. 21–44). Washington, DC: American Psychiatric Press.

Beitman, B., Blinder, B., Thase, M., Riba, M., & Safer, D. (2003). *Integrating Psychotherapy and Pharmacotherapy: Dissolving the Mind-Brain Barrier.* New York: Norton.

Bender, D., Donan, R., Skodol, A., Sanislow, C., et al. (2001). Treatment utilization by patients with personality disorders. *American Journal of Psychiatry, 158* (2), 295–302.

Benjamin, L. (1993). *Interpersonal diagnosis and treatment of personality disorders.* New York: Guilford.

Benjamin, L. (2003). *Interpersonal reconstructive therapy.* New York: Guilford.

Bernstein, D. (2002). Cognitive therapy of personality disorders in patients with histories of emotional abuse or neglect. *Psychiatric Annals, 32* (10), 618–628.

Bernstein, D., Stein, J., & Handelsman, L. (1998). Predicting personality pathology among adult patients with substance disorders: Effects of childhood maltreatment. *Addictive Behavior, 23,* 855–868.

Binder, J. (2004). *Key competencies in brief dynamic psychotherapy: Clinical practice beyond the manual.* New York: Guilford.

Bishop, S. (2002). What do we really know about mindfulenss-based stress reduction? *Psychosomatic Medicine, 64,* 71–84.

Bornstein, R. (1993). *The dependent personality.* New York: Guilford.

Bornstein, R. (1994). Dependency in psychotherapy: Effective therapeutic work with dependent patients. In L. Vandecreek, S. Knapp, & T. Jackson (Eds.), *Innovations in clinical practice: A sourcebook* (Vol. 13, pp. 139–150). Sarasota, FL: Professional Resource Press.

Bornstein, R. (1995). Sex differences in dependent personality disorder prevalence rates. *Clinical Psychology: Science and Practice, 3* (1), 1–12.

Bornstein, R. (1997). Dependent personality disorder in the DSM-IV and beyond. *Clinical Psychology: Science and Practice, 4* (2), 175–187.

Brennan, K., & Shaver, P. (1998). Attachment styles and personality disorders: Their connection to each other and to parental divorce, parental death, and perceptions of parental caregiving. *Journal of Personality, 66,* 835–878.

Bricker, D., Young, J., & Flanagan, C. (1993). Schema–focused cognitive therapy: A comprehensive framework for characterological problems. In K. Kuehlwein & H. Rosen (Eds.), *Cognitive therapies in action. Evolving innovative practice* (pp. 88–125). San Francisco, CA: Jossey-Bass.

Buie, D., & Adler, G. (1983). The definitive treatment of the borderline personality. *International Journal of Psychoanalytic Psychotherapy, 9,* 51–87.

Cadenhead, K., Light, G., Geyer, M., et al. (2002). Neurobiological measures of schizotypal personality disorder. *American Journal of Psychiatry, 159* (5), 869–871.

Clarkin, J., Foelsch, P., Levy, K., et al. (2001). The development of a psychodynamic treatment for patients with borderline personality disorder: A preliminary study of behavior change. *Journal of Personality Disorders, 15* (6), 487–495.

Clarkin, J., & Lenzenweger, M. (Eds.). (1996). *Major theories of personality disorders.* New York: Guilford.

Cloninger, C. (Ed.). (1999). *Personality and psychopathology.* Washington, DC: American Psychiatric Press.

Cloninger, C. (2004). *Feeling good: The science of well-being.* New York: Oxford.

Cloninger C.R. (2000). A practical way to diagnosis of personality disorders: A proposal. *Journal of Personality Disorders, 14,* 99–108.

Cloninger, R. (1987). A systematic method for clinical description and classification of personality variants. *Archives of General Psychiatry, 44*, 573–588.

Cloninger, R., Svrakic, D., & Prybeck, T. (1993). A psychobiological model of temperament and character. *Archives of General Psychiatry, 50*, 975–990.

Coccaro, E. (1993). Psychopharmacologic studies in patients with personality disorders: Review and perspectives. *Journal of Personality Disorders, 7* (Supplement), 181–192.

Coccaro, E., & Kavoussi, R. (1991). Biological and pharmacological aspects of borderline personality disorder. *Hospital and Community Psychiatry, 42,* 1029–1033.

Costello, C. (Ed.). (1996). *Personality characteristics of the personality disordered.* New York: Wiley.

Crits-Christoph, P., & Barber, J. (2002). Psychological treatment for personality disorders. In P. Nathan & J. Gorman (Eds.). *A guide to treatments that work* (2nd ed., pp. 611–624). New York: Oxford Press.

Deltito, J., & Stam, M. (1989). Psychopharmacological treatment of avoidant personality disorder. *Comprehensive Psychiatry, 30*, 498–504.

Derogatis, L. (1983). SCL-90: Administration, scoring and procedures manual for the Revised Edition, Baltimore, MD: Clinical Psychometric Research.

Dolan, M., & Park, I. (2002). The neuropsychology of antisocial personality disorder. *Psychological Medicine, 32* (3), 417–427.

Driscoll, K., Cukrowicz, K., Reardon, M., & Joiner, T. (2004). *Simple treatment for complex problems: A flexible cognitive behavioral analysis approach to psychotherapy.* Mahweh, NJ: Lawrence Erlbaum Associates.

Eagle, M. (1986). The psychoanalytic and the cognitive unconscious. In R. Stern (Ed.), *Theories of the unconscious* (pp. 155–190). Hillsdale, NJ: Analytic Press.

Eckstein, D., Baruth, L., & Mahrer, D. (1992). *An introduction to life-style assessment* (3rd ed.). Dubuque, IA: Kendall-Hunt.

Ellis, A. (1979). *Reason and emotion in psychotherapy.* New York: Citadel.

Erdman, P., & Caffery, T. (Eds.). (2003). *Attachment and family systems: Conceptual, empirical and therapeutic relatedness.* New York: Brunner/Routledge.

Everett, S., Halperin, S., Volgy, S., & Wissler, A. (1989). *Treating the borderline family: A systematic approach.* Boston: Allyn & Bacon.

Fawcett, J. (2002). Schemas or traits and states: Top down or bottom up? *Psychiatric Annals, 32* (10), 567.

Fernando, J. (1998). The etiology of the narcissistic personality disorder. *Psychoanalytic Study of the Child, 53*, 141–158.

First, M. (2002). A research agenda for DSM-V: Summary of the white papers. *Psychiatric Research Report, 18* (2), 10–13.

Fossatti, A., Madeddu, F., & Maffei, C. (1999). Borderline personality disorder and childhood sexual abuse: A meta-analytic study. *Journal of Personality Disorders, 13*, 2268–2280.

Francis, A., Clarkin, J., & Perry, S. (1984). *Differential therapeutics in psychiatry: The art and science of treatment selection.* New York: Brunner/Mazel.

Freeman, A. (1992a). Developing treatment conceptualizations in cognitive therapy. In A. Freeman & F. Datillo (Eds.). *Comprehensive casebook of cognitive therapy* (pp. 13–26). New York: Plenum.

Freeman, A. (1992b). Dysthymia. In A. Freeman & F. Datal (Eds.), *Comprehensive casebook of cognitive therapy* (pp. 129–138). New York: Plenum.

Freeman, A., & Davison, M. (1997). Short-term therapy for the long-term patient. In L. Vandecreek, S. Knapp, & T. Jackson (Eds.), *Innovations in clinical practice: A sourcebook* (Vol. 15, pp. 5–24). Sarasota, FL: Professional Resource Press.

Freeman, A., & Jackson, J. (1996). Single session treatment of a borderline personality disorder. *Cognitive and Behavioral Practice, 3*, 183–208.

Gabbard, G. (2000). *Psychodynamic psychiatry in clinical practice* (3rd ed.). Washington, DC: American Psychiatric Press.

Gabbard, G. (2005). *Psychodynamic psychiatry in clinical practice* (4th ed.). Washington, DC: American Psychiatric Press.

Glantz, K., & Goisman, R. (1990). Relaxation and merging in the treatment of the personality disorders. *American Journal of Psychotherapy, 44,* 405–413.

Glick, I., Clarkin, J., & Goldsmith, S. (1993). Combining medication with family psychotherapy. In J. Oldham, M. Riba, & A. Tasman, (Eds.), *American psychiatric press review of psychiatry* (Vol. 12, pp. 585–610). Washington, DC: American Psychiatric Press.

Graham, J. (2000). *MMPI-2: Assessing personality and psychopathology.* New York: Oxford University Press.

Graybar, S., & Boutilier, L. (2002). Nontraumatic pathways to borderline personality disorder. *Psychotherapy: Theory/Research/Practice/Training, 39* (2), 152–162.

Grossman, P., Niemann, L., Schmidt, S., & Walach, H. (2004). Mindfulness-based stress reduction and health benefits: A meta-analysis. *Journal of Psychosomatic Research, 57,* 35–43.

Gunderson, J. (1989). Borderline personality disorder. In T. Karasu (Ed.), *Treatments of psychiatric disorders* (pp. 2749–2758). Washington, DC: American Psychiatric Press.

Gunderson, J., & Chu, J. (1993). Treatment implications of past trauma in borderline personality disorder. *Harvard Review of Psychiatry, 1,* 75–81.

Harbir, H. (1981). Family therapy with personality disorders. In J. Lion, (Ed.), *Personality disorders: Diagnosis and management* (2nd ed.). Baltimore: Williams & Wilkins.

Hayes, S. (2004). Acceptance and commitment therapy and the new behavior therapies: Mindfulness, acceptance, and relationship. In S. Hayes, V. Follette, & M. Linehan, (Eds). *Mindfulness and acceptance: Expanding the cognitive-behavioral tradition* (pp. 1–29). New York: Guilford.

Hayes, S., Follette, V., & Linehan, M. (Eds). (2004). *Mindfulness and acceptance: Expanding the cognitive-behavioral tradition.* New York: Guilford.

Holmes, S., Slaughter, J., & Kashani, J. (2001). Risk factors in childhood lead to the development of conduct disorder and antisocial personality disorder. *Child Psychiatry and Human Development, 31* (3), 183–193.

Horowitz, L. (1987). Indications for group psychotherapy with borderline and narcissistic patients. *Bulletin of the Menninger Clinic, 51,* 248–318.

Horowitz, M. (1988). *Introduction to psychodynamics: A new synthesis.* New York: Basic Books.

Horowitz, M. (1995). Histrionic personality disorder. In G. Gabbard (Ed.), *Treatment of psychiatric disorders* (2nd ed., pp. 2311–2326). Washington, DC: American Psychiatric Press.

Imbesi, E. (2000). On the etiology of narcissistic personality disorder. *Issues in Psychoanlytic Psychology, 22* (2), 43–58.

Inderbitzin, L., & James, M. (1994). Psychoanalytic psychology. In A. Stoudemire (Ed.), *Human behavior: An introduction for medical students* (2nd ed., pp. 107–142). Philadelphia, PA: Lippincott.

Jenike, M. (1991). Obsessive compulsive disorder. In B. Beitman & G. Klerman (Eds.), *Integrating pharmacotherapy and psychotherapy* (pp. 183–210). Washington, DC: American Psychiatric Press.

Jones, S. (1987). Family therapy with borderline and narcissistic patients. *Bulletin of the Menninger Clinic, 51,* 285–295.

Kabat-Zinn J. (1994.). *Wherever you go, there you are: mindfulness meditation in everyday life.* New York: Hyperion.

Kalojera, I., Jacobson, G., Hoffamn, G., et al. (1999). The narcissistic couple. In J. Carlson & L. Sperry (Eds.), *The disordered couple* (pp. 207–238.). New York: Brunner/Mazel.

Kavoussi, R., Liu, J., & Chaucer, E. (1994). An open trial of sertraline in personality disordered patients with impulsive aggression. *Journal of Clinical Psychiatry, 55,* 137–141.

Keller, M., McCullough, J., Klein, D., Arnow, B., et al. (2000). A comparison of nefazodone, the cognitive behavioral analysis system or psychotherapy, and their combination for the treatment of chronic depression. *The New England Journal of Medicine, 342,* 1462–1470.

Kennedy, J. (1992). *Fundamentals of Psychiatric Treatment Planning.* Washington, DC: American Psychiatric Press.

Kernberg, O. (1984). *Severe personality disorders: Psychotherapeutic strategies.* New Haven, CT: Yale University Press.

Klein, R. (1989). Diagnosis and treatment of the lower-level borderline patient. In J. Masterson & R. Klein (Eds.), *Psychotherapy of disorders of the self* (pp. 69–122). New York: Brunner/Mazel.

Klosko, J., & Young, J. (2004). Cognitive therapy of borderline personality disorder. In R. Leahy (Ed.), *Contemporary cognitive therapy: Theory, research and practice* (pp. 269–298). New York: Guilford.

Koenigsberg, H. (1991). Borderline personality disorder. In B. Beitman & G. Klerman (Eds.), *Integrating pharmacotherapy and psychotherapy* (pp. 271–290). Washington, DC: American Psychiatric Press.

Koenigsberg, H. (1993). Combining psychotherapy and pharmacotherapy in the treatment of borderline patients. In J. Oldham, M. Riba, & A. Tassman (Eds.), *American psychiatric press review of psychiatry* (Vol. 12, pp. 541–564). Washington, DC: American Psychiatric Press.

Koenigsberg, H., Woo-Ming, A., & Siever, L. (2002). Pharmacological treatment for personality disorders. In P. Nathan & J. Gorman (Eds.), *A guide to treatments that work* (2nd ed., pp. 625–641.). New York: Oxford Press.

Kristeller, J., & Hallet, B (1999). An exploratory study of meditation-based intervention for binge eating disorder. *Journal of Health Psychology* (Vol. 4, 357–363).

Kyrios, M. (1999). A cognitive-behavioral approach to the understanding of obsessive-compulsive personality disorder. In C. Perris & P. McGorry (Eds.), *Cognitive psychotherapy of psychotic and personality disorders* (pp. 351–378). New York: Wiley.

Lachkar, J. (1998). Narcissistic/borderline couples: A psychodynamic approach to conjoint treatment. In J. Carlson & L. Sperry (Eds.), *The disordered couple* (pp. 254–284). New York: Brunner/Mazel.

Lachkar, J. (1999). Narcissistic/borderline couples: A psychodynamic approach to conjoint treatment. In J. Carlson & L. Sperry (Eds.), *The disordered couple* (pp. 259–284). New York: Brunner/Mazel.

Layden, M., Newman, C., Freeman, A., & Morse, S. (1993). *Cognitive therapy of borderline personality disorder.* Boston: Allyn & Bacon.

Lazarus, A. (1981). *The practice of multimodal therapy.* New York: McGraw-Hill.

Leichsenring, F., & Leibing, E. (2003). The effectiveness of psychodynamic therapy and cognitive behavior therapy in the treatment of personality disorders: A meta-analysis. *American Journal of Psychiatry, 160,* 1223–1232.

Lieberman, R., DeRisi, W., & Mueser, K. (1989). *Social skills training for psychiatric patients.* New York: Pergamon.

Liebowitz, M., Schneier, F., Hollander, E., et al. (1991). Treatment of social phobia with drugs other than benzodiazepines. *Journal of Clinical Psychiatry, 52* (11, Supplement), 10–15.

Linehan, M. (1993). *Cognitive-behavioral treatment of borderline personality disorder.* New York: Guilford.

Linehan, M., Armstrong, H., Suarez, A., et al. (1991). Cognitive-behavioral treatment of chronically parasuicidal borderline patients. *Archives of General Psychiatry, 48,* 1060–1064.

Linehan, M., Heard, H., & Armstrong, H. (1993). Naturalistic follow-up of a behavioral treatment for chronically parasuicidal borderline patients. *Archives of General Psychiatry, 50,* 971–974.

Lyddon, W., & Sherry, A. (2001). Developmental personality styles: An attachment theory conceptualization of personality disorders. *Journal of Counseling & Development, 79* (4), 405–414.

Mann, J. (1973). *Time-limited psychotherapy.* Cambridge, MA: Harvard University.

Marlatt, G. (1994). Addiction, mindfulness and acceptance. In S. Hayes, N. Jacobson, V. Follette, & M. Dougher (Eds.), *Acceptance and change: Content and context in psychotherapy* (pp. 175–197). Reno, NV: Context Press.

Marlatt. G., & Kristeller, J. (1999). Mindfulness and meditation. In. W. Miller (Ed.), *Integrating spirituality into treatment: Resources for practitioners* (pp. 67–84). Washington, DC: American Psychological Association.

Marra, T. (2005). *Dialectic behavior therapy in private practice: A practical and comprehensive guide.* Oakland, CA: New Harbinger Publications.

Martin, J. (1997). Mindfulness: A proposed common factor. *Journal of Psychotherapy Integration, 7,* 291–312.

Masterson, J. (1993). *The emerging self: A developmental, self, and object relations approach to the treatment of the closet narcissistic disorder of self.* New York: Brunner/Mazel.

Masterson, J., & Klein, R. (Eds.). (1989). *Psychotherapy of the disorders of the self.* New York: Brunner/Mazel.

McCullough, J. (2000). *Treatment for chronic depression: cognitive behavioral analysis system of psychotherapy.* New York: Guilford Press.

McCullough, J. (2001). *Skills training manual for diagnosing and treating chronic depression: Cognitive behavioral analysis system of psychotherapy.* New York: Guilford.

McCullough, J. (2002). What kind of questions are we trying to answer with our psychotherapy research? *Clinical Psychology: Science and Practice, 9,* 447–452.

Meares, R., Stevenson, J. & Comerford, A. (1999). Psychotherapy with borderline personality patients: 1. A comparison between treated and untreated cohorts. *Australian & New Zealand Journal of Psychiatry, 33,* 467–472.

Meichenbaum, D. (1977). *Cognitive-behavior modification: An integrated approach.* New York: Plenum.

Messina, N., Wish, E., Hoffman, J., & Nemes, S. (2002). Antisocial personality disorder and TC treatment outcomes. *American Journal of Drug and Alcohol Abuse, 28* (2), 197–212.

Miller, M., Useda, J., Trull, T., et al. (2001). Paranoid, schiperwsonality disorder. In P. Sutker & H. Adams (Eds.), *Comprehensive handbook of psychopathology* (3rd ed., pp. 535–559). New York: Plenum.

Miller, W., & Rollnick, S. (1991). *Motivational interviewing.* New York: Guilford.

Millon, T. (1981). *Disorders of personality: DSM-III Axis II.* New York: Wiley.

Millon, T. (1996). *Disorders of personality: DSM-IV and beyond* (2nd ed.). New York: Wiley.

Millon, T. (1999). *Personality guided therapy.* New York: Wiley.

Millon, T., & Davis, R. (2000). *Personality disorders in modern life.* New York: Wiley.

Nehls, N., & Diamond, R. (1993). Developing a systems approach to caring for persons with borderline personality disorder. *Community Mental Health Journal, 29,* 161–172.

Nurse, A. (1998). The dependent/narcissistic couple. In J. Carlson & L. Sperry (Eds.), *The disordered couple* (pp. 315–332). New York: Brunner/Mazel.

Oldham, J., Gabbard, G., Goin, M., et al. (2001). Practice guidelines for the treatment of patients with borderline personality disorder. *American Journal of Psychiatry, 158,* 1–52.

Oldham, J., & Skodol, A. (2000). Charting the future of Axis II. *Journal of Personality Disorders, 14,* 17–29.

Osterbaan, D., vanBalkom, A., Sinhoven, P., et al. (2002). The influence of treatment gain on comorbid avoidant personality disorder in patients with social phobia. *Journal of Nervous and Mental Disease, 190* (1), 41–43.

Othmer, E., & Othmer, S. (1994). *The clinical interview using DSM-IV. Volume 1: Fundamentals.* Washington, DC: American Psychiatric Press.

Othmer, E., & Othmer, S. (2002). *The clinical interview using DSM-IV: Volume 1: Fundamentals, 2nd Ed.* Washington DC: American Psychiatric Press.

Paris, J. (2002). Commentary on the American Psychiatric Association Clinical practice guidelines for borderline personality disorder: Evidence-based psychiatry and the quality of evidence. *Journal of Personality Disorders, 16* (2), 130–134.

Perry, J. (1995). Dependent personality disorder. In G. Gabbard (Ed.), *Treatment of psychiatric disorder* (2nd ed., pp. 2355–2366). Washington, DC: American Psychiatric Press.

Perry, J. (2004). Review: Psychodynamic therapy and cognitive behavioural therapy are effective in the treatment of personality disorders. *Evidence-Based Mental Health, 7*, 16–17.

Perry, J., Herman, J., Van der Kolk, B., et al. (1990). Psychotherapy and psychological trauma in borderline personality disorder. *Psychiatric Annals, 20*, 33–43.

Pretzer, J., & Beck, J. (2004). Cognitive therapy of personality disorders: Twenty years of progress. In R. Leahy (Ed.), *Contemporary cognitive therapy: Theory, research and practice* (pp. 299–318). New York: Guilford.

Prochaska, J., & DiClementi, C. (1982). Transtheoretical therapy: Toward a more integrative model of change. *Psychotherapy, 19*, 276–288.

Pukrop, R. (2002). Dimensional personality profiles of borderline personality disorder in comparision with other personality disorders and healty controls. *Journal of Personality Disorders, 16* (2), 135–147.

Reich, J. (2000). The relationship of social phobia to the personality disorders. *European Psychiatry. 15*, 151–159.

Reich, J. (2002). Drug treatment of personality disorder traits. *Psychiatric Annals, 32* (10), 590–600.

Reich, J. (2005). Drug treatment of personality disorder traits. In J. Reich (Ed.), *Personality disorders: Current research and treatments* (pp. 127–146). New York: Routledge.

Reid, W. (1998). Personality disorders. In W. Reid (Ed.), *The treatment of psychiatric disorders—Revised for the DSM-III-R* (pp. 332–351). New York: Brunner/Mazel.

Roemer, L., & Orsillo, S. (2002). Expanding our conceptualization of and treatment for generalized anxiety disorder: Integrating mindfulness/acceptance-based approaches with existing cognitive-behavioral models. *Clinical Psychology: Science and Practice, 9* (1), 54–68.

Salzman, L. (1980). *Treating the obsessive personality.* New York: Jason Aaronson.

Salzman, L. (1989). Compulsive personality disorder. In T. Karasu (Ed.), *Treatment of psychiatric disorder* (pp. 2771–2782). Washington, DC: American Psychiatric Press.

Sanislow, C., Grilo, C., Morey, L, Bender, D., et al (2002). Confirmatory factor analysis of DSM-IV criteria for borderline personality disorder: Findings from the collaborative longitudinal personality disorders study. *American Journal of Psychiatry, 159* (2), 284–290.

Schmidt, N., Joiner, T., Young, J., & Telch, M. (1995). The schema questionnaire: Investigation of psychometric properties and the hierarchical structure of a measure of maladaptive schemas. *Cognitive Therapy and Research, 19*, 295–321.

Schwartz, J., & Begley, S. (2002). *The mind and the brain: Neuroplasticity and the power of mental force.* New York: HarperCollins.

Segal, Z. Williams, J., & Teasdale, J. (2002). *Mindfulness- based cognitive therapy of depression.* New York: Guilford.

Segal, Z. Williams, J., Teasdale, J., & Williams, M. (2004). Mindfulness-based cognitive therapy: Theoretical and empirical status. In S. Hayes, V. Follette, & M. Linehan, (Eds.), *Mindfulness and acceptance: Expanding the cognitive-behavioral tradition* (pp. 45–65). New York: Guilford.

Shapiro, E. (1982). The holding environment and family therapy for acting out adolescents. *International Journal of Psychoanalysis, 9*, 209–226.

Sharoff, K. (2002). *Cognitive coping therapy.* New York: Brunner/Routledge.

Siever, L., & Davis, K. (1991). A psychological perspective on the personality disorders. *American Journal of Psychiatry, 148*, 37–48.

Siever, L., Koenigsberg, H., Harvey, P., et al. (2002). Cognitive and brain function in schizotypal personality disorder. *Schizophrenia Research, 54*, 157–167.

Silk, K. (1996). Rational pharmacotherapy for patients with personality disorders. In P. Links (Ed.), *Clinical assessment and management of severe personality disorders* (pp. 109–142). Washington, DC: American Psychiatric Press.

Silk, K. (2002). Borderline personality disorder: The lability of psychaitric diagnosis. *Current Psychiatry, 1* (11), 25–33.

Skodol, A., Gunderson, J., McGlashan, Dyck, I., et al. (2002). Functional impairment in patients with schizotypal, borderline, avoidant or obsessive-compulsive personality disorder. *American Journal of Psychiatry, 159* (2), 276–282.

Slap, J., & Slap-Shelton, L. (1981). *The schema in clinical psychoanalysis.* Hillsdale, NJ: Analytic Press.

Smucker, M. (1999). *Cognitive behavioral treatment for adult survivors of childhood trauma: Imagery rescripting and reprocessing.* New York: Jason Aronson.

Snyder, M. (1994). Couple therapy with narcissistically vulnerable clients: Using the relationship enhancement model. *The Family Journal: Counseling and Therapy for Couples and Families, 2,* 27–35.

Soloff, P., Lynch, K., & Kelly, T. (2002). Childhood abuse as a risk factor for suicidal behavior in borderline personality disorder. *Journal of Personality Disorders, 16* (3) 201–214.

Solomon, M. (1989). *Narcissism and intimacy: Love and marriage in an age of confusion.* New York: Norton.

Solomon, M. (1998). Treating narcissistic and borderline couples. In J. Carlson & L. Sperry (Eds.), *The disordered couple* (pp. 239–258). New York: Brunner/Mazel.

Sperry, L. (1995a). *Handbook of the diagnosis and treatment of DSM-IV personality disorders.* New York: Brunner/Mazel.

Sperry, L. (1995b). *Psychopharmacology and psychotherapy: Strategies for maximizing treatment outcomes.* New York: Brunner/Mazel.

Sperry, L. (1999). *Cognitive behavior therapy of DSM-IV personality disorders: Highly effective interventions for the most common personality disorders.* New York: Brunner/Mazel.

Sperry, L. (2002). From psychopathology to transformation: Retrieving the developmental focus in psychotherapy. *Journal of Individual Psychology, 58,* 398–421.

Sperry, L. (2003). *Handbook of the diagnosis and treatment of DSM-IV-TR personality disorders* (2nd ed.). New York: Brunner-Routledge.

Sperry, L., Carlson, J., & Kjos, D. (2003). *Becoming an effective therapist.* Boston, MA: Allyn & Bacon.

Sperry, L., Brill, P., Howard, K., & Grissom, G. (1996). *Treatment Outcomes and Psychiatric Interventions.* New York: Brunner/Mazel.

Sperry, L., & Maniacci, M. (1998). The histrionic-obsessive couple. In J. Carlson & L. Sperry (Eds.), *The disordered couple.* New York: Brunner/Mazel.

Sperry, L., & Mosak, H. (1996). Personality disorders. In L. Sperry & J. Carlson (Eds.), *Psychopathology and psychotherapy: From DSM-IV diagnosis to treatment* (2nd ed., pp. 279–336). Washington, DC: Accelerated Development/Taylor & Francis.

Stein, D., & Young, J. (1992). Schema approach to personality disorders. In D. Stein & J. Young (Eds.), *Cognitive science and clinical disorders* (pp. 272–288). San Diego: Academic Press.

Stone, M. (1993). *Abnormalities of personality: Within and beyond the realm of treatment.* New York: Norton.

Svartberg, M., Stiles, T., & Seltzer, H. (2004). Randomized, controlled trial of the effectiveness of short-term dynamic psychotherapy and cognitive therapy for Cluster C personality disorders. *American Journal of Psychiatry, 161,* 810–818.

Thaker, G., Adami, H., & Gold, J. (2001). Functional deterioration in individuals with schizophrenia spectrum personality symptoms. *Journal of Personality Disorders, 15,* 229–234.

Turner, R. (1992). Borderline personality disorder. In A. Freeman & F. Dattilio (Eds.), *Comprehensive casebook of cognitive therapy* (pp. 215–222). New York: Plenum.

Vaughn, B., & Bost, K. (1999). Attachment and temperament: Redundant, independent, or interacting influences on interpersonal adaptation and personality development? In P. Cassidy & P. Shaver (Eds.). *Handbook of attachment: Theory, research and clinical applications* (pp. 198–225). New York: Guilford.

Wachtel. P. (1982). *Resistance: Psychodynamics and behavioral approaches.* New York: Plenum.

Waldeck, T., & Miller, L. (2000). Social skill deficits in schizotypal personality disorder. *Psychiatry Research, 93* (3) 237–246.

Waldinger, R. (1987). Intensive psychodynamic therapy with borderline patients: An overview. *American Journal of Psychiatry, 144,* 267–274.

Waldo, M., & Harman, M. (1993). Relationship enhancement therapy with borderline personality. *Family Journal, 1,* 25–30.

Waldo, M., & Harman, M. (1998). Borderline personality disorders and relationship enhancement therapy. In J. Carlson & L. Sperry (Eds.), *The disordered couple* (pp. 285–298). New York: Brunner/Mazel.

Wells, M., Glickhauf-Hughes, C., & Buzzel, V. (1990). Treating obsessive-compulsive personalities in psychoanalytic/interpersonal group therapy. *Psychotherapy, 27,* 366–379.

Westin, D., & Shedler, J. (2000). A prototype matching approach to personality disorders. *Journal of Personality Disorders, 14,* 109–126.

Widiger, T., & Bornstein, R. (2001). Histrionic, dependent and narcissistic personality disorders. In P. Sutker & H. Adams (Eds.), *Comprehensive handbook of psychopathology* (3rd ed., pp. 509–531). New York: Plenum.

Widiger, T., Costa, P., & McCrae, R. (2002). A proposal for Axis II: Diagnosing personality disorders using the five factor model. In P. Costa & T. Widiger (Eds.), *Personality disorders and the five factor model of personality* (2nd ed., pp. 431–456). Washington, DC: American Psychological Association.

Winer, J., & Pollack, G. (1989). Psychoanalysis and dynamic psychotherapy. In T. Karasu (Ed.), *Treatment of psychiatric disorders* (pp. 2639–2648). Washington, DC: American Psychiatric Press.

Wolff, S. (2000). Schizoid pesonality in childhood and Asperger syndrome. In A. Klin, F. Volkmar, & S. Sparrow (Eds.), *Asperger syndrome* (pp. 278–305). New York: Guilford.

Woodward, B., Duckworth, K., & Guthiel, T. (1993). The pharmacotherapist-psychotherapist collaboration. In J. Oldham, M. Riba, & A. Tassman (Eds.), *American psychiatric press review of psychiatry* (Vol. 12, pp. 631–649). Washington, DC: American Psychiatric Press.

Yalom, I. (1985). *The theory and practice of group psychotherapy* (3rd ed.). New York: Basic Books.

Young, J. (1994). *Cognitive therapy for personality disorders: A schema-focused approach* (rev. ed.). Sarasota, FL: Professional Resource Exchange.

Young, J. (1999). *Cognitive therapy for personality disorders: A schema-focused approach* (3rd ed.) Sarasota, FL: Professional Resource Press.

Young, J., Klosko, J., & Weishaar, M. (2003). *Schema Therapy: A practitioner's guide.* New York: Guilford.

INDEX

A

abandonment/instability schema, 29t
abandonment/loss schema, 29t, 104, 114, 127t
acceptance and commitment therapy, 7
Adler, A., 22, 24
Adler, G., 100
affective instability, 11, 99, 113, 116, 154, 172
affective style, 6, 41, 42
    avoidant personality, 82, 95t
    borderline personality, 103, 127t
    histrionic personality, 181t
    narcissistic personality, 163t
    obsessive-compulsive, 189, 190, 201t
aggressivity, 4, 38, 40, 69, 113, 117, 154
agoraphobia, 137, 141
Alberti, R., 47
Alcoholics Anonymous (AA), 75
Alden, L., 85, 87
Allen, D., 175
Allnut, S., 81, 103, 151, 169, 188
Alonso, A., 154
Altamura, A., 9
American Psychiatric Association (APA), 79, 99, 131, 149, 166, 185
anger management training, 43–44, 43t, 154, 163t
    resources, 44
antisocial personality disorder, 6, 11
anxiety management training, 43t, 45–46, 47, 136, 145t
    resources, 46
approval-seeking/recognition-seeking schema, 29t, 78, 130, 166, 172
Armstrong, H., 12, 13

assertiveness training, 37, 43t, 46–47, 106, 137, 143, 144, 145t
    resources, 47
assessment
    changes in, 6–7
    schema, 24–25
automatic thoughts, 31, 145
avoidant personality disorder, 6, 9, 11, 77–95
    case example, 90–94
    clinical conceptualization, 77–78
    cognitive behavior analysis system of psychotherapy (CBASP), 84–85
    collaboration, facilitating, 79–80
    combined treatment strategies, 87–89
    countertransference, 80–81, 95t
    DSM-IV description/criteria, 78–79t
    engagement strategies, 79–81, 91, 95t
    group treatment strategies, 83, 84, 86–87
    marital/family therapy strategies, 87
    medication strategies, 86
    pattern analysis strategies, 81–82, 91–92, 95t
    pattern change strategies, 83–89, 92–94, 95t
    pattern maintenance, 89–90, 94, 95t
    relapse prevention strategies, 90
    schema change, 83, 95t
    schemas, 82, 95t
    temperament/style change strategies, 85–86
    temperament/style dimensions, 82, 92f, 95t
    termination strategies, 89, 94, 95t
    transference, 80–81, 95t
    triggers, 77, 82

B

Baer, L., 190
Barlow, D., 137, 138
Baruth, L., 24
Beck, A., 4, 13, 22, 24, 26, 27, 30, 31, 37, 82, 83, 135, 153, 168, 171, 172, 190
behavioral/relational style, 41, 42, 135
    avoidant personality, 85, 87, 95*t*
    borderline personality, 127*t*
    dependent personality, 145*t*
    histrionic personality, 181*t*
    narcissistic personality, 154, 163*t*
    obsessive-compulsive personality, 190, 201*t*
Beitman, B., 10, 14
biosocial formulations, 4
Bishop, S., 36
borderline personality disorder, 6, 11, 18, 97–127
    case example, 121–126
    clinical conceptualization, 97–98
    cognitive behavior analysis of psychotherapy (CBASP), 108–109
    collaboration, facilitating, 100–102
    combined treatment strategies, 117
    countertransference, 102, 127*t*
    dialectical behavior therapy, 106–108
    DSM-IV description/criteria, 98–99*t*
    engagement strategies, 99–102, 122–123, 127*t*
    group treatment strategies, 114–115
    intervention targets, 111–113*t*
    marital/family therapy strategies, 100, 115–117
    medication strategies, 113–114
    pattern analysis strategies, 102–104, 123, 127*t*
    pattern change strategies, 104–119, 123–125, 127*t*
    pattern maintenance strategies, 119–121, 125–126, 127*t*
    relapse prevention strategies, 120–121, 126
    schema change strategies, 105, 110, 114
    schemas, 103–104, 127*t*
    schema therapy, 105–106
    temperament/style change strategies, 109–113
    temperament/style dimensions, 104, 124*f*, 127*t*
    termination strategies, 119, 125–126, 127*t*
    transference, 102, 127*t*

    triggers, 97, 103
Bornstein, R., 139
Bricker, D., 82, 152, 170, 188
Brill, P., 74
Brown, G., 25, 105
Buie, D., 100
Buzzel, V., 191

C

case examples
    avoidant personality, 90–94
    borderline personality, 121–126
    dependent personality, 140–144
    histrionic personality, 176–179
    Narcissistic personality, 158–162
    obsessive-compulsive personality, 195–200
character, 3, 4, 21–22
Chaucer, E., 172
Chu, J., 100
Clark, D., 62, 68
Clarkin, J., 3, 18, 101, 116
Cloninger, C., 4, 6, 22, 39, 40, 41
cognitive awareness training, 43*t*, 47–48, 110, 127*t*, 136, 154, 160, 163*t*
    resources, 48
cognitive behavior analysis system of psychotherapy (CBASP) strategies, 33–34
    avoidant personality, 84–85
    borderline personality, 108–109
cognitive behavior therapy, 7–8, 23–24
cognitive coping therapy, 37
cognitive restructuring, 37
cognitive style, 6, 12, 38, 41, 42, 69
    avoidant personality, 78, 82, 85, 95*t*
    borderline personality, 98, 103, 126, 127*t*
    dependent personality, 129, 134, 136, 145*t*
    histrionic personality, 165, 167, 170, 172, 179, 181*t*
    narcissistic personality, 148, 153, 163*t*
    obsessive-compulsive personality, 184, 189, 192, 197, 201*t*
cognitive therapy, 25–26
    vs. dialectic behavior therapy, 30–31
    mindfulness-based, 7, 36, 60–61
Cognitive Therapy of Personality Disorders, 26, 30
collaboration, 15
    avoidant personality, 79–80

borderline personality, 100–102
contract, 186, 201*t*
dependent personality, 131–132
histrionic personality, 167–168
narcissistic personality, 150
obsessive-compulsive personality, 186–187
pseudocollaboration, 186
combined treatment strategies, 9–10, 11, 18
avoidant personality, 87–89
borderline personality, 117
dependent personality, 138
histrionic personality, 174
narcissistic personality, 156–157
obsessive-compulsive personality, 192–193
Compass-OP, 74
coping styles, 28
Costello, C., 4, 41
countertransference
avoidant personality, 80–81, 95*t*
borderline personality, 102, 127*t*
dependent personality, 132–133, 145*t*
histrionic personality, 168, 181*t*
narcissistic personality, 150–151, 163*t*
obsessive-compulsive personality, 187, 201*t*
Cukrowicz, K., 34, 84, 108

D

Davis, D., 13, 24, 26, 153, 168, 170, 172, 190
Davis, K., 11, 125
Davison, M., 12
defectiveness/shame schema, 29*t*, 82, 92, 95*t*
Deffenbacher, J., 46
dependence/incompetence schema, 29*t*, 114, 143
dependent personality disorder, 6, 11, 129–145
case example, 140–144
clinical conceptualization, 129–130
collaboration, facilitating, 131–132
combined treatment strategies, 138
countertransference, 132–133, 145*t*
DSM-IV description/criteria, 130–131*t*
engagement strategies, 131–133, 141, 145*t*
group treatment strategies, 136–137
marital/family therapy strategies, 137–138
medication strategies, 136

pattern analysis strategies, 133–134, 141–142, 145*t*
pattern change strategies, 135–138, 142–144, 145*t*
pattern maintenance strategies, 138–140, 144, 145*t*
relapse prevention strategies, 140
schema change, 135
schemas, 134, 145*t*
temperament/style change strategies, 135–136
temperament/style dimensions, 134, 142*f*, 145*t*
termination strategies, 138–140, 144, 145*t*
transference, 132–133, 145*t*
triggers, 129, 133–134
depressive personality disorder, 7, 9, 11, 18
DeRisi, W., 38, 40, 41
Derogatis, L., 74
Desyrel, 125
Diagnostic and Statistical Manual of Mental Disorders, 3, 79, 99, 131, 149, 166, 185
dialectic behavior therapy, 7, 25, 30–33, 40
borderline personality, 106–108
vs. cognitive therapy, 30–31
mindfulness skills, 57–60
Diamond, R., 119
DiClementi, C., 15
distress tolerance skill training, 43*t*, 48–49, 54, 110, 115, 124, 127*t*
resources, 49
Driscoll, K., 34, 84, 85, 108, 109
Duckworth, K., 118

E

Eagle, M., 23
Eckstein, D., 24
Ellis, A., 24
emotional deprivation schema, 29*t*, 98, 148, 166, 170, 171, 177, 179, 181*t*
emotional inhibition schema, 29*t*, 184, 188, 190, 197, 200, 201*t*
emotion awareness training, 110, 127*t*, 171, 181*t*, 190, 201*t*
emotion regulation training, 43*t*, 49–51, 110
resources, 51
empathy training, 43*t*, 51–52, 154, 156, 157, 161, 163*t*, 172, 179, 181*t*
resources, 52

engagement strategies, 14–16, 72
  avoidant personality, 79–81, 91, 95*t*
  borderline personality, 99–102, 122–123,
    127*t*
  dependent personality, 131–133, 141, 145*t*
  histrionic personality, 167–168, 176, 181*t*
  narcissistic personality, 149–151, 159–160,
    163*t*
  obsessive-compulsive personality,
    185–187, 195–196, 201*t*
enmeshment/undeveloped self schema,
    29*t*, 116
entitlement/grandiosity schema, 29*t*, 148,
    152, 153, 160, 163*t*, 169, 170, 177,
    179, 181*t*
escape behaviors, 111*t*
Everett, S., 116

F

failure schema, 29*t*, 134
Fawcett, J., 40
Flanagan, C., 82, 152, 170, 188
Fleming, B., 190
Fluoxetine, 113, 154, 172
Follette, V., 7
Francis, A., 18, 101
Freeman, A., 12, 13, 17, 24, 25, 26, 37, 83, 153,
    168, 170, 172, 179, 190
Freud, S., 5, 22, 23

G

Gabbard, G., 10, 80, 81, 150, 151, 168, 173, 187
Glantz, K., 138
Glick, I., 116
Glickhauf-Hughes, C., 191
Global Assessment of Functioning, 10, 42, 74
Goisman, R., 138
Goldsmith, S., 116
Green, S., 57
Grisson, G., 74
Grossman, P., 36
group treatment strategies
  avoidant personality, 83, 84, 86–87
  borderline personality, 114–115
  dependent personality, 136–137
  histrionic personality, 172–173
  narcissistic personality, 154–155

obsessive-compulsive personality,
    191–192
Guerney, B., 52
Gunderson, J., 100, 114
Guthiel, T., 118

H

Halperin, S., 116
Handbook of DSM-IV-TR Personality Disorders,
    72
Harbir, H., 137, 173, 192
Harman, M., 117
harm avoidance, 41
Hawton, K., 62, 68
Hayes, S., 7
Heard, H., 12
histrionic personality disorder, 6, 11, 165–181
  case example, 176–179
  clinical conceptualization, 165–166
  collaboration, facilitating, 167–168
  combined treatment strategies, 174
  countertransference, 168, 181*t*
  DSM-IV description/criteria, 166*t*
  engagement strategies, 167–168, 176, 181*t*
  group treatment strategies, 172–173
  marital/family therapy strategies, 173
  medication strategies, 172
  pattern analysis strategies, 169–170,
    177–178, 181*t*
  pattern change strategies, 170–174, 179,
    181*t*
  pattern maintenance strategies, 174–176,
    179, 181*t*
  relapse prevention strategies, 175–176
  schema change, 171, 181*t*
  schemas, 169–170, 181*t*
  temperament/style change strategies,
    171–172
  temperament/style dimensions, 170, 178*f*,
    181*t*
  termination strategies, 174–175, 179, 181*t*
  transference, 168, 181*t*
  triggers, 169
Hoffman, G., 156
holding environment, 74, 101–102, 124, 127,
    156
Horowitz, L., 155
Horowitz, M., 4, 22, 23, 167
Howard, K., 74

I

impulse control training, 43*t*, 53–54, 110,
    125, 127*t*, 154, 160, 172, 181*t*
    resources, 54
impulsivity, 4, 9, 11, 38, 40, 49, 69, 86
    avoidant personality, 86
    borderline personality, 98–99*t*, 104, 113,
        115, 116, 125
    dependent personality, 136
    narcissistic personality, 153, 154
Inderbitzin, L., 23
individuation, 116
insomnia, 9, 90, 93, 121, 125, 159, 195, 200
insufficient self-control/self-discipline
        schema, 29*t*, 98, 148, 152, 160, 163*t*
integrative treatment. *see* combined
        treatment strategies
interpersonal skills training, 43*t*, 54–55, 86,
        87, 110, 115, 127*t*, 190, 199, 201*t*
    resources, 55
intervention strategies, 42–68, 43*t*
    anger management training, 43–44, 43*t*,
        154, 163*t*
    anxiety management training, 43*t*, 45–46,
        47, 136, 145*t*
    assertiveness training, 37, 43*t*, 46–47, 106,
        137, 143, 144, 145*t*
    cognitive awareness training, 43*t*,
        47–48, 110, 127*t*, 136, 154, 160, 163*t*
    distress tolerance skill training, 43*t*,
        48–49, 54, 110, 115, 124, 127*t*
    emotion regulation training, 43*t*, 49–51,
        110
    empathy training, 43*t*, 51–52, 154, 156,
        157, 161, 163*t*, 172, 179, 181*t*
    impulse control training, 43*t*, 53–54, 110,
        125, 127*t*, 154, 160, 172, 181*t*
    interpersonal skills training, 43*t*, 54–55,
        86, 87, 110, 115, 127*t*, 190, 199, 201*t*
    limit-setting, 43*t*, 56–57, 101, 118
    mindfulness training, 34–36, 43*t*, 57–61
    problem-solving training, 43*t*, 61–62, 136,
        145*t*, 171, 179, 181*t*
    self-management training, 43*t*, 48, 49,
        62–64, 127*t*, 170
    sensitivity reduction training, 43*t*, 65–66,
        85, 95*t*, 163*t*
    symptom management training, 43*t*,
        66–67, 125, 179
    thought-stopping, 37, 43*t*, 67–68, 190, 200,
        201*t*

J

Jacobson, G., 156
James, M., 23
Jenike, M., 5, 190
Joiner, T., 34, 84, 108
Jones, S., 156

K

Kabat-Zinn, J., 34, 36
Kalojera, I., 156
Kanfer, F., 39
Karoly, P., 46
Kavoussi, R., 172
Keller, M., 33
Keller, P., 44
Kennedy, J., 74
Kernberg, O., 102
Kirk, J., 62, 68
Klein, R., 114, 118
Klosko, J., 22, 24, 25, 27, 28, 30, 39, 105, 152,
        171, 188, 190
Koenigsberg, H., 117, 118, 119

L

lability, 6, 9, 13, 37, 38, 49, 50, 99, 121
Lachkar, J., 116, 156
Layden, M., 17, 104, 114
Lazarus, A., 137
Leibing, E., 8
Leichsenring, F., 8
Lenzenweger, M., 3
Lieberman, R., 38, 40, 41, 42
lifestyle, 24
limit-setting, 43*t*, 56–57, 101, 118
    resources, 57
Linehan, M., 7, 12, 30, 31, 33, 35, 36, 40, 57,
        101, 106, 107, 110, 115
Links, P. S., 81, 103, 151, 169
Liu, J., 172

M

Mahrer, D., 24
maladaptive schemas, 27–28, 29*t*
    abandonment/loss schema, 29*t*, 104, 114,
        127*t*

approval-seeking/recognition-seeking schema, 29t, 78, 130, 166, 172
defectiveness/shame schema, 29t, 82, 92, 95t
dependence/incompetence schema, 29t, 114, 143
emotional deprivation schema, 29t, 98, 148, 166, 170, 171, 177, 179, 181t
emotional inhibition schema, 29t, 184, 188, 190, 197, 200, 201t
enmeshment/undeveloped self schema, 29t, 116
entitlement/grandiosity schema, 29t, 148, 152, 153, 160, 163t, 169, 170, 177, 179, 181t
failure schema, 29t, 134
insufficient self-control/self-discipline schema, 29t, 98, 148, 152, 160, 163t
mistrust/abuse schema, 29t, 98, 152, 163t
negativity/pessimism schema, 29t
punitiveness schema, 29t, 184
self-sacrifice schema, 29t, 78, 130, 141, 143
social isolation/alienation schema, 29t, 78, 82, 92, 95t, 98
subjugation schema, 29t
unrelenting standards/hypercriticalness schema, 29t, 148, 184
vulnerability to harm/illness schema, 29t
Maniacci, M., 173, 192
Mann, J., 139
marital/family therapy strategies
avoidant personality, 87
borderline personality, 100, 115–117
dependent personality, 137–138
histrionic personality, 173
narcissistic personality, 155–156
obsessive-compulsive personality, 192
psychodynamically oriented approach, 116
relationship enhancement therapy, 117
structural family approach, 117
Marra, T., 30, 31, 33, 57, 104, 106, 107, 171
Masterson, J., 114, 147
McCullough, J., 33, 34, 40, 84, 108
medication strategies, 9
avoidant personality, 86
borderline personality, 113–114
dependent personality, 136
histrionic personality, 172
narcissistic personality, 154

obsessive-compulsive personality, 190–191
meditative practices, 60–61
Meichenbaum, D., 24
Mellaril, 122
Miller, W., 16
Millon, T., 4, 6, 13
Millon Multiaxial Clinical Inventory, 6, 137
mindfulness-based cognitive therapy, 7, 36, 60–61
mindfulness-based stress reduction, 36
mindfulness training, 34–36, 43t, 57–61
resources, 61
mirroring, 4, 22, 150, 151, 155, 156, 157, 159, 160, 162, 163t
mistrust/abuse schema, 29t, 98, 152, 163t
modification guidelines, 73–75
modulation, 12, 17
Morse, S., 17
Mosak, H., 103, 152, 169, 188
motivational counseling, 16
Mueser, K., 38, 40, 41
multiple personality disorders, 13–14

N

narcissistic personality disorder, 6, 11, 147–163
case example, 158–162
clinical conceptualization, 147–148
collaboration, facilitating, 150
combined treatment strategies, 156–157
countertransference, 150–151, 163t
DSM-IV description/criteria, 148–149t
engagement strategies, 149–151, 159–160, 163t
group treatment strategies, 154–155
marital/family therapy strategies, 155–156
medication strategies, 154
pattern analysis strategies, 151–153, 160, 163t
pattern change strategies, 153–157, 160–162, 163t
pattern maintenance strategies, 157–158, 162, 163t
relapse prevention strategies, 158
schema change, 153–154, 163t
schemas, 152, 163t
temperament/style change strategies, 154

temperament/style dimensions, 152–153, 161*f*, 163*t*
termination strategies, 157–158, 162, 163*t*
transference, 150–151, 163*t*
triggers, 147, 152
National Depressive and Manic Depressive Association, 75
negativity/pessimism schema, 29*t*
Nehls, N., 119
neurobiological formulations, 4
Newman, C., 17
Niemann, L., 36
Novaco, R., 44, 48
novelty seeking, 41
Nurse, A., 137, 156

O

obsessive-compulsive personality disorder, 5, 6, 11, 183–201
    case example, 195–200
    clinical conceptualization, 183–184
    collaboration, facilitating, 186–187
    combined treatment strategies, 192–193
    countertransference, 187, 201*t*
    DSM-IV description/criteria, 184–185*t*
    engagement strategies, 185–187, 195–196, 201*t*
    group treatment strategies, 191–192
    marital/family therapy strategies, 192
    medication strategies, 190–191
    pattern analysis strategies, 187–189, 196–198, 201*t*
    pattern change strategies, 189–193, 198–200, 201*t*
    pattern maintenance strategies, 193–195, 200, 201*t*
    relapse prevention strategies, 194–195
    schema change, 190, 201*t*
    schemas, 188, 201*t*
    temperament/style change strategies, 190
    temperament/style dimensions, 188–189, 198*f*, 201*t*
    termination strategies, 193–194, 200, 201*t*
    transference, 187, 201*t*
    triggers, 183, 188
Othmer, E., 79, 99, 103, 149, 167, 168, 169, 186, 188
Othmer, S., 79, 99, 103, 149, 167, 168, 169, 186, 188

P

panic personality disorder, 9
paranoid personality disorder, 6, 11
parasuicidal symptoms, 56, 107, 110, 111*t*, 121
passive-aggressive personality disorder, 6–7, 11
patient readiness, 10–11, 15–16, 110, 111–113*t*
pattern, defined, 81, 103, 151, 169, 188
pattern analysis strategies, 16, 72, 81, 103
    avoidant personality, 81–82, 91–92, 95*t*
    borderline personality, 102–104, 123, 127*t*
    dependent personality, 133–134, 141–142, 145*t*
    histrionic personality, 169–170, 177–178, 181*t*
    narcissistic personality, 151–153, 160, 163*t*
    obsessive-compulsive personality, 151–153, 160, 163*t*
pattern change strategies, 16–17, 72–73
    avoidant personality, 83–89, 92–94, 95*t*
    borderline personality, 104–119, 123–125, 127*t*
    dependent personality, 135–138, 142–144, 145*t*
    histrionic personality, 170–174, 179, 181*t*
    narcissistic personality, 153–157, 160–162, 163*t*
    obsessive-compulsive personality, 189–193, 198–200, 201*t*
pattern maintenance, 14, 17, 72, 73
    avoidant personality, 89–90, 94, 95*t*
    borderline personality, 119–121, 125–126, 127*t*
    dependent personality, 138–140, 144, 145*t*
    histrionic personality, 174–176, 179, 181*t*
    narcissistic personality, 157–158, 162, 163*t*
    obsessive-compulsive personality, 193–195, 200, 201*t*
Perry, J., 8, 117
Perry, S., 18, 101
personality disorders
    assessment, 6–7
    changes in conceptualization, 4–5
    classification, 11
    criteria, 5–6
    treatment changes, 7–10
Pollack, G., 10
Pretzer, J., 30, 190
problem-solving training, 43*t*, 61–62, 136, 145*t*, 171, 179, 181*t*
    resources, 62

Prochaska, J., 15
Prybeck, T., 39
pseudocollaboration, 186
psychoanalytic therapy, 4, 8, 10, 23, 117
psychodynamic therapy, 8–9, 23, 87, 114, 116, 157
psychopharmacological treatment, 9
punitiveness schema, 29t, 184

R

rational emotive therapy, 24
Reardon, M., 34, 84, 108
Recovery, Inc., 75
Reich, J., 9, 11, 40, 86, 113, 114, 154, 191
relapse prevention strategies
    avoidant personality, 90
    borderline personality, 120–121, 126
    dependent personality, 140
    histrionic personality, 175–176
    narcissistic personality, 158
    obsessive-compulsive personality, 194–195
relationship enhancement therapy, 117
reward dependence, 4, 40, 41
Ritt, L., 44
Rollnick, S., 16

S

sadistic personality disorder, 6
Salkovskis, J., 62
Salkovskis, P., 68
Salzman, L., 192, 193
Sank, L., 47
schema assessment, 24–25
schema camouflage, 13
schema change strategies, 13, 22
    avoidant personality, 83, 95t
    borderline personality, 105, 110, 114
    dependent personality, 135
    histrionic personality, 171, 181t
    narcissistic personality, 153–154, 163t
    obsessive-compulsive personality, 190, 201t
Schema Questionnaire, 25, 105
schemas, 4, 22–23, 72
    avoidant personality, 82, 95t
    borderline personality, 103–104, 127t
    cognitive-behavioral tradition, 23–24

dependent personality, 134, 145t
    histrionic personality, 169–170, 181t
    narcissistic personality, 152, 163t
    obsessive-compulsive personality, 188, 201t
    psychoanalytic tradition, 23
    psychodynamic tradition, 23
schemas, maladaptive. *see* maladaptive schemas
schema therapy, 26–30
    borderline personality, 105–106
    coping styles, 28
    domains, 27–28, 29t
    maladaptive, 27–28, 29t
    modes, 28
schizoid personality disorder, 6, 11
schizotypal personality disorder, 6, 11
Schmidt, N., 25
Schmidt, S., 36
SCID-II, 6
SCL-90R, 74
Segal, Z., 7
selective serotonin reuptake inhibitor (SSRI), 86, 114, 125, 136, 172, 190, 191
self-control, 17
self-defeating personality disorder, 6
self-instructional training, 24
self-management training, 43t, 48, 49, 62–64, 127t, 170
    resources, 64
self-sacrifice schema, 29t, 78, 130, 141, 143
Seltzer, H., 8
sensitivity reduction training, 43t, 65–66, 85, 95t, 163t
    resources, 66
Shaffer, C., 47
Sharoff, K., 37, 40
Siever, L., 11, 125
Silk, K., 125
Simon, K., 190
skill deficits, 41–42
skills training, 32, 37, 38, 54–55
Slap, J., 22, 23
Slap-Shelton, L., 22, 23
Snyder, M., 156
social isolation/alienation schema, 29t, 78, 82, 92, 95t, 98
Solomon, M., 116, 156
somatic treatments, 18

Sperry, L., 5, 9, 10, 12, 18, 37, 38, 40, 74, 80, 82, 87, 88, 100, 103, 117, 137, 138, 150, 152, 153, 155, 157, 167, 169, 170, 173, 186, 188, 189, 192
SSRI, 86, 114, 125, 136, 172, 190, 191
Stein, D., 4, 22–23
Stiles, T., 8
Stone, M., 4, 8, 10, 11, 12
stress-inoculation, 24
structured interventions. *see* intervention strategies
style. *see* temperament/style change strategies; temperament/style dimensions
subjugation schema, 29*t*
Suinn, R., 46
Svartberg, M., 8
Svrakic, D., 39
symptom management training, 43*t*, 66–67, 125, 179
  resources, 67

T

Teasdale, J., 7, 61
telephone contact, 31, 32, 106–107
temperament, 4, 37–38, 40–69, *see also* temperament/style change strategies; temperament/style dimensions
Temperament Character Inventory, 6, 22, 41
temperament/style change strategies
  avoidant personality, 85–86
  borderline personality, 109–113
  dependent personality, 135–136
  histrionic personality, 171–172
  narcissistic personality, 154
  obsessive-compulsive personality, 190
temperament/style dimensions, 40–41
  avoidant personality, 82, 92*f*, 95*t*
  borderline personality, 104, 124*f*, 127*t*
  dependent personality, 134, 142*f*, 145*t*
  histrionic personality, 170, 178*f*, 181*t*
  narcissistic personality, 152–153, 161*f*, 163*t*
  obsessive-compulsive personality, 188–189, 198*f*, 201*t*
termination strategies, 72, 73
  avoidant personality, 89, 94, 95*t*
  borderline personality, 119, 125–126, 127*t*
  dependent personality, 138–140, 144, 145*t*
  histrionic personality, 174–175, 179, 181*t*

narcissistic personality, 157–158, 162, 163*t*
  obsessive-compulsive personality, 193–194, 200, 201*t*
therapeutic confrontation, 15, 37, 100, 114
thought-stopping, 37, 43*t*, 67–68, 190, 200, 201*t*
  resources, 68
transference, 16
  avoidant personality, 80–81, 95*t*
  borderline personality, 102, 127*t*
  dependent personality, 132–133, 145*t*
  histrionic personality, 168, 181*t*
  narcissistic personality, 150–151, 163*t*
  obsessive-compulsive personality, 187, 201*t*
treatment, *see also* treatment goals; treatment strategies
  basic premises, 10–14
  contracting, 15, 101, 127*t*, 158, 160, 162
  modification guidelines, 73–75
  "no treatment" option, 18, 101
  stages, 14–17
  tailoring, 11, 17–18
treatment goals, 11–13
  avoidant personality, 81, 85, 95*t*
  borderline personality, 107, 116, 127*t*
  dependent personality, 132, 137, 145*t*
  histrionic personality, 169, 172, 181*t*
  narcissistic personality, 151, 157, 163*t*
  obsessive-compulsive personality, 186, 188, 189, 201*t*
treatment strategies, 71–72
  avoidant personality, 95*t*
  borderline personality, 127*t*
  bottom-up, 40
  dependent personality, 145*t*
  histrionic personality, 181*t*
  narcissistic personality, 163*t*
  obsessive-compulsive personality, 201*t*
  top-down, 37, 40
treatment threatening behavior, 111*t*
triggers, 25, 30, 43, 44, 45, 46, 68
  avoidant personality, 77, 82
  borderline personality, 97, 103
  dependent personality, 129, 133–134
  histrionic personality, 169
  narcissistic personality, 147, 152
  obsessive-compulsive personality, 183, 188
Turkat, I., 54, 66
Turner, R., 114

U

undesireability/alienation schema, 29*t*, 78, 82, 92, 95*t*, 98
unlovability/defectiveness schema, 104, 114, 127*t*
unrelenting standards/hypercriticalness schema, 29*t*, 148, 184

V

validation, 32, 35, 107
Volgy, S., 116
vulnerability to harm/illness schema, 29*t*

W

Wachtel, P., 23

Waddell, M., 137, 138
Walach, H., 36
Waldinger, R., 100
Waldo, M., 117
Weishaar, M., 25, 27, 30, 39, 105, 152, 171, 188, 190
Wells, M., 191
Williams, J., 7
Williams, M., 7
Winer, J., 10
Wissler, A., 116
Woodward, B., 118

Y

Yalom, I., 136
Young, J., 4, 22–23, 24, 25, 26, 27, 28, 30, 39, 82, 104, 105, 106, 152, 170, 171, 188, 190

Z

Zimbardo, P., 55
Zoloft, 122, 125